imes

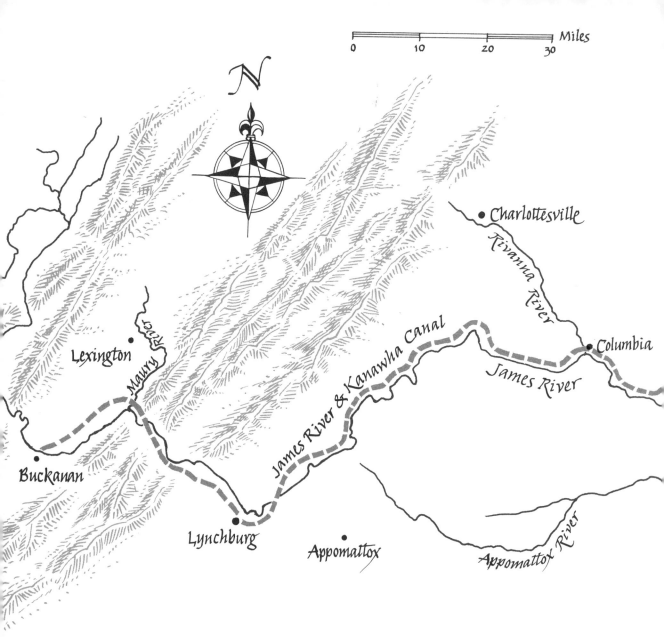

*B*ETWEEN the older colonial America
and the later industrial America stand the ideals
of the Old Dominion, more humane and generous
than either. . . . The nineteenth century first entered
America by way of the James River.

Vernon Louis Parrington

The James

Where A Nation Began

By PARKE ROUSE, Jr.

Essays from the
Newport News *Daily Press*
and other periodicals

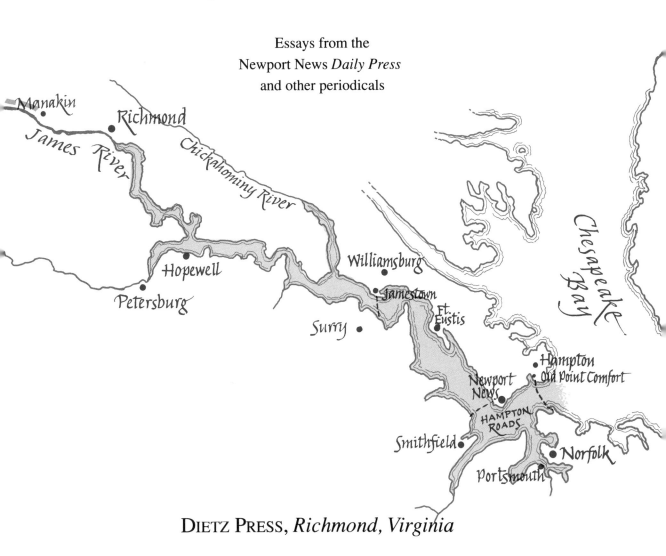

DIETZ PRESS, *Richmond, Virginia*

COVER PRINT: *"View of Richmond from Gamble's Hill," 1857,*
              by Edward Beyer. Courtesy Virginia State Library

Design by Stinely Associates

For my devoted brother,
William Dashiell Rouse

Contents

Introduction

This book is made up from columns by the author published in the Newport News *Daily Press* since 1980 plus other essays first printed in *The Virginia Magazine of History and Biography, Chesapeake Bay Magazine, The Iron Worker,* and *Early American Life.*

After decades of pollution and defacement, the James shows signs of regaining its natural beauty. Many individuals, governmental agencies, and other organizations have devoted themselves to this effort, including:

Anheuser-Busch Corporation, Williamsburg
Association for the Preservation of Virginia Antiquities, Richmond
Chesapeake Bay Foundation, Baltimore
Chippokes Foundation, Surry County
Colonial National Historical Park, Jamestown–Williamsburg–Yorktown
Dominion Resources, Richmond
Ethyl Corporation, Richmond
Flowerdieu Hundred, Prince George County
Historic Richmond Foundation, Richmond
Historic Scottsville, Scottsville
James River Corporation, Richmond
Jamestown-Yorktown Foundation, Jamestown
Lower James River Association, Richmond
Mariners Museum, Newport News
Newport News Shipbuilding, Newport News
Reynolds Metals Company, Richmond
Richmond Renaissance Incorporated, Richmond
United States Army Corps of Engineers, Norfolk
Virginia Canals and Navigations Society, Richmond
Virginia Department of Transportation, Richmond
Virginia Institute of Marine Science, Gloucester Point

I hope these pages may help readers appreciate the James and its wealth of history and beauty.

Parke Rouse, Jr.

Sailboats were America's chief links from Jamestown's day to the Civil War.
When Fort Monroe was sketched at the outset of the Civil War, steamers were few.

I

The Age
of Sail

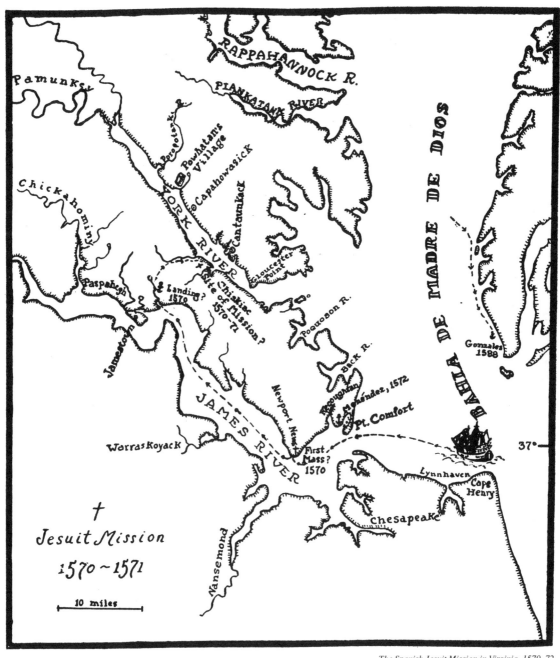

The Spanish Jesuit Mission in Virginia, 1570–72
U.N.C. Press

Jesuit missionaries settled on the James in 1570 and crossed the Peninsula to start a mission on the York.

Spanish ships visited Virginia in 1570 and brought a short-lived Jesuit mission.

1. *When the Spaniards Came to Virginia*

IT'S a little-known fact that Spanish settlers came to Virginia well before the first English adventurers arrived in 1607. Not only that, but the site they chose as their settlement in 1525 may have been the same James River peninsula which the British were to choose 81 years later.

Spain made two known attempts to settle Virginia. The first was led from Santo Domingo in 1525 by Lucas Vasquez de Ayllon, who had been authorized by King Carlos I of Spain to settle the North American mainland. From Vasquez de Ayllon's descriptions, he must have settled on the peninsula which the English later named Jamestown. The Spaniards called it "Guandape," a name the Virginia Indians were still using in 1607.

What happened to the Spanish? Vasquez de Ayllon died of fever, and his successors finally gave up and sailed back to Santo Domingo. Only in 1565 did the Spanish finally gain a foothold in Florida by settling at St. Augustine—now the oldest continuous European settlement in what is now the United States.

Another Spanish settlement was attempted in Virginia in 1570. This time it was a small Jesuit missionary expedition, sent by Spain's governor of Florida, Captain Pedro Menendez de Aviles in hopes of Christianizing the Indians.

The story of the Jesuit settlement called "Ajacan" was published in 1953 by the Virginia Historical Society in a book titled *The Spanish Jesuit Mission in Virginia, 1570–1572*. It was written by two Jesuit scholars, Fathers Clifford Lewis and Albert Loomie, with an introduction by Earl Gregg Swem, librarian of the College of William and Mary and an ardent student of Virginia history.

The book recounts the sad story of eight Jesuit missionaries and a Spanish boy, Alonso, who debarked near the mouth of College Creek, two miles below Jamestown. They found the red men suffering from prolonged drought and famine, but the Spanish leader, Father Juan Baptista de Segura, decided to land anyway. The Spanish ship returned to Florida, leaving the missionaries on their own.

The Jesuits were aided at first by an Indian, Don Luis, whom they had brought with them as an interpreter. However, Don Luis soon deserted them and joined the natives. The Jesuits, in search of a place to build their mission, crossed the Peninsula near the present Williamsburg and settled on the York near Queen's Creek and the

Algonquin warriors were depicted by early artist John White, much as John Smith later knew them.

Indian village of Kiskiack. There the Indians murdered them, with the help of the treacherous Don Luis.

When Governor Menendez sent ships from St. Augustine back to Virginia to see how the mission fared, the Spaniards found Indian braves dressed in the dead priests' cassocks. At last they rescued the boy Alonso, the only survivor, and took him back to St. Augustine.

Such early English historians as Richard Hakluyt left fragmentary records of several Spanish and British voyages in the Chesapeake Bay, but they somehow missed the Jesuits' effort to settle the Virginia area. Several European and American scholars made further studies in the nineteenth century. The fullest report yet is the Loomie and Lewis book. So detailed is it that Dr. Swem felt he could even identify the areas traveled by the Spaniards.

The authors searched the Spanish archives in Madrid to discover early Spanish maps of the Chesapeake and accounts written by explorers. Particularly relevant are the accounts of Fathers Segura and Luis de Quiros, who wrote home to their Jesuit superiors in Florida and in Spain.

One priest was impressed by the numerous Indians of the Peninsula. "There are more people here than in any of the other lands I have seen so far along the coast explored," wrote Father Juan Rogel from Virginia to Florida. "It seemed to me that the natives are more settled than in other regions I have been, and I am confident that should Spaniards settle here, (provided they would frighten the natives that threaten harm), we could preach the Holy Gospel more easily than elsewhere."

Spain still hoped to claim the Chesapeake region as late as 1607, when the London Company's settlers planted the English flag here. However, King Philip III of Spain was not sufficiently impressed with Virginia's prospects for gold to risk an attack on Jamestown. Besides, the British had so badly defeated the Spanish Armada in 1588 that Spain was reluctant to tackle the British again.

Thus it was that the Chesapeake region was settled as Virginia instead of as Ajacan. Had the Indians not killed the Jesuit settlers of 1570, America north of Mexico might have developed as a Spanish civilization instead of an English- and French-speaking one. The world would have been very different.

Engraving by DeBry from John White watercolor

James River Indians used log canoes to pursue fish, which were abundant in colonial times.

*The chief reminder of the Jamestown settlement is the 1639 church tower.
The church is reconstructed.*

2. *The First Englishmen at Jamestown*

EVEN by the standards of their time the *Susan Constant, Godspeed,* and *Discovery* were not large ships. To bring the three of them together across the Atlantic in winter was a difficult feat in 1607, as it would be today.

Yet by their crushing defeat of the Spanish Armada, English sailors had shown themselves to be the masters of any sea-going men in Europe. Now they were sailing to follow up their Spanish victory with a claim to North American lands, in defiance of the decree of Pope Alexander VI, who in 1493 had divided the New World between the Roman Catholic monarchs of Spain and Portugal.

It was far from England's first attempt. Sir Walter Raleigh tried to settle a colony in 1584 on the North Carolina coast, then part of the unexplored lands between latitudes 34 and 45 degrees North which Raleigh had designated as "Virginia" to honor the "virgin Queen" Elizabeth. The effort met failure, and Raleigh was now a prisoner in the Tower of London, charged with intriguing with Spain. The English flag had reached North America again when English fishermen spent several summers along the Maine coast, but no permanent settlement had come of that.

The Virginia Company chose winter for its voyage in order to put the settlers ashore in Virginia at planting time. From several dozen previous English voyages to North America, they knew the outward passage would take from four to five months, using the preferred South Atlantic crossing. (The return would be quicker because of favorable winds.)

Into the hold of the *Susan Constant,* the 100-ton flagship of the force, the crew stowed oats, barley, and wheat (they called it "corn") for seed. Tools and provisions were part of the cargo, together with beer and wine and the makings of the watery gruel which was to feed crew and passengers on the long voyage out.

It is one of the ironies of history that Raleigh, in the Tower, could not see the history-making ships as they sailed on the outbound tide for the English Channel and the open sea. A bend in the Thames hid them from his view, but no doubt he heard the news from his jailers. To Raleigh, who first dreamed of "a new English nation" in North America, this voyage was to be a vindication.

Records of the passage are sketchy. The fullest account was written by George Percy, a younger son of the Duke of Northumberland, who remained at Jamestown until 1612. After a

9

slow voyage down the Thames, past Queen Elizabeth's erstwhile palace at Greenwich, they finally reached the English channel and anchored in the Downs.

Wrote Percy: "the winds continued contrarie so long that we were forced to stay there some time, where we suffered great stormes, but by the skilfulnesse of the Captaine we suffered no great losse or danger." In these agonizing weeks, when diminishing supplies threatened to end the voyage, Chaplain Robert Hunt inspired his shipmates by refusing to turn back in spite of deathly seasickness.

After six weeks the weather improved, and Captain Newport in the *Susan Constant* gave signal to Captains Bartholomew Gosnold in the *Godspeed* and John Ratcliffe in the *Discovery* to set sail southward, along the coasts of France and Spain. It was a monotonous voyage. One night the crewmen on watch (passengers stayed below for fear of rheumy night air) saw a falling star, followed by a storm. A day or so later the ships put in at the Canary Islands to fill their water casks.

Then, just below the Tropic of Cancer, Newport changed course and the ships veered from the African coast and headed westward across the Atlantic. On March 23, more than three months out of London, they reached Martinique. The first half of the voyage was safely past.

How could the three sailing ships of different size and speed have kept together on so long an ocean voyage? The question remains unresolved to this day. No accounts left by the crew or passengers reveal the technique. Perhaps the 100-ton *Susan Constant* towed the 20-ton *Discovery* and thus enabled the 40-ton *Godspeed* to keep pace. It is known, however, that in the sixteenth-century English navy an admiral's ship carried a cresset astern in which lightwood was burned at night to guide accompanying vessels. Perhaps Newport used some such device with his merchant ships, though it only could have been of slight help. Whatever the case, the crews showed superb seamanship in

crossing relatively uncharted waters together and with no loss of life.

In rapid sequence Newport's force put in at Dominica, Guadeloupe, Nevis, Mona, and Monito. To walk on solid earth was a welcome change indeed for the 105 passengers, who had spent three months in dark holds. At Dominica natives brought them pineapples, potatoes, bananas, tobacco, and leather in return for knives, hatchets, beads, and copper jewelry. Two days later they sighted the small island of Marie Galante, and the next day they visited Guadeloupe and were fascinated by a hot spring which cooked pork in half an hour.

Newport sailed his ships past the then uninhabited islands of Montserrat and St. Kitts and landed at Nevis, where passengers and part of the crew camped six days. Then back to sea on April 4, past the islands of St. Eustatius and Saba and another which Percy called the "Ile of Virgines," probably St. John or St. Thomas.

On past Vieques and Puerto Rico they sailed to tiny Mona, where occurred the death of Edward Brooke, the first of the settlers to lose his life in the enterprise. Percy recorded that after a journey over the island's terrain, Brooke's "fat melted within him by the great heate and drought of the Country." A small party of the settlers went by small boat from Mona to the nearby island of Monito and brought back to their ship two hogsheads full of wildfowl and eggs.

Thus provisioned and refreshed, the settlers turned north and began the final crucial leg of their journey. A spring squall hit them, and the crew lowered sail to avert grounding, believing themselves near Virginia. Their hopes were premature, however, for five days must pass before they would see its headlands. "The six and twentieth day of Aprill," wrote Percy, "about foure a 'clocke in the morning, wee descried the Land of Virginia; the same day wee entred the Bay of Chesupioc directly. . . ." The day was Sunday, April 26, 1607.

As the sun rose over the dark waters, sailors could make out the low, pine-forested shore of

Virginia, which poet Michael Drayton had ambitiously proclaimed "earth's only paradise." Landing on a promontory, they cautiously began to explore the rim of Chesapeake Bay. Percy was entranced with "faire medowes and goodly tall trees with such Fresh-waters running

Helmet found near Jamestown survives the 1607 settlement

through the woods, as I was almost ravished at the first sight thereof." But pleasure turned to pain when Indians suddenly emerged and drove the exploring party back aboard ship, wounding settler Gabriel Archer and sailor Mathew Morton. Such was the settlers' ominous welcome to Virginia.

During the 10 weeks under sail, Newport had been the unquestioned master of the ships, the 39 seamen, and the settlers, now reduced to 104 by Brooke's death. However, that evening at Cape Henry the sealed box of instructions from the Virginia Company was opened and Newport was forced to share his primacy with Gosnold and Ratcliffe, together with Edward Maria Wingfield, John Martin, George Kendall, and the most controversial hero in all American legend, Captain John Smith. No longer could Newport reign supreme; hereafter he must abide by the wishes of the quarrelsome Council.

Thus in Virginia's April of redbud and dogwood, the argonauts reached their goal. So rich and numerous were Virginia's charms that they were filled with desire to hasten ashore and find the gold and jewels which must abound in so favored a country.

Exploring parties spent the next two days reconnoitering Virginia Beach, Lynnhaven Inlet, and Point Comfort. On Wednesday, April 29, they erected a cross and gave thanks to God on the land where they stood, naming it Cape Henry in honor of one of the sons of King James.

They hoisted sail and headed up the James, following it instead of Chesapeake Bay, in anticipation of finding the long hoped for westward passage through North America to the Pacific. They were also obeying instructions from His Majesty's Council for Virginia to settle 30 or 40 miles upriver from the Atlantic so that coast watchers, later stationed at Point Comfort, could warn the colony by runner if Spanish marauders approached.

To explore the shoals of the James, too shallow for the ships, the settlers used a shallop or rowboat, brought from England in sections and assembled at Cape Henry. At each protected place until they reached the confluence of the Appomattox, now Hopewell, the ships paused while the shallop nosed ashore, seeking a deep-water landing. Then, dissatisfied, they went back downriver and examined a point near the present Williamsburg, which Gabriel Archer so championed they named it "Archer's Hope." They rejected it because supply ships "could not ride neere the shoare," but next day found a peninsula two miles away with water so deep their vessels could approach its bank.

Mooring the weary ships to trees overhanging the river, the settlers prepared to go ashore. The long voyage was over. On May 13, 1607, the site for Jamestown was found.

Next day the settlers left the ships and began to build the triangular palisade which was to enclose England's first permanent settlement overseas. While the Council elected Wingfield president, others cleared a site and cut clapboard as cargo for the ship's return voyage. In a few days English wheat, oats, and barley were germinating in small clearings around the camp.

A feeling of optimism surged through the settlement. Captain Newport felt that the "new English nation overseas" also had begun to germinate, and he ordered his crews back to their ships and set sail for England, leaving the *Discovery* for the colonists' use in their vain search for a westward passage to the Pacific.

Although the *Susan Constant* and *Godspeed* were to return to the New World as supply ships, they were never again to make so historic a voyage as that to Virginia in 1607. As the British political scientist Sir James Bryce declared, "The landing at Jamestown was one of the great events in the history of the world —an event to be compared for its momentous consequences with the overthrow of the Persian empire by Alexander; with the destruction of Carthage by Rome; with the conquest of Gaul by Clovis; with the taking of Constantinople by the Turks—one might almost say with the discovery of America by Columbus. . . ."

The James River would long remain England's main highway into Virginia.

The James River appeared as the westernmost estuary of Chesapeake Bay in John Smith's map of Virginia, which put north to the right.

3. *Meet Christopher Newport*

NOBODY knows precisely how the James River entrance got the name Newport News Point (called Newport's News until the 1900s). Annie Jester wrote in her Newport News history in 1961, "Presumably, the name was given to the location as the source of the first news of Captain Newport's several arrivals in Virginia. He made four voyages to the newly established colony subsequent to that in 1607, kept the struggling settlement supplied, landed new colonists, and equally important, brought the news, including official communications from England. For four difficult years he supplied that vital link with the homeland that kept the colony alive."

In Allan Jones's 1957 Newport News library mural the one-armed captain is shown standing on Newport News Point while his crewmen drink from a spring, noted by early mariners, in the city's present dockside area. He made his last Jamestown voyage in 1611, bringing over Sir Thomas Dale to be governor. The following year he entered service for England's famous East India Company. He died on a voyage in 1617.

Christopher Newport was born in the reign of England's Queen Elizabeth I, when the island nation was exploring the world and grabbing what land it could. Those were the years of captains like Drake, Hawkins, Frobisher, and other piratical explorers trying to excel the Spanish, Portuguese, Dutch, and French.

Born in the poor Limehouse section of London, Newport went to sea as a cabin boy. On an early voyage to Brazil he was cast away from his ship with two other discontented sailors. After several years he was carried back to England on a ship by the Earl of Cumberland.

He went back to sea as captain of a privateer, permitted under the then-current European law, to seek reprisal against vessels of enemy powers. Captured enemy vessels became prizes whose contents were sold for benefit of the monarch, the captain, and the crew. Captured seamen were treated as prisoners. Many became galley slaves.

Newport sailed as captain of a privateer under Sir Francis Drake in 1587, attacking Spanish ships in Cadiz awaiting the Spanish Armada's expedition to England. In "singeing the beard of the King of Spain," Drake sank or took more than 30 Spanish vessels. It hastened the end of Spanish sea power.

Christopher Newport in 1607 halted his ships at Newport News Point to drink from a spring.

In his next privateering venture, to the West Indies to capture Spanish silver trade vessels, Newport lost his right arm. It didn't stop him. He spent the next 13 years plundering Spanish ships in the Caribbean. His biggest prize was the Spanish carrack *Madre di Dios* in 1592, loaded with spices, gems, silks, and other goods valued at a half-million pounds.

When the *Madre di Dios* first appeared on the horizon, Newport called his crew on deck and told them, "Masters, now the time is come that either we must end our days or take the said carrack." Then he "wished all the company to stand to their charge like men, and if any displeasure were amongst any of them, to forget or forgive one another."

After toasting healths, the crew attacked the Spanish ship and captured her.

When the Virginia Company of London sought a seaman to get its settlers to Virginia, it found that Newport knew the New World better than most others. He had what one historian called "an unrivalled experience of the Atlantic crossing by the Canaries, of West Indies waters, and watering places, and of the Florida Channel and the homeward passage by Newfoundland or by Bermuda and the Azores." As a fellow captain wrote, he was "a mariner well practised for the western parts of America."

In his four years as Virginia's chief supplier, Newport had only one serious misadventure. In 1609 several of his vessels were lost, and his *Sea Venture* was wrecked at Bermuda. But he and his shipwrecked crew built smaller ships and completed the voyage to Jamestown.

In his last trips to the Orient, Captain Newport had to go ashore and bargain with natives for silks, porcelains, and other oriental products sought by the East India Company. So well did he bargain that the company gave him a bonus of 50 gold coins. After he died in Java, the Virginia Company gave his widow 3,500 acres of land in Virginia.

In her history of Newport News, Mrs. Jester points out that Newport News Point became an early Jamestown coast-watcher's site. This was in response to the Virginia Company's instruction of 1606. They said in part:

> When you have made choice of the river on which you mean to settle . . . and to the end that you be not surprised as the French were in Florida by [Menendez, the Spanish leader] . . . you shall do well to make this double provision. First, erect a little store at the mouth of the river that may lodge some ten men, with whom you shall be in sight, they may come with speed to give you warning. . . ."

Thus, Christopher Newport not only helped John Smith to settle Jamestown, but he apparently helped establish the first European settlers of Newport News. As Mrs. Jester noted, "The look-out point . . . marks the harbor of the greater city of Newport News. . . ."

Daily Press

At Jamestown Settlement over 300,000 view reconstructed ships annually, near the ferry docks.

Painting by Sidney King from Berkeley

After Berkeley was settled in 1619, sailing ships were built on its James River shoreline.

4. *The Settlement of Berkeley*

WELVE years after Jamestown and two years before New England's birth, an important Virginia settlement was made at Berkeley Hundred, 30 miles up the James.

The 38 pioneers who came ashore that December 4, 1619, had sailed from England aboard the *Margaret* under the leadership of Captain John Woodlief, who had come to Jamestown briefly in 1608.

"The Town and Hundred of Berkeley" had been conceived by four well-to-do English venturers who lived in England's West Country, near Bristol and Bath. They were John Smythe of Nibley (no kin to John Smith of Jamestown), Sir William Throckmorton, Richard Berkeley, for whom the company was named, and the Reverend George Thorpe, an Anglican clergyman.

When the *Margaret* sailed into Jamestown, Captain Woodlief received from Governor Sir George Yeardley a patent from the Virginia Company of London for 8,000 acres of highly desirable land fronting three miles along the James in the shire which had been designated as Charles City. The tract lay 80 miles from the Chesapeake Bay between Jamestown and the falls of the James, later to develop as Richmond. Many such villages were then developing along the James near Jamestown.

The first act of Woodlief and his settlers on the arrival of their ship was to kneel and give thanks for their safe deliverance. This was in compliance with their charter, which had directed that the day of their arrival and its anniversary "shall be yearly and perpetually kept holy as a day of thanksgiving to Almighty God."

This thanksgiving anniversary was observed at Berkeley each year until the Indian massacre along the James in 1622 interrupted it. A commemorative service is now held annually at Berkeley in November.

Like the Jamestown settlers, the Berkeley venturers cut tree trunks to erect a palisade against the Indians and the possible attack of Spanish colonists from Florida. Then, for years they cleared lands, planted tobacco, and created a farm village.

The colony expanded in 1622 with the arrival of two supply ships bearing 90 more settlers, including the wives and children of some of the earlier pioneers. The most important of the arrivals was the Reverend George Thorpe, one of the company's four stockholders, who came to take over leadership from Captain Woodlief.

Thorpe was a thoughtful and educated man, and he proved an energetic leader. He took great interest in a school or college in Virginia to educate settlers' sons and to Christianize the Indians. He also learned from the Indians to distill corn into whiskey, a predecessor of the bourbon which later became the favorite alcoholic beverage of early Virginians and other Southerners.

"We have found a way to make so good a drink of Indian corn," the cleric wrote, "as I protest I have divers times refused to drink good strong English beer and chosen to drink that."

By the time King James I in London in 1625 declared Virginia to be a crown colony, many of Berkeley's settlers were dead of disease or Indian attack, and its investors had sadly abandoned hope of profit. But the seed had been sown for the colony which would become Great Britain's largest, most populous, and most profitable in the New World.

Berkeley was a stepping stone towards that "new English nation" in North America which Sir Walter Raleigh envisioned as Great Britain's hope for the future.

Berkeley

Several smaller frame houses preceded Benjamin Harrison's eighteenth-century Berkeley mansion.

5. *When the Indians Wrote in Blood*

LOST towns are romantic, and Virginia is discovering many of them through the laborious efforts of archaeologists. One of the most exciting discoveries of recent years was the finding of Wolstenholm Town, a village on the James near Williamsburg that was wiped out in the Powhatan Indians' uprising of 1622.

Wolstenholm was a primitive, palisaded settlement near the present Carter's Grove mansion in James City County. It was accidentally discovered in 1970 by an archaeological team under Ivor Noël Hume from Colonial Williamsburg, that was seeking remains of early Carter's Grove outbuildings. What they found were the long-lost skeletons of men, women, and children who died cruelly in the massacre.

Since discovery, Wolstenholm Town has become internationally known. It was the subject of an article by Noël Hume in the *National Geographic* magazine and of a book by him, *Martin's Hundred*, published by Alfred Knopf in 1982. It has also been the subject of highly popular television programs.

Wolstenholm Town lay within an English land grant in James City County called Martin's Hundred. Most of the land was later absorbed in the Burwell family's plantation, called Carter's Grove.

A Virginia highway marker at the Route 60 entrance to Carter's Grove reads:

Martin's Hundred: On both sides of this road and extending west was the plantation known as Martin's Hundred, originally of 80,000 acres. Settled in 1619, this hundred sent delegates to the first legislative assembly in America, 1619. In the Indian massacre of 1622, 78 persons were slain here.

Noël Hume and his diggers stumbled across skeletons of Wolstenholm residents lying as they fell when attacked by the Indians long ago. In many cases their skulls had been pierced by tomahawks and their scalps removed.

Visitors to Carter's Grove may see the Wolstenholm site on a brief walk from the plantation house towards the James River. The palisade and houses built by the settlers have rotted away, but drawings, photographs, and Carter's Grove guides point out the salient points of the findings.

Wolstenholm was typical in its brief and tragic history of most of the dozen or so settle-

Archeologist Ivor Noël Hume recovers fragments of Wolstenholm Town from Carter's Grove site.

ments then established along the James. We know that 11 of these "particular plantations" elected delegates to the first assembly at Jamestown in 1619. They included Argall's Gift, where the suburb of Williamsburg called First Colony now stands; Flowerdew Hundred in Prince George County, which is being excavated and exhibited; Lawne's plantation in a wilderness area on the river shore in Isle of Wight County; and Martin's Brandon in Prince George, where Brandon plantation now stands.

Another "particular plantation" was Berkeley, in Charles City County. A little-known set-tlement area was Archer's Hope, on the James, at the mouth of College Creek. Historian Charles E. Hatch, Jr., learned that it was once a small seaport with several structures, now long gone.

How many more of Virginia's lost towns will be found in future years? As suburbs spread, no doubt others await discovery. However, I doubt if any has a more dramatic story to tell than Ivor Noël Hume, his wife Audrey, and their fellow diggers have turned up at Martin's Hundred. They've shown us the human drama that lies in our midst on the shores of our own James River.

One third of Virginia's 1,200 James River settlers died in the Powhatan Indians' 1622 insurrection.

English settlers at Wolstenholm Town were among those killed in the massacre.

6. *From the James River to England*

FTER Virginia was settled, Englishmen immediately became curious about what grew there. A few daring English explorers and naturalists even crossed the ocean and brought back animal and plant specimens to the British Isles to be admired and identified.

One of the most appealing of the voyaging naturalists was John Tradescant the Younger. (The name is pronounced Tra-DES-cant.) He was a royal gardener to England's Kings Charles I and II, and he braved the Atlantic at least three times.

Now John Tradescant and his father—who was also a gardener to the king—have been honored by the formation of a Tradescant research group and an international horticultural museum at St. Mary's Church in Lambeth, in London. Plant and animal exhibits in this Tradescant Gardeners Museum include some that John Tradescant the Younger brought back.

Current interest in the little-known Tradescants began in 1964, when naturalist Mea Allen published in London the first study of their lives. Titled *The Tradescants: Their Plants, Gardens, and Museum, 1570–1662*, it helps to explain how Europeans came to know such

New World oddities as the opossum, raccoon, and such plants as the climber Englishmen called the Virginia creeper.

It is believed by some that the younger Tradescant is responsible for the presence in England for nearly 400 years of "Powhatan's mantle," a deerhide hanging decorated with small shells. It is one of the many early Virginia items Tradescant contributed to what in 1683 became the Ashmolean Museum at Oxford University.

Because their lives spanned 92 eventful years of Virginian and English history, the Tradescants have become an important international cultural link. The Tradescants gained their odd name in medieval England, when they "treaded" or tanned skins, or hides.

The elder John was born in London in 1570 and developed gardens which still survive at Hatfield House, the seat near London of the Cecil family. To landscape the gardens, Tradescant journeyed over Europe and collected exotic species of plants and trees to bring to England.

The self-taught naturalist also collected stuffed animals, natural oddities, and other "rarities," as he called them, to exhibit at his house and garden in the South Lambeth part of London. Eventually he opened his house to the public as a "Closett of Rarities"—the first public museum in the British Isles.

The elder Tradescant was a friend of Captain John Smith, of the Jamestown settlement. When Smith returned from his last North American expedition and died in England, he left Tradescant senior several books from his sea chest. It is thought that these inspired John Tradescant junior—born in 1608—to come to Virginia and see it for himself.

Little is known of the three trips young John made to Virginia, except the dates. However, Sir Joseph Williamson, the keeper of King Charles II's library at Whitehall, wrote that "In 1637 John Tradescant was in the colony, to gather all rarities of flowers, plants, shells, etc."

After Tradescant senior died, the younger returned to Virginia twice—in 1642 and again in 1654. In October of 1642 he was granted headrights for 650 acres of land on the north side of the Charles River, now the York. They were located on "Payanketank" or Piankitank Creek in what is now Gloucester County. The grant acknowledged that Tradescant had brought 13 new settlers to Virginia, for each of whom he received 50 acres.

Scholars believe the naturalist was encouraged to visit Virginia and was hosted here by Edward Digges, a planter who lived near the present Yorktown. Digges was the son of Sir Dudley Digges of Kent, England, with whom Tradescant senior had voyaged to Russia. Edward Digges was helpful in recording facts about New World animals and plants. His "sweet-scented" tobacco, which he developed in early Virginia and sent to England, brought the highest prices of any Virginia leaf.

Like a few other amateur naturalists of the time, the Tradescants sought to classify plants and animals scientifically. In this they anticipated the binomial method introduced by the Swedish botanist, Karl Linnaeus, in his *Systema naturae* in 1735. Wrote their biographer, Mea Allen: "The Tradescants in their work, which was truly scientific, were far ahead of

scientists in other fields, for those were still in their crude beginnings."

The Tradescant museum at "The Ark," in London's section called Lambeth, grew to contain many curiosities to attract visitors. One observer wrote of John junior, "Of flowers he has a good choice; and his Virginia and other

Author's collection

John Tradescant the Younger made three or four voyages to Virginia to collect curiosities.

birds in a great variety, with his glass hive, add much to the pleasure of his garden." An adventurer named Peter Munday, who had sailed for England's East India Company and was about to depart for China, wrote thus about his visit:

I was invited by Mr. Thomas Barlow (whoe went into India with my Lord of Denbigh and returned with us on the *Mary*) to view some rarities at John Tredescans, soe went with him and one friend more, there to spend the whole day in peruseings and that superficially, such as hee had gathered together. . . . Moreover, a little garden with divers outlandish herbes and flowers, whereof some that I had not seene elsewhere but in India, being supplyed by Noblemen, Gentlemen, Sea Commanders, etts . . . .

Author's collection

John Tradescant the Elder began a London museum later given to Oxford as the Ashmolean Museum.

One of the plants in the Tradescant garden was "Silke Grasse that groweth" in Virginia. We know it today as spiderwort, or flower-of-a-day. In England it came to be known as "Tradescant his Spiderwort" and was catalogued later by Linnaeus as Tradescantia virginiana. It is currently used by botanists in experiments to determine factors in plant heredity.

Some of the exotic plants catalogued by the Tradescants in their Lambeth museum were Virginian cranesbill, persimmon, New England strawberry, Virginia creeper, Virginian yucca, Virginian nettle tree or hackberry, Virginian mulberry, Virginian arsmart, tulip tree, Virgini-

an evergreen thorn, Virginian crowfoot, Virginian bladdernut, riverbank grape, and Virginian fox grape.

Before he died, John Tradescant junior made a catalogue of his "rarities" in 1656, published as *Musaeum Tradescantianum.* Among his "Principall Benefactors," he lists many early patrons or explorers of Virginia including Sir Thomas Smythe, onetime head of the Virginia Company; Sir Dudley Digges; and 11 ship's captains. Some benefactors reflect the esteem the Tradescants enjoyed as men of science. These include King Charles I and his queen; George Villiers, Duke of Buckingham; William Laud, Archbishop of Canterbury; two successive Earls of Salisbury; and Viscount Falkland, for whom the Falkland Islands were named.

The Tradescants' lives reveal that Englishmen were not only concerned to add wealth but also to learn more about the brave new world of Virginia and the other British colonies abroad.

In London today, the visitor to the Tradescants' Gardeners Museum at Lambeth will

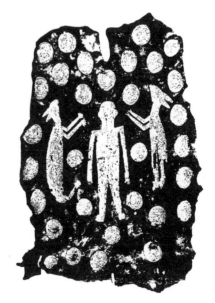

Author's collection

An early Virginia deerskin mantle in Oxford's museum was probably found by Tradescant Jr.

encounter the tombstone in St. Mary's Churchyard of three generations of John Tradescants
—the last one the son of John junior, who died
as a boy. The handsome seventeenth-century
memorial bears these words:

Know, stranger, ere thou pass, beneath this
   stone,
Lye John Tradescant, grandsire, father, son,
The last dy'd in his spring, the other two
Liv'd till they had travell'd Orb and Nature
   through,
As by their choice Collections may appear,
Of what is rare, in land, in sea, in air:
Whilst they (as Homer's Iliad in a nut)

A world of wonders in one closet shut,
These famous Antiquarians that had been
Both Gardiners to the Rose and Lily Queen,
Transplanted now themselves, sleep here:
   and when
Angels shall with their trumpets waken men,
And fire shall purge the world, these three
   shall rise
And change this garden then for Paradise.

Like Charles Darwin and his voyage on the
Beagle more than a century later, the Tradescants helped us know our universe. Their
"world of wonders" has become ours.

The James River was Virginia's highway in colonial times,
when British ships hauled tobacco to Europe.

7. *Dividing the James by Counties*

FOR its first 170 years colonial Virginia modeled itself after England. That's why the General Assembly, meeting at Jamestown in 1634, divided the colony into eight shires, like the counties of Mother England. We started in 1607 as a farm society and we stayed so well into this century.

Virginia's first eight counties were the beginning of county government in North America. Counties are still the principle unit of local life in 49 of the 50 states, and they still contain more people than America's cities, though cities are now growing faster.

The tiny population of those original counties is hard to believe. When a census was made in the colony in 1625 and sent to England, James City had only 465 English settlers and 10 blacks. (Indians weren't included in the count.) Of the 465 settlers, 204 were free men and women, 226 were indentured servants, and 35 were children.

Elizabeth City in 1625 was the second most populous community of English Virginia. It had 435 English people plus six blacks and two domesticated Indians. Of its settlers, 235 were free men and women, 157 were indentured servants, and 43 were children.

Charles City was the third most populous area in 1625, with 229 English settlers and seven blacks. Of its settlers, 119 were free men and women, 84 were indentured, and 26 were children.

All of those original counties except Accomack lay close to Jamestown. They were James City (including Jamestown and later Williamsburg), Charles City, Henrico, Warwick, Elizabeth City, York, and Warrosquoyoake, whose harsh Indian name was changed to Isle of Wight.

Today six of those eight counties survive. Warwick became a city in 1952 and merged with Newport News six years later. Elizabeth City merged with Hampton in 1952. The other six have lost much of their original acreage to other counties or cities, but they're still going.

County government didn't change much in Virginia from 1634 until the Model T began to revolutionize life in the early 1900s. But automobiles soon changed everything. They reduced travel time between counties, made it possible for men to commute to work, and led to consolidated schools, churches, and shopping centers. Most important, they erased the insular social effect of waterways, which had once made each Virginia peninsula a law unto itself.

"Virginia society was much like early England's," the Rev. Clayton Torrence, director of the Virginia Historical Society, used to say. "Each county had its own ruling families. The links between them gradually built up the planter dynasties that led Virginia and the nation in the Revolution."

If you go to a rural Virginia courthouse today like Charles City or New Kent, you can judge what early counties were like. The courtroom is the focal center of the county, where the county board, then called justices of the peace, met on specified "court days" each month to transact county business. Originally justices of the peace also sat as judges, in addition to other duties, but as Virginia grew bigger, men trained in the law were named as judges to hold court.

Those justices of the peace—nearly all farm-ers—made the local laws and decisions that our county boards of supervisors do now, in addition to their judicial duties. They oversaw roads, bridges, ferries, and taverns, and they directed a handful of county officers: a sheriff (who roughly corresponded to our county manager), a clerk of courts, a jailer, and a county lieutenant (pronounced "leftenant"), who commanded the militia.

Early Tidewater and Piedmont courthouses contained a courtroom where county board meetings were also held and business transacted, a clerk's office, a sheriff's office, and a jail. Today you can see those functions well in old courthouses like New Kent, Charles City, and Hanover.

The casual style of early government is surprising. Taverns often served as part time courthouses. Before a county built its court-

Colonial National Historical Park

At Jamestown and elsewhere on the James, creeks harbored boats and home sites

house, court was sometimes held in a private house or even outdoors. The clerk of court often kept his county records in his own house, lacking a courthouse. (Thomas Ludwell, who was secretary of the Virginia colony at Jamestown, kept his records for a while at his plantation, Richneck, on College Creek near Williamsburg.)

Writers on early Virginia life, like Thomas Nelson Page, have described the attractions of monthly "court days" in Virginia's county seats. Everybody who could make it came to the

Hill Carter

At Shirley, the James divides to encircle Eppes Island, a haven for wildlife.

courthouse for there you saw your friends. Land and goods were sold, livestock was traded, horse races were run, gamecocks were fought, and inside the courthouse the county board wrangled over county business. "Court days" were like the larger "public times," held when the Assembly met at Jamestown and later at Williamsburg.

We didn't have statewide public schools till 1872 in Virginia, but a few colonial ministers also taught schools. These Anglican ministers were part of the county government. They and their parish vestries were a sort of county welfare department, responsible for orphans, the insane, paupers, and derelicts.

A lot of Virginia statesmen got their start on parish vestries. And men like Patrick Henry and George Washington were trained in the militia.

Taverns grew up close to courthouses to house county officers and lawyers when court was in session. Sykes's Inn at Smithfield is typical of them, having been built next door to the first brick Isle of Wight courthouse on Smithfield's Main Street about 1749. The Isle of Wight government was later moved about 10 miles south of Smithfield, near Windsor, to be closer to more people.

Since our first eight counties began in 1634, 158 others have been created by the General Assembly. Ninety-six of the total of 166 are still in existence in Virginia, while 61 survive as parts of West Virginia and Kentucky. Since the 1950s Virginia has been slowly losing counties, as urban counties like Elizabeth City, Warwick,

Princess Anne, and Arlington have become cities. My guess is that more will convert as their population grows, particularly in our eastern corridor from Norfolk through northern Virginia.

Counties vary as widely in personality as people do. In Tidewater, most go back to colonial days and are named for English shires, monarchs, or noblemen. (King and Queen, Surry, Essex.) A few, like Accomack and Powhatan, bear Indian names. Further west, they're apt to honor Revolutionary figures or early governors, like Washington, Lee, or Henry.

Courthouse architecture varies widely, too. Especially appealing are a few surviving eighteenth-century brick structures with Italianate arches in Hanover, Charles City, and in the original Isle of Wight courthouse at Smithfield. In the Piedmont and the Shenandoah Valley, courthouses are neo-classical temples with white columns. It's safe to say that most Virginia courthouses have a monument in the yard or on a wall to Confederate soldiers who died in the Civil War.

Important lore is preserved in many old courthouses. You'll find portraits of judges, tablets honoring early citizens, and even flags of the Confederacy. County judges are still the reigning squires of rural counties.

Despite the bright lights of the city, many people prefer rural life. And so long as they do, counties will serve them. From Accomack westward to Cumberland Gap, they've helped make Virginia a pleasant place to live.

8. *Plants from the New World*

ONE of the better known early tycoons of Williamsburg was Colonel John Custis, an eccentric Eastern Shore planter who built a fine house about 1715 on Francis Street and developed the most beautiful garden in town.

Custis is known as the father-in-law of Martha Dandridge, who later became Martha Washington, but the old boy is interesting in his own right.

Custis's transatlantic exchange of flowers and shrubs with Peter Collinson, an English naturalist, went on from the 1730s until 1746— three years before Custis died and left one of the largest fortunes in Virginia. The Custis-Collinson exchanges introduced to Virginia plants from Europe hitherto unseen in America. In turn, Custis sent to England hitherto unfamiliar New World flora.

You can see some of the Custis and Collinson species when you visit the gardens of England's stately homes today.

Letters written by the Virginia planter and the English botanist to accompany their plant shipments were collected by Earl Gregg Swem of William and Mary. He published them in 1957 in a book entitled *Brothers of the Spade*,

and thereby spurred interest in Custis and other naturalists in Virginia before Thomas Jefferson. These included John Clayton of Gloucester, Dr. John Mitchell of Urbanna, John Randolph, "the Tory," of Williamsburg, and William Byrd of Westover.

Custis and Collinson were very different men, despite their love for nature. Collinson was a Quaker from Middlesex, England, who had inherited with a brother a drygoods and haberdashery business that traded with the British colonies. In his colonial dealings Collinson had correspondents send him plants, seeds, and bulbs. He gave many to form Sir Hans Sloane's natural history collection, now a part of the British Museum.

Collinson explained, "In the very early part of my life, I had a love for gardening. This with my years, my public station in business brought me acquainted with persons that were natives of Carolina, Virginia, Maryland, Pennsylvania and New England. My love for new and rare plants put me often in soliciting their acquaintance for seeds or plants from new countries."

Collinson's chief American connection was John Bartram, a self-taught Quaker botanist in

Many Virginia plants and animals, unknown in England, were sent back by early settlers.

Chester, Pennsylvania. Bartram occasionally traveled to collect American specimens for Collinson. Several wealthy Englishmen financially supported the project.

Custis, a powerful dynasty builder and member of the Virginia Council, traveled from Williamsburg often to his nearby plantations. These included Arlington on the Eastern Shore, where he was born; Queen's Creek in York County, now part of the Naval Weapons Station; White House in New Kent; and another in King William County. But he stayed mostly at "Six Chimneys," his house in Williamsburg, and at his 3,330-acre Queen's Creek plantation between Williamsburg and Yorktown. He often sent plants from these to Collinson.

In his book on Collinson and Custis, Swem printed more than 50 letters or fragments, about half from each man. They were sent via captains of ships sailing the England-Virginia route. Often the sender cited the captain's name. Plants and seeds usually went with each letter, impelling the sender to pay the captain to water the plants en route. Too often they weren't watered, however, arriving dead and provoking dismay and a request for more plants.

A Collinson letter of 1735 to "My Worthy Good Friend Mr. Custis" says, "Mr. [Mark] Catesby tells mee there is a very pretty plant that he calls a sorrell Tree that grows between Williamsburgh & York. Some seed will be acceptable." Custis in turn requested striped lilies, "being a great admirer of all the tribe striped gilded and variegated plants . . . I am told those things are out of fashion; but I do not

*Col. John Custis IV of Williamsburg
exchanged plants with English scholars.*

mind that I allways make my fancy my fashion."

With a shipment of persimmon seed, bayberry, white mulberry seed, and Angola peas, Custis explained, "Wee have them from Angola a place in guinea I am told when dryd as you do coco they make a rich chocolate." Custis wasn't much on spelling or punctuation.

Then Collinson asked for a walking stick made of sorrell wood. He also wanted chinquapins, swamp cypress cones, willow oak acorns, tulip tree cones, sweet gum burrs, and fringe tree seeds. In exchange he sent cowslips, peach stones, Italian evergreen oaks, damsons, bullice, sloes, pistachio nuts, and tuberoses.

When Custis died in 1749, he left his garden and all the rest to his son Daniel Parke Custis, who was himself to die soon after he married Martha. The widowed Martha and second husband George Washington sold the property. Today, the site is owned by Colonial Williamsburg and occupied by a grove of trees. The garden is gone, alas.

*Wild deer graze Jamestown Island's sightseers' road against
the backdrop of a historic marker.*

9. *"The Green Path" to Carolina*

MOST former Indian trails in eastern America are unmarked, but many are becoming better known. Virginia was criss-crossed in prehistoric times by forest paths used by aborigines in their migrations, trading, and wars. Many major highways today follow those primeval redmen's trails. Many important early trails developed around the James.

One of the most-used Virginia-North Carolina trails on early maps was called "Green's Path." It was named for the Reverend Roger Green of Nansemond County, who successfully petitioned the Virginia Assembly in 1653 for nearly 11,000 acres of land below the Roanoke River for the first 100 settlers who would claim them. The route Green's settlers followed south became "Green's Path."

From 1653 onward, more Virginians dared to go to Carolina and brave the Indians of the region. The route they used is much the same as U.S. Route 95. It goes south from Petersburg to Emporia, Roanoke Rapids, Rocky Mount, Wilson, Smithfield in North Carolina, and Fayetteville.

Early English maps identify Green's Path as a trading path once used by Indians roaming from Virginia to the Cherokee forests of western North Carolina. Apparently Roger Green's settlers followed an old Indian trail.

In North Carolina's Indian Wars of 1711, one Colonel Barnwell of South Carolina is described as leading South Carolina men up Green's Path to help North Carolina settlers fight the Tuscarora tribe.

Green's Path was also used in the seventeenth century by Virginia traders on their pack train trips to the Great Smoky Mountains to barter metal trinkets for the furs of beavers, martens, or other pelts in demand in England.

In 1676 Nathaniel Bacon and his men interrupted that Indian trade by burning the Indian town of Occonneechee, near the present Clarksville, Virginia. Bacon felt that Governor Sir William Berkeley, who had an interest in a British fur-importing firm, was in collusion with the Indians, so Bacon took the matter in his hands.

One result of the use of Green's Path by Virginians is the survival in the Carolina country along it of many early Virginia family names. Because colonial North Carolina had no deepwater port to dock English ships, most early North Carolina settlement was by families who

Much of Jamestown Island eroded after the capital's removal in 1699, but Ambler plantation (at right) remained.

had come to Jamestown, Yorktown, Hampton, Norfolk, and other Virginia ports and gone south on foot or by boat.

Anyone from Virginia who travels today through this Carolina region will note many Southside names: Bunkley, Brinkley, Crumpler, Pittman, Chapman, Battle, Darden, Morrisette, Norfleet, Underwood, Pretlow, Gwaltney, Cofer, Crocker, Durham, Duke, Bridger, Holland, and others. Many Carolinians in this area trace their families to Virginia.

I found many Southside Virginia names among a list of Johnston County, North Carolina, families in the U.S. Census of 1850. Johnston County centers around Smithfield, North Carolina. Among Southside names along the present Green's Path I find Pulley, Raper, Rhodes, Pace, Speight, Stallings, Whitehead, Whitley, Blalock, Bugg, Hinton, House, Jeffrey, Lashley, Parker, Strickland, Fulghum, Womble,

Jordan, and many others. State lines don't mean much.

Several early Southside trails led west to the Indians. One, called by Virginia fur traders the "Occonneechee Path," was similar to Green's Path. It also ran from the south shore of the James, opposite Jamestown, southwestward to the Roanoke River, where the Occonneechee Indians lived.

Explorers from Tidewater were impressed by the natives' commercial enterprise. They were described as collecting furs from as far south as the Gulf of Mexico. At Occonneechee Town, the Indians exchanged them to fur buyers from Jamestown and Bermuda Hundred, who sent their trains of pack horses over the Occonneechee Path each fall and spring, when travel was easiest.

Among early fur traders were William Byrd I, who lived at Shockoe's, now Richmond;

Thomas Batte and Peter Poythress, who lived in the present Surry or Prince George; Abraham Wood, who lived near Petersburg; and Edward Bland, who lived near Jordan's Point in Prince George. Bland, whose family had moved across the James from Kimages Creek in Charles City County, was said to have acquired Spanish horses in the 1650s from the Occonneeches, who may have got them by trade as a result of the visit of Spanish explorer Hernando de Soto to the Gulf Coast in 1539–1542.

Traders who adventured from Southside to Occonneechee Town faced a five- or six-day ride over a narrow forest path, beset by dangers. The trader usually rode at the head of a train of horses, each tied to the horse ahead of it. Every horse had a saddlebag across it, packed with mirrors, cheap jewelry, cloth, and other objects desired by Indians in exchange for furs. The horses had bells on their bridles in case the packtrain was dispersed and the horses strayed.

One early trader wrote that the Occonnee-chees claimed that within five days journey from the James to the south, "there is a great

Cook photo collection, Valentine Museum

An ox-drawn cart unloads bagged grain onto a rowboat
at Upper Brandon on the James in an 1890 photo.

high mountain, and at the foot thereof, great rivers that run into a great sea; and that there are men that come thither in ships . . . and have reed caps on their heads, and ride on beasts like horses, but have much longer ears. . . ."

Apparently the Indians were describing the Spanish in Florida, who had settled at Saint Augustine. However, Florida actually proved a much longer journey than five days.

The most heavily traveled early road in Virginia was the coastal route which in 1762 was chosen as part of the colonial post road. It led from Annapolis south to Alexandria, Fredericksburg, Williamsburg, and then across Burwell's Ferry on the James to Isle of Wight County and southward to Edenton, North Carolina, avoiding the Dismal Swamp.

The most colorful of all colonial Virginia routes was the so-called "Appalachian Warriors' Path" or "Iroquois Traders' Path," which followed the lowest ground of the Valley of Virginia from the Potomac River west and then veered south at the present city of Roanoke through North Carolina and on to Augusta, Georgia. It was designated by later maps as the "Great Philadelphia Wagon Road." A western branch of this path crossed Cumberland Gap into Kentucky and was called the "Wilderness Road."

But for Virginia's first century, the James River was the principal highway, crossed by many ferries. Most have been replaced by highway bridges, but the long-running ferry service at Jamestown still operates.

10. *When Arthur Allen Built His Castle*

AS you drive along Route 10 in Surry County, south of the James, you pass the entrance to a road which leads to Hog Island, where the Virginia Power Company nuclear power plant stands. Close by, in the flat pineland of Southside, you come upon one of the oldest houses in North America. It's Bacon's Castle, and it has been recently restored.

Bacon's Castle is an unusual bit of Americana. The original brick house, built in 1665, has Dutch-gabled ends and tall triple chimneys. Alongside it is a nineteenth-century house, connected by a hyphen to the older dwelling. There are many such houses in England, but few in the United States.

A lot of questions are asked about Bacon's Castle. How did it get its name? It's because troops of Nathaniel Bacon holed up there in his 1676 rebellion, making the house famous ever after. And why was it built so far from the James River shore? Probably because the land was rich and water available there. Surry was one of the best farm counties in Virginia's pioneer age.

"The Castle," as Surry folk call it, is now open to the public from Garden Week through September 30. Many visit it to see its unusual architecture, but to me the house is chiefly interesting as hub of Southside life for over 300 years. Rural life has survived with less change in Southside than in most of our industrialized coastal areas.

Surry is a poor county today, with no major industry except the nuclear power plant, but it had productive plantations and farms until the Civil War. Along its James River boundary lived such planters as the Harrisons, Allens, and Cockes. After Appomattox, many of these old families moved out.

For the last 125 years, Surry's predominantly black population has been trying to survive on small farms. In recent years it has become a county of commuters. Many Surry people drive daily to Petersburg or Smithfield for jobs. A few take the ferry to Jamestown every workday.

An emigrant from England named Arthur Allen built the oldest part of Bacon's Castle. The house had become the property of his son, another Arthur, by the time Nathaniel Bacon staged his rebellion against Governor Sir William Berkeley. Allen had been appointed by Berkeley as one of Surry's justices, and he stayed loyal to the governor despite Southside

Bacon's Castle in Surry survives from 1665 to illustrate English farm life in early America.

support of Bacon, the rabble-rousing rebel. As a result, 70 of Bacon's followers seized Allen's plantation and lived there for three months, destroying Allen's livestock and crops.

When Berkeley triumphed over Bacon, Allen returned home and sued the rebels, recovering most of his losses. He rose to be Speaker of the House of Burgesses at Jamestown before he died. He left Bacon's Castle to his son, Arthur Allen III, who remained prominent in colonial affairs until his death in 1727.

When William Byrd led an expedition to run the North Carolina–Virginia boundary in the 1730s, he enjoyed the widow Allen's hospitality at Bacon's Castle. "She entertained us elegantly and seemed to pattern Solomon's housewife, if one may judge by the neatness of her house

and the good order of her family," Byrd wrote in his diary.

Elizabeth Allen's second husband was another Southsider. He was Arthur Smith II, who lived in Windsor Castle, a house still surviving in Smithfield. Smith about 1750 divided his Isle of Wight plantation into city lots to create the new town of Smithfield. That made Smith wealthy. Elizabeth Allen Smith in 1753 endowed a primary school in Smithfield—the boys to be schooled three years and the girls two. Then the boys were to learn a trade and the girls to learn "household affairs."

Following the Allens, the next Bacon's Castle owners were the Cockes. Allan Cocke, grandson of Elizabeth Allen Smith, inherited Bacon's Castle on his grandmother's death. He kept a stable of thoroughbred racehorses. It was one of many farms which gave Surry fame as a horse-raising county, continuing till the early 1900s.

The Cockes of Bacon's Castle conducted a stagecoach line from Petersburg to Portsmouth in the 1820s and '30s. After the family lost the estate in 1843, it was bought by the Hankins family from James City County across the James. Their gifted daughter Virginia was courted by the Georgia poet Sidney Lanier when he was stationed nearby as a Confederate soldier, but the two never married. The Hankins family lost Bacon's Castle, as so many Southerners lost their lands, during Reconstruction, lacking money to pay taxes.

Bacon's Castle was owned for nearly a century after 1880 by the Warrens, another large Southside clan. The third generation of the

family there were the Walker Pegram Warrens, who lived chiefly at Smithfield and summered there until they died in 1972. Then the Association for the Preservation of Virginia Antiquities bought the house and outbuildings, together with 40 acres, and restored Bacon's Castle as a house and as a museum of its period.

In many ways I find the old house cramped and unexciting. It has none of the grandeur of two nearby houses, the Cockes' Mount Pleasant in Surry, and the Allens' Claremont Manor in Prince George. But "the Castle" tells us a lot about farm life in early Virginia. Once a prosperous plantation, it slowly succumbed to the lower prices of new farms in the Ohio Valley and deep South. Today, like many farms, its fields are growing in timber. Farming is a vanishing way of life in eastern Virginia.

APVA

One of the oldest houses on the James is Smith's Fort plantation in Surry County.

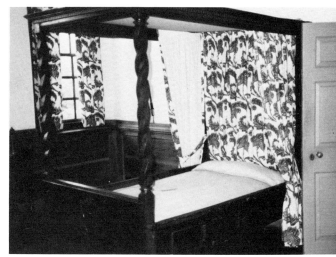

Dorothy Grubbs

Seventeenth-century furniture adorns Smith's Fort plantation, like this walnut bed.

Colonial Dames

*Wilton was the Randolph plantation house
moved from Varina on the James
to west Richmond.*

Colonial Williamsburg

*Knighted for service to Virginia's trade
with England was Sir John Randolph
of Williamsburg.*

11. *The Randolphs of Virginia*

IT doesn't happen often now, but in the years before World War II people along the James often bought and moved historic houses to new suburbs and restored them to live in. Richmond was especially infected with this bug, and several of the city's finest mansions—Wilton, Virginia House, Ampthill, Agecroft Manor—were removed from England or rural Virginia to be re-erected there on the James River.

Today several of these showplaces are open to the public. Virginia House, the most famous, was brought from England by the late Ambassador and Mrs. Alexander Weddell and is exhibited by the Virginia Historical Society. Agecroft, another medieval English manor, is now also a museum. Wilton, the smallest of the three open to the public, is a typical eighteenth-century Virginia plantation manor. It is owned by the Society of Colonial Dames and used as their Virginia headquarters. About 25,000 visitors a year see the house.

Of all Virginia's colonial houses, Wilton is the most livable. It isn't huge or breathtaking. Instead, it's a classic Georgian brick rectangle with wide central halls and four generous rooms on each floor. Each room has a fireplace. The house today has no outbuildings, for none from the original house was still standing when Wilton was bought by the Colonial Dames and moved, brick by brick, from rural Henrico to Richmond.

You can visit the house from 10 A.M. to 5 P.M. throughout the year, for a small admission charge. It is at the end of South Wilton Road, off Cary Street Road, in Richmond's Westhampton suburbs.

The rebuilt house again looks out over the James from a bluff, as it did originally. The façade gazes eastward down the cascading falls of the river past downtown Richmond. Shielding Wilton from nearby mansions, including the well-known colonial mansion, Ampthill—also moved from a rural site to Richmond—are five acres of woodland.

Wilton is a remnant of days when the numerous Randolph dynasty of Virginia dominated social life on the lower James. A recent writer has called William Randolph and Mary Isham Randolph, who came from England to settle on Turkey Island along the lower James, "the Adam and Eve of Virginia society." Many famous Americans stem from their union: not only Peyton, Edmund, and John Randolph, but

41

Colonial Williamsburg

Peyton Randolph of Williamsburg was the first president of the Continental Congress.

Thomas Jefferson and John Marshall were descendants through their mothers. Robert E. Lee was another.

Even California's millionaire newspaper publisher, William Randolph Hearst, claimed to be kin to the family, though wrongly.

It was William Randolph III and his wife, the former Anne Carter Harrison of Berkeley, who built Wilton in 1750–1753. A parlor cornice bears the inscription, "Samson Darrell put up this cornish in the year of our Lord 1751." Unfortunately, William and Anne chose a remote Henrico site on the James near Varina, about 15 miles east of Richmond, on which to build their dream house. It was good farming but far from other houses. That's one reason Wilton was later deserted.

The Randolphs were members of the pre-Revolutionary James River society that dominated early Virginia: The Allens of Bacon's Castle and Claremont Manor, the Byrds of Westover, the Harrisons of Berkeley and Bran-don, the Hills and Carters of Shirley, the Burwells of Carter's Grove, the Cockes of Mount Pleasant, and many others.

Of course, William Randolph III knew his Jefferson and Marshall cousins as well as his numerous kinsmen named Randolph. George Washington spent the night several times at Wilton. So did Lafayette, when he was leading his army onto the Peninsula during the Revolution, harrying the British under Banastre Tarleton. In fact, Peyton Randolph II, the son of Wilton's builder, was an aide to Lafayette in the Revolution. Lafayette made Wilton his headquarters for a short time in 1781, before he met the British in the battles of Greenspring and Yorktown.

After restoring Wilton in 1933–35, the Colonial Dames furnished it with all the original Randolph furniture they could find, though not much was to be had. They still haven't located that "picture of the Washington family" listed in an early inventory, but they do have 10 original portraits of three Randolph generations, most of them by the well-known John Wollaston. These include not only Wilton's builders, William III and Anne, but also three of their eight children.

Wilton fell prey to decay in the nineteenth-century decline of Virginia's tobacco economy, along with most other tobacco plantations. It was sold by its last Randolph owner in 1859. After Virginians lost their slaves in the Civil War, it changed hands frequently. The old house was a ruin when a Colonial Dame from Richmond, the late Mrs. Granville Valentine, persuaded the society to buy it and move it piecemeal to Richmond as a museum and meeting place.

Wilton's move owes much to John D. Rockefeller, Jr.'s revival of Williamsburg, which was underway when Wilton was restored. That was also when Mr. and Mrs. Archibald McCrea were restoring Carter's Grove, the Malcolm Jamiesons were reviving Berkeley, and the Hill Carters were preserving Shirley, all on the James River below Richmond. All are open to the public today.

Wilton's rebuilder was the late Herbert Claiborne, Richmond antiquarian and longtime head of Claiborne and Taylor, contractors.

Wilton's greatest distinction is the panelling throughout its two floors, even in closets. Wood panelling had gone out of style in the colonies when the house was built, but the Randolphs evidently liked it. Only Drayton Hall near Charleston, built about 1738, has panelling as beautiful as Wilton's.

Also exceptional is the parlor, with its 12 Corinthian pilasters and handsome woodcarving. It has been called "one of the most important rooms of this period," built when such nearby Virginia houses as Tuckahoe, Ampthill, and the Wythe House, President's House, and Brafferton Hall—the latter three in Williamsburg—were springing up.

Wilton has strong historical connections with the Peyton Randolph house in Williamsburg and Tazewell Hall in Newport News. These were the pre-Revolutionary houses of the brothers Peyton and John Randolph "the Tory," cousins and contemporaries of Wilton's builder Peyton Randolph II.

The Randolphs were preeminent among the James River dynasties that helped to shape colonial and Revolutionary America.

Courtesy of Anne M. Faulconer

Among several Randolph houses is Tazewell Hall, moved from Williamsburg to Newport News.

12. *Revolution in Hampton Roads*

ALTHOUGH the first American blood in the Revolution was shed in Massachusetts, Virginia was not far behind. Eight months after the battles of Lexington and Concord, Virginia's citizen soldiers got their baptism of fire.

The date was December 9, 1775, and the place was an unlikely marsh south of Norfolk, on the dirt road leading to North Carolina. It was an important battle, for it helped dislodge the repudiated royal governor, Lord Dunmore, from Virginia. It also showed the British that Virginians were ready to die for independence.

Dunmore had taken to the sea in June after arousing Virginia by his seizure of the gunpowder in the colony's Magazine at Williamsburg. Once aboard the British warship, H.M.S. *Fowey*, he sent world through Tidewater Virginia that loyal Britons should join him and that slaves should desert their masters to join his "Ethiopian Regiment."

Lord Dunmore's activities worried George Washington, who had just become commander-in-chief of the American forces. From the North, he wrote that "The arch traitor to the rights of humanity, Lord Dunmore, should be instantly crushed if it takes the force of the whole colony to do it."

When Dunmore moved his fleet to Norfolk, a stronghold of English and Scottish merchants loyal to King George III, Washington wrote to Peyton Randolph of Williamsburg, who was the first president of the Continental Congress: "I do not mean to dictate, I am sure they will pardon me from freely giving them my Opinion, which is, that the fate of America a good deal depends on his [Dunmore's] being obliged to evacuate Norfolk this winter. . . ."

Virginia's Revolutionary government quickly moved to dislodge Dunmore from Norfolk. To that area it dispatched Colonel William Woodford's 2nd Virginia Regiment, recently organized in the counties of Culpeper, Caroline, and Orange.

Anticipating an assault on Norfolk by Patriot forces, Dunmore in November built a wooden fort along the causeway which crossed the south branch of the Elizabeth River, 12 miles from Norfolk. A few days later, Woodford and his new regiment crossed the James near Williamsburg and marched southward to Dunmore's fort at Great Bridge.

On the morning of December 9, Dunmore ordered 120 men of the British forces to attack Woodford. He had heard that Woodford's troops would shortly be reinforced by North

Carolina soldiers, and he hoped to catch the Virginians unprepared.

But Dunmore's plan misfired. As his Britishers attacked, they were answered by murderous crossfire from Woodford's militiamen. Of the 120 Britishers, 17 were killed, 48 wounded, and one captured. Only one Virginian was hurt.

Soon reinforcements reached Woodford from North Carolina and Williamsburg, bringing the Patriot army to 1,200 men. With that, they marched into the Tory stronghold of Norfolk on December 14, forcing Dunmore's friends to hastily join him aboard the half-dozen British ships in the Elizabeth River off Norfolk's shore.

In terms of troops, the battle of Great Bridge was small potatoes, but it was a good omen for Virginia's citizen soldiers. Six years later, at nearby Yorktown, their ordeal was vindicated with the victory over Cornwallis.

Colonial Williamsburg

The Jefferson-Fry map of Virginia, first published in 1752, depicted shippers. This version appeared in 1775.

*Canal boats at Richmond discharged wheat at the Gallego,
Haxall, Rutherfoord and Dunlop flour mills on the river.*

13. *Building the Great Canal*

GEORGE WASHINGTON, who devoted much of his life to America's expansion, was one of the first Virginians to see the importance of the James as a highway into western Virginia —in his lifetime the boundary of Virginia stretched to the Mississippi River.

Even before the Revolution, Washington urged that Virginia should invest colonial funds in canals to open the upper James and Potomac for navigation. By that means, he proposed to link the wide tidal stretches of the two rivers, below their falls at Richmond and Georgetown, with the rocky upriver portions.

Looking further ahead, enterprising Virginians envisioned a connecting canal system through the Kanawha River, on the western slope of the Alleghenies, in what later became West Virginia. The projected James River-Kanawha Canal system was to have been 485 miles long, but only the James River section was ever completed.

To undertake the first part of this project, the Virginia General Assembly in 1785 chartered the James River Company and invested state money to cut the canal around Richmond. In appreciation for Washington's wartime leader-

ship, Virginia gave its favorite son 100 shares of its James River canal stock. Washington, in turn, bestowed the $50,000 gift on the tiny Presbyterian school called Liberty Hall Academy in Rockbridge County—the first institution of higher learning to take root west of the Alleghenies, beginning about 1749. The trustees immediately renamed the school Washington Academy. Today it is Washington and Lee University.

Building the canal proved slow, but work went on. At first the canal was used chiefly by shallow draft tobacco boats carrying hogsheads of leaf. Sometimes two barges were lashed together as a catamaran for stability. Later passenger "packets," two decks high, carried passengers, freight, and mail between Richmond and Lynchburg, with a connecting service up the North or Maury River to Lexington.

By 1805 100 miles of the canal had been built, permitting long, snub-nosed canal boats to travel easily. By 1826 work was underway westward of Lynchburg to Buchanan. The success of New York state's Erie Canal, opened in 1824, gave a boost to Virginia's efforts.

At Buchanan the canal finally ended, dogged by floods and lack of funds. And by the 1850s railroads were clearly the transportation mode

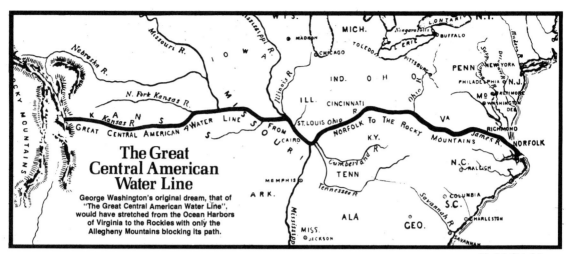

George Washington favored "Central American Water Line"
up the James to connect by canals with the Rocky Mountains.

of the future. As one example, the Baltimore and Ohio Railroad in the 1830s had run its line from Wheeling on the Ohio River through Western Virginia to Baltimore, greatly expanding that port. Virginia realized it was backing the wrong horse.

Yet the James's canal days were a prosperous era in the life of the region. Slaves became skillful mariners, poling tobacco boats down the

James to Richmond. Passenger traffic grew. Canal boats were towed upstream by horses or mules, which walked along the towpath adjoining the canal, while passengers lounged on the upper deck by day or slept on the lower by night.

Canal boats were shallow vessels about 15 feet wide and up to 100 feet long, designed to fit into the 20-foot wide canal and its locks.

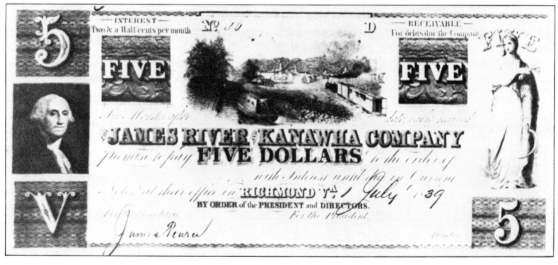

George Washington was honorary head of the James River
canal company, which issued its own money.

Most of them carried 25 to 100 tons of cargo. On the eastward voyage from Lynchburg to Richmond, they carried coal, grain, hay, tobacco, iron ore, salt, and stone. Going westward from Richmond they hauled flour, ironware, machinery, and manufactured wares. The Richmond to Lynchburg voyage, against the current, took three and a half days, while the downstream voyage with the current took only three.

Many canal passengers left accounts of voyages, which cost $5.27 from Richmond to Lynchburg in 1845, including meals and a bunk for the night. Wrote Richmond journalist George Bagby, recalling a trip he made from Richmond to Lynchburg as a lad:

> The packet landing at the foot of Eighth Street presented a scene of great activity. Passengers on foot and in vehicles continued to arrive up to the moment of starting. . . . At last we were off, slowly pushed under the bridge at Seventh Street; then the horses were hitched; then slowly along, until at length, with a lively jerk as the horses fell into a trot, away we went, the cutwater throwing up the spray as we rounded the Penitentiary hill, and the passengers lingering on deck to get a last look at the fair city of Richmond. . . . There was abundant leisure to enjoy the scenery, that grew more and more captivating as we rose, lock after lock, into the rock-bound eminences of the upper James . . . All the scenery in the world . . . avail not to keep a Virginian away from a julep on a hot summer day. From time to time he would descend from the deck of the packet and refresh himself. The bar was small, but vigorous and healthy. . . . "Gentlemen, your very good health"; "Colonel, my respects to you"; "My regards, Judge." "When shall I see you again at my house? Can't you stop now and stay a little while, if it is only a week or two?" "Sam" (to the barkeeper), "duplicate these drinks". . . . After supper, men talked and smoked on deck while women played cards and sewed. Gam-

The heaviest canal traffic was from Lynchburg to Richmond, connecting with coastal boats.

blers were avoided. At bedtime a curtain was drawn across the lower-deck saloon to separate the quarters of men and women. Berths were stacked three high.

As George Washington foresaw, the canal made Virginia's post-Revolutionary capital at Richmond a livelier trading center than isolated Williamsburg had ever been. Iron ore from the valley fed Richmond's Tredegar Iron Works, and vast amounts of upcountry wheat were ground into flour in the nineteenth century at Richmond's huge Gallego, Haxall, Dunlop, and Rutherfoord mills, turned by power from the waters of the James River canal. By the time of the Civil War, Richmond was the leading industrial city of the South.

After Appomattox the James River canal was a ghost of its former self. Its slow transport gave way to railroads and then to highways. At deserted moorings all along the river towpath, abandoned canal boats rotted into nothingness.

After the Chesapeake and Ohio Railway developed its Richmond division in the 1880s, it bought up part of the abandoned canal land at Shockoe Bottom for its tracks and station. It also acquired the towpath west of Richmond for its Balcony Falls railroad line.

Not until this century has the James River canal been recognized as a valuable keepsake. Several Richmond locks have been rediscovered and put to use as parks. Some canal enthusiasts hope for the eventual restoration of the lower end of the system as a recreational waterfront, as canal boaters have done in England and France. But to most people the canal today is a forgotten remnant of the past.

---

250   RICHMOND BUSINESS DIRECTORY.

FOR SCOTTSVILLE & COLUMBIA.

On and after Monday, January 8th, our Packet,

FARMER,

CAPT. G. WYTHE MUNFORD, Jr.

Will leave Richmond for Scottsville, every MONDAY, WEDNESDAY and FRIDAY, at 5 o'clock, P. M., and arrive at Scottsville at 11 o'clock, A. M., the next day. Returning, will leave Scottsville every TUESDAY and THURSDAY. at 2 o'clock, P. M., and arrive in Richmond at 8 o'clock, A. M., the next day,—and SUNDAYS at 10 o'clock, A. M., and arrive in Richmond at 4 o'clock, A. M., on MONDAYS.

THE PLOUGH-BOY

Will leave Richmond every TUESDAY, THURSDAY and SATURDAY, at 7 o'clock, A. M., and arrive at Columbia at 7½ o'clock, P. M.   Returning, will leave Columbia at 7 o'clock, A. M., and arrive in Richmond at half past 7 o'clock, P. M.

Persons traveling on these Packets can get all their Meals on Board

FROM SCOTTSVILLE. TO	HOURS OF PASSING. Tuesdays and Thursdays.	Sundays.	FROM SCOTTSVILLE. TO	HOURS FOR PASSING. Tuesdays and Thursdays.	Sundays.
New Canton,	5 P. M.	1 P. M.	Michaux Ferry,	1 P. M.	9 A. M.
Columbia,	7¼ "	3¼ "	Beaver Dam,	1½ "	9½ "
Elk Hill,	8¼ "	4¼ "	Dover Mills,	3¼ "	11¼ "
Pemberton,	9¼ "	5¼ "	Manakin,	4 "	17 M.
Rock Castle,	10¾ "	6¾ "	Tuckahoe,	5 "	1 A. M,
Bowling Hall,	12 M.	8 "	Richmond,	8 "	4 "
Cedar Point,	12½ A. M.	8½ "			

CROUCH & HOOPER.

Richmond Business Directory from Virginia State Library

Weekday packet boat service was from Scottsville to Richmond with 13 stops.

Virginia's Canal Travelers in Their Nineteenth-Century Glory

Harper's Weekly

A packet boat ready to leave the landing at Richmond's 8th Street.

Passenger boats pause along the upper James canal to rest their horses and to exchange news.

Virginia State Library

Heavy boat traffic near Lynchburg sometimes caused a backup of vessels waiting to go through the locks.

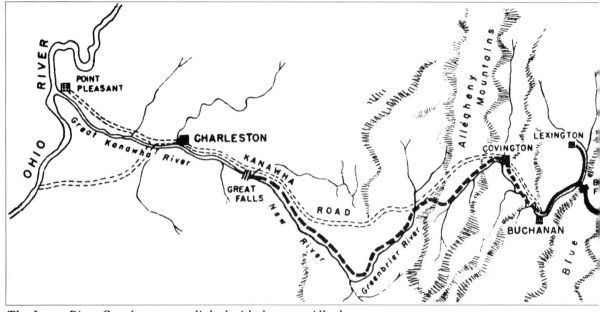

The James River Canal never was linked with the trans-Allegheny Kanawha Canal in West Virginia, as intended.

Shipping on Richmond's canal made it the South's top industrial city before the Civil War.

Canal travelers approaching Richmond from the west could see the Capitol, church spires, and industry.

RICHMOND

JAMES RIVER & KANAWHA CANAL

James River

CHESAPEAKE BAY

Hampton Roads

...HBURG

LEGEND

━━━ COMPLETED CANAL
━ ━ ━ PROPOSED CANAL
‑ ‑ ‑ ‑ WAGON ROADS

In the Piedmont foothills near Lynchburg the canal resembled the Rhine River through Germany.

53

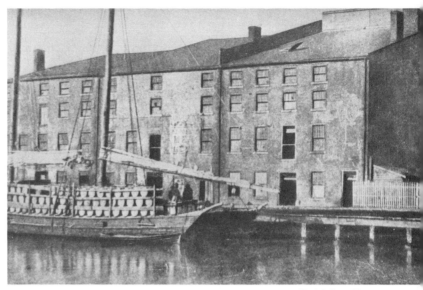

Along the canal at Richmond was the tobacco warehouse used as Libby Prison in the Civil War.

Virginia State Library

Valentine Museum

Past Richmond's Hollywood Cemetery ran the James and its canal, with the C & O tracks in between.

14. *The Day They Burned Norfolk*

THE year 1776 began ominously for Virginia. Frowning at Norfolk from the Elizabeth River were the naval guns of Governor Lord Dunmore and his British siege vessels. Inside the town were 1,500 militiamen from Virginia and North Carolina, who had forced Dunmore to seek the safety of the ships.

Captain Matthew Squire, in command of His Majesty's sloop *Otter*, awaited a signal from Dunmore. Along with two other Royal Navy warships and a half-dozen other vessels, his mission was to recapture Norfolk and hold Virginia loyal to King George III.

In his log, Captain Squire noted, under date of January 1, 1776: "Mostly little wind and fair."

Then, in the afternoon, came the signal. "At 4 P.M. began a brisk fire from the squadron on the town," the *Otter* recorded. Together with H.M.S. *Kingfisher* and H.M.S. *Liverpool*, she continued shelling until 11 that night. Then the British sent marines ashore in small boats and set fire to the food in Norfolk's warehouses.

Thus began Norfolk's burning. For three days British ships and American soldiers fought over the town. By January 4, Norfolk was a smoking ruin, intensifying Virginians' hatred of Dunmore and stiffening Americans' determination to separate from Britain. In Philadelphia, the Continental Congress tried vainly to send ships to Virginia. But all it could do was to appropriate funds to build 13 frigates to strengthen the "mosquito fleet" of Virginia merchantmen assembled to oppose the British.

Norfolk had felt itself doomed ever since Virginia soldiers overwhelmed the British at Great Bridge on December 9 and captured Norfolk from Royalist forces on December 14. Dunmore then appealed to Loyalists to join with him to repulse the revolutionary Virginia government at Williamsburg.

The fires set on January 1 were burning hotly next day. "It is now become general," wrote Colonel Robert Howe, a North Carolinian in command of colonial forces at Norfolk, to the Virginia Convention at Williamsburg on January 2. "The whole town will, I doubt not, be consumed in a day or two.

"The burning of the town has made several avenues . . ." Howe explained in a letter to Edmund Pendleton, president of the Virginia Convention, "so that they may now fire with greater effect. The tide is now rising, and we expect at high water another cannonade. . . . We have not one man killed, and but a few wounded. I cannot enter into the melancholy consideration of the women and children running through a crowd of shot to get out of the tòwn, some of them with children at their breasts; a few have, I hear, been killed."

Howe's soldiers continued to fire at the British ships, but the British had bigger guns. "At 7 A. M. the rebels began to fire upon us with musketry," the log of H.M.S. *Liverpool* recorded on January 2. "We returned with great guns until they dispersed."

Tobacco hogsheads were shipped on paired log canoes and on narrow James River boats.

Norfolk's fire spread as colonial troops set fire to houses and stores owned by any persons suspected of being loyal to the king. By Wednesday, January 3, a Loyalist aboard H.M.S. *Otter* wrote home to England:

I have the pleasure to assure you that this rebel town of Norfolk is in ashes. It is glorious to see the blaze of the town and shipping. I exult in the carnage of these rebels. The signal was given from the *Liverpool*, and in an instant the place was in flames. We

are now proceeding on this business, and will burn every port on the sea shore.

Writing to Lord Dartmouth, British Secretary of State for the Colonies, on January 4, Dunmore expressed surprise that the "Rebels" had joined in burning Norfolk—their own city. "They appear to me to have nothing more at heart than the utter destruction of this once most flourishing country," he wrote. "Conscious, I suppose, that they cannot long enjoy it themselves, they wish to make it of as little use as possible to others."

Aboard H.M.S. *Fowey* with the Governor were Virginia Loyalists who had chosen to stay with the British. A few suspected Royalists who remained in Norfolk, Dunmore wrote Dartmouth, fared worse. "They are imprisoning every man that they even suppose wishes well to government. Nay, the ladies who have dared to write or speak disrespectfully of them have not been exempted."

A midshipman aboard H.M.S. *Liverpool* also wrote back to England an account of the battle, later published in London's *Public Advertiser*:

The Rebels have been in possession of Norfolk three weeks, when Lord Dunmore was forced to retire afloat, with all the inhabitants that were well affected to Government. . . . The town is still burning, as it will be for three or four days. The Rebels are called "Shirtmen" for their uniforms, being a long shirt down to their heels, with a leaden medal at their breasts in the shape of an old English Shield, on which is inscribed, "Liberty or Death."

In the weeks preceding and during Norfolk's siege, the Continental Congress in Philadelphia tried to assemble a naval force to prevent Dunmore's burning of other Virginia towns. The Naval Committee on January 5 wrote to the Virginia Convention in Williamsburg:

The Congress, attentive to the safety and security of every party of the united colonies

Painting by Latrobe, Maryland Historical Society

Sailing ships clustered at Norfolk's Town Point in the 1790s, many serving the James River.

and observing the peculiar distresses that the Colony of Virginia is liable to from a marine enemy, have with all possible expedition fitted out a small fleet of armed vessels, which they have ordered in the first place to the Bay of Chesapeake, if the winds and weather permit, there to seize and destroy as many of the enemies' ships and vessels as they can. . . .

Virginia was instructed to station a reliable agent at Cape Henry to meet the incoming fleet "and furnish the Commander-in-Chief with the most accurate information on the then strength and situation of Lord Dunmore's fleet and land forces." Though Norfolk waited, the relief force did not come.

An attack on Yorktown was feared as an aftermath of Norfolk's burning. An express rider hastened from Yorktown to Williamsburg on January 4 with news that two vessels thought to be British men-of-war were coming up the York. After the first alarms, however, Colonel Patrick Henry at Yorktown relieved the capital

with news that the two were merchant ships, one from Ireland and one from Grenada, loaded with food. They were welcomed.

The *Virginia Gazette* of January 6, published in Williamsburg, carried a highly congratulatory account of the Virginian troops' behavior at Norfolk:

> Six of the enemy were left dead on the shore and great numbers were supposed to be carried off in their boats. We did not lose a man; but had six or seven wounded.
>
> Some poor women were killed in endeavoring to move out of town. It was a shocking scene to see the poor women and children, running about through the fire, and exposed to the guns from the ships, and some with children at their breasts. Let our countrymen view and contemplate the scene!

The *Gazette* also paid credit to the Virginians' marksmanship:

> It is affirmed that one hundred cannon played on the town almost incessantly for

twenty five hours, and express says he heard firing all the way on the road. Notwithstanding this heavy firing, and the town in flames around them, our men had the resolution to maintain their posts, and the coolness to aim as usual. They seem animated in their glorious cause, and appear to be shielded as the favorites of heaven.

Was worse to come? Writing from Williamsburg on January 6, Samuel Inglis, a Norfolk merchant, painted this picture to Robert Morris in Philadelphia:

His Lordship, it seems, had given notice to the inhabitants of Portsmouth to remove out of town, as he intended to fire it next, and then Yorktown. . . . No pen can describe to you the horrid situation the inhabitants of Norfolk are drove to. The country about there was miserably poor at best. The army lately sent there has drained it of any provisions or necessaries the inhabitants had, so that now these poor wretches who have been fired from their houses (many of them as genteel people as any in the Colony) must absolutely perish for the mere want of covering and victuals.

Still cooped up aboard H.M.S. *Fowey* in the Elizabeth River, Lord Dunmore on January 9 reported to Lord Dartmouth the rising hunger of Norfolk's citizens.

I am happy to have it in my power to inform your Lordship that [I am] depriving the Rebels from every supply of salt, rum or sugar in my power. . . . I think the want of rum will damp their courage more ways than one, and I know they will feel the want of the last article, though only a luxury of life.

Norfolk was indeed a shambles. A midshipman aboard H.M.S. *Otter* wrote on January 9: "The detested town of Norfolk is no more! Its destruction happened on New Year's Day! . . .

Nor are the flames yet extinguished. But no more of Norfolk remains than about twelve houses which have escaped the flames!"

On January 10, the *Virginia Gazette* reported the burning by American forces of Gosport, the home of the wealthy Scottish trader Andrew Sprowle and of other suspected Tories. "Gosport, since our last, is burnt by our people, on which account old Sprowle has lost considerable property," the *Gazette* exulted.

With Norfolk's burned-out citizens huddled in makeshift shelters, British ships continued to stand by in the Elizabeth River. Then on Sunday, January 21, the conflict renewed.

"About 4 this afternoon," wrote Colonel William Woodford to the Virginia Convention in Williamsburg,

another heavy cannonading began from the *Liverpool* and *Otter,* during which the enemy landed and set fire to some houses that remained unhurt, near to what is called Town Point wharf. I sent strong parties to reinforce our water guards. We had three fine men killed with cannon shot, and one wounded, who, it is thought, will lose his arm. We have found one sailor and two Negroes dead, and supposed many others were killed and wounded, that were carried off in their boats. . . .

The next night, sailors from British ships went ashore to bring aboard some tobacco belonging to Scottish merchants. The *Liverpool's* log recorded that "At 3 A.M. the Rebels fired on a party of Volunteers. . . . Fired several shot and dispersed them. . . ."

Norfolk remained an unhappy host to the British ships for five months. On February 1 the *Liverpool's* log recorded that:

The Lieutenant went on shore with a party of armed men in conjunction with some men belonging to the *Otter,* and brought off nine bullocks and some pigs, fired several shot at a party of Rebels, who fired on a party of

[Royalist] Volunteers that were bringing some tobacco belonging to merchants here.

Virginians were increasingly angry. Adam Stephen on February 1 wrote from his home at Berkeley to Richard Henry Lee at the Continental Congress in Philadelphia: "I think the Congress should apply for foreign assistance, as the bloody violence of King and Ministry and the apathy of the people of Britain seem incurable. Every sinew must be exerted."

By February 6, Virginia and Carolina forces under Colonels Howe and Woodford withdrew from Norfolk. Reported the *Virginia Gazette* in Williamsburg on February 9:

We learn that [the colonial troops] abandoned Norfolk last Tuesday [February 6] after removing the poor inhabitants, with what effects they could carry along with them, and demolishing the Entrenchments which Lord Dunmore threw up a little before he fled aboard the fleet now lying before that place. What few houses remained after the late bombardment were likewise destroyed, after being valued, to prevent our enemies taking shelter in them.

Thus, in the course of five weeks, was a town which contained upwards of 6,000 inhabitants, many of them in affluent circumstances—a place that carried on an extensive

Virginia-grown cotton was a James River export till the 1930s, as a Norfolk cargo dock reveals.

trade and commerce, consequently affording bread to many thousands—been reduced to ashes and become desolate through the wicked and cruel machinations of Lord North and juncto, aided by their faithful servants, my Lord Dunmore with his motley army and renowned Capt. Henry Bellow, commodore of his Britannic Majesty's fleet in Virginia, and his generous and valiant crew. Truly may it be now said:

Never can true reconcilement grow
Where wounds of deadly hate have pierced
    so deep. . . .

We hear Lord Dunmore and his friends are exceedingly uneasy, and a good deal frightened, upon hearing that the continental fleet is designed against them, and indeed they have a very good reason, for, as sure as a rifle (and that, they well know, is pretty sure, Commodore [Esek] Hopkins will pay them a visit so soon as he is joined by the Maryland squadron. . . .

Worn out with his long wait in Norfolk's harbor, Lord Dunmore was at last overjoyed on February 18 to hear of the arrival in Chesapeake Bay of a fleet bearing the British army of General Sir Henry Clinton, which had come down from the north. But his joy was brief. Clinton was headed for North Carolina. Deeply angered, Dunmore dashed off a letter to Lord Dartmouth:

This moment General Clinton is arrived, and to my inexpressible mortification [I] find he is ordered by your Lordship to North Carolina, a most insignificant province, when this, which is the first colony on the continent, both for its riches and power, is totally neglected. Had North Carolina been your object, policy, in my poor opinion, ought to have induced your Lordship to have ordered your army to have rendezvoused here, for many reasons. . . .

To see my government thus totally neglected, I wot, is a mortification I was not prepared to meet with after being imprisoned on board a ship between eight and nine months and now left without a hope of relief either to myself or the many unhappy friends to government that are now afloat, suffering with me, but I have none.

With Norfolk shattered but still unconquered, Dunmore finally sailed from the Elizabeth River in May. On July 8 and 9, in the battle of Gwynn's Island, his fleet was so severely damaged that he left Virginia, never to return.

As for Norfolk, it rebuilt with surprising speed. It had lost half its 6,000 population and every building. But thanks to the energies of a young and vital nation, the city rose from its ashes bigger and better than ever before.

15. *Dynasties of the James*

THE James is famed for many things, but none more than its eighteenth-century plantations, whose families ruled Virginia in colonial times and took a lead in winning the Revolution.

Until recent years, the James River shore from Jamestown to Richmond seemed a community of interlocking families: Randolphs, Byrds, Hills, Carters, Cockes, Burwells, Allens, Tylers, Douthats, and others. Virginia's first leaders came from the James River, around Jamestown and Williamsburg. Some of these families had died off or lost influence well before the Revolution in 1776. By that time Virginia had a new cast of dynasties, many from the uplands: Washingtons, Jeffersons, Madisons, Monroes, Cabells, Marshalls, Prestons, Breckenridges, Pattons, Lewises, and the like.

Virginians were once the most dynastic people in America because they emulated the English families that Virginia planters admired. They built family seats to declare their importance. Houses such as Mount Vernon and Monticello proclaim Washington and Jefferson as great men, born to rule.

The best of Virginia's dynasts set high standards for themselves and their offspring. I think of George Mason in his library at Gunston Hall, pondering world history and listing what he regarded as each American's inalienable rights. No more search and seizure. No more imprisonment without trial.

But preserving dynastic seats like Gunston Hall is too great a burden today for most families. Plantations are an intolerable expense. Most big James River houses are being bought by corporations or exhibited as museums, kept up by admission fees.

Dynasties were finished when our Revolution forswore aristocracy in favor of democracy. No more primogeniture. No more entail. Lacking these supports for the eldest son's inheritance, the dynastic concept after 1776 had rough going. Though some parents still favor sons over daughters in bequeathing wealth, few family houses in Virginia remain in the original family's hands.

Another anti-dynastic force is Americans' desire to marry for love rather than for money. In Washington's time, many sensible folk carefully chose wealthy mates. Both Washington and Jefferson, for example, wed rich widows.

As a basis for comparing Virginia's colonial families, the *Virginia Magazine of History and*

Biography in 1954 ran a study by historian Jackson T. Main of "Virginia's 100 Richest," based on state tax records of 1787 and 1788.* Land, slaves, livestock, and vehicles were the chief possessions in 1788, for cash money and securities were scarce in the Southern states. Few Virginians owned more than 100 slaves, and only 12 had 300 or more.

Virginia Museum

Elizabeth Jacquelin was depicted by a visiting limner, probably at Jamestown.

In fact, the richest—merchant and planter David Ross of Richmond—in 1789 owned 100,000 acres and 400 slaves. With land averaging $10 an acre, Ross owned about $1 million worth. And with slaves worth about $200 then, he added another $80,000 for a worth of $1,080,000 not counting his house, livestock, or securities. And one dollar at that time would buy as much as $50 today.

Virginia's economy 200 years ago was strictly agricultural, with little ready money or securities. Farmers had been impoverished by the drop of tobacco sales in the Revolution, but

most held on to land. As for slaves, some from Virginia were being sold to new settlers in Kentucky and Tennessee. After the invention of the cotton gin by Eli Whitney in 1783 spurred cotton-growing in South Carolina and Georgia, other Virginia slaves would be sold down south.

Most of Virginia's Revolutionary leaders were among its richest residents in 1788. They included Washington, Jefferson, Henry, Benjamin Harrison, Henry "Light Horse Harry" Lee, George Mason, Thomas Nelson, John Page, Edmund Randolph, and Edmund Pendleton.

George Washington was about the twentieth richest Virginian, with over $200,000 in taxable wealth; he had 352 slaves on his Fairfax County plantations. Washington also owned 32,373 acres in the west, presumably a Revolutionary bounty.

Jefferson ranked about 28th, Pendleton 39th, and Patrick Henry 90th. James Madison of Orange County, St. George Tucker of Williamsburg, and other Revolutionary figures fell just below the first 100.

The Byrd family was no longer conspicuously rich, after the gambling losses and suicide of William Byrd III. However, other First Families of Virginia were prominent among the richest. Main's list includes nine Cockes, eight Carters, Washingtons, Fitzhughs, and Lees; and seven Harrisons.

Professor Main found the 10 richest Virginians of 1788, judging from tax records, were David Ross of Richmond, Robert Beverley of Blandfield, Robert Carter of Westmoreland, Charles Carter of Shirley, William Fitzhugh of Chatham, William Allen of Claremont, Alexander Spotswood of Spotsylvania, Roger Atkerson of Dinwiddie, Benjamin Harrison of Berkeley, and Thomas Nelson of Yorktown.

Virginia's richest were clustered chiefly in 35 of Virginia's oldest and easternmost counties. There were a few in Warwick and Elizabeth City counties, and even fewer in Southside, Piedmont, and western Virginia. Between them, the James and Northern Neck held about 80 of the 100 richest. Many of the others clus-

* See appendix

tered near the fall line on the James, Mattaponi, Pamunkey, Rappahannock, and Potomac rivers.

Virginia's 100 richest planters averaged about 3,000 acres of land; a few such as David Ross (100,000 acres) and Thomas Fairfax (116,000 acres) held much more. Owners averaged 80 slaves apiece, including both house servants and field hands.

Main notes that most planters held land in several counties and owned on average one slave for every 30 acres. The largest slaveholder was Charles Carter of Shirley, who owned 785. Close behind was William Allen of Claremont with 700.

All of the planters owned and were taxed on livestock, four-wheel carriages, two-wheel "chariots," and securities. The "average" rich planter had 32 horses, but George Washington owned over a hundred.

After the Revolution, Main notes, eastern Virginia plantations began to decline. Many young Virginians moved south of the James or into the Piedmont and beyond to Kentucky, Tennessee, and the Deep South.

The old plantations' breakup was hastened by Virginia's abolition of the law of primogeniture, which had once favored the oldest son in the bequeathing of property. Main writes: "Even prior to the abolition of primogeniture in 1785, the division of huge estates . . . had already begun, and the process . . . meant the decline of the aristocracy of Virginia."

Surry County in 1788 held several of the richest Virginians, including William Allen, Allen Cocke, John Cocke, and John Hartwell Cocke. Williamsburg was the home of two

planters, William Southall and John Paradise of the Ludwell-Paradise House, and James City the home of four: John Ambler of Jamestown, Nathaniel Burwell of Carter's Grove, William Lee of Greenspring, and Richard Taliaferro of Powhatan plantation.

Jackson Main's study reveals the simplicity of Virginia's tobacco-based economy, before the

Colonial Williamsburg

William Byrd II lived in London and on the James River at Westover.

industrial era and its formation of capital. Yet even then the wealth was becoming almost essential to political office-holding America.

Plantation Houses on the James, Homes of Early American Leaders

APVA

BAÇON'S CASTLE, Surry County, Allen family

Jamestown-Yorktown Foundation

GREENSPRING, James City County, Berkeley, Ludwell, and Lee families

POWHATAN, James City County, Taliaferro family

Colonial Williamsburg

CARTER'S GROVE, James City County, Carter and Burwell families

SHERWOOD FOREST, Charles City County, Tyler family

Virginia Chamber of Commerce

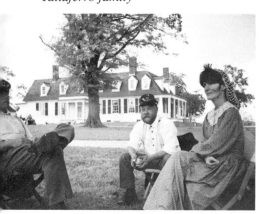

Hopewell Promotion & Tourism Office

APPOMATTOX MANOR, Prince George County, Eppes family

*SMITH'S FORT, Surry County,
Rolfe and Warren families*

*SHIRLEY, Charles City County,
Hill and Carter families*

*WEYANOKE, Charles City County,
Douthat and Lewis families*

BERKELEY, Charles City County, Harrison family

*UPPER BRANDON, Prince George
County, Harrison and Byrd families*

*WESTOVER, Charles City County,
Byrd family*

16. *Low Tide at Hampton Roads*

INVASION!!! Yesterday several expresses arrived from the Bay Side of Princess Anne County, giving the long anticipated intelligence of a British Squadron entering our waters. . . ." So the *Norfolk Herald* announced on February 5, 1813. As many Americans feared, it was a prelude to the blockade of Chesapeake Bay and the invasion of Washington 18 months later by red-coated marines of King George III. The infant United States navy was challenged in the War of 1812 by the greatest naval power in the world. How could a handful of American warships hold off such an enemy?

Yet Britain's victory did not come without a fight. Norfolk did not fall like a ripe plum, as Admiral Sir John Warren had expected. The British invasion of Norfolk—the first amphibious landing attempted on United States shores—was foiled by the heavy gunfire of Virginia militiamen and U. S. naval forces. The American victory at Craney Island slowed up and almost stopped Britain's conquest of the Chesapeake.

When word of the enemy's approach reached the U.S.S. *Constellation*, that frigate was grounded by low tide at Willoughby Spit, opposite Old Point Comfort, between the Virginia Capes and Norfolk. Desperately, the *Constellation*'s crew worked to float her as the British squadron—two 74-gun men-of-war, three frigates, a brig, and a schooner—came through the capes toward Hampton. At last the tide floated her free, and Captain Charles Stewart, USN, raced his ship safely into the Elizabeth River toward Norfolk, mooring between Fort Norfolk and Fort Nelson. Gunboats from the nearby Naval Yard were then brought up to protect the river's mouth.

The British did not pursue the *Constellation*. Instead, they formed a barrier at Lynnhaven Roads, near Cape Henry, to halt all commerce. "This port is now effectually blockaded by the enemy's squadron under Admiral Warren," reported the *Norfolk Herald* on February 8. "Not a vessel can pass from Hampton Roads, either up or down the Bay, without being intercepted." For two years no tobacco, wheat, or cotton was to move through Hampton Roads.

Fear of attack ran high. Governor John Barbour came down the James from Richmond to inspect defenses. U. S. Navy recruits from the barracks at Gosport Naval Yard were stationed at Fort Norfolk. The Virginia militia was called into service, under command of Brigadier General Robert Barraud Taylor, a Norfolk attorney.

Ten thousand militiamen from Tidewater counties packed their rifles and hurried to Norfolk, Portsmouth, and Hampton, the most vulnerable Chesapeake ports.

One militiaman was a 22-year-old orderly sergeant in the Portsmouth Rifles named James Jarvis. Describing General Taylor's immediate attempt to instill order among the militiamen, he wrote:

It is a fact that most of the members of the militia companies were blood relations. In some of the companies, the captains would have at least three brothers, one or two uncles, and perhaps ten or fifteen cousins; then, in consequence of later marriages, the balance of the company were half brothers, etc., to the brothers, cousins, and uncles. Here was a pretty mess of discipline. It was not unusual for a private to sing out to his captain, "Nat, what in the devil do you keep us marching all day for?" General Taylor soon discovered that this kind of soldiering would not answer and determined on the celebrated Organization. He saw that for this time "Auld Acquaintance" must be forgot.

Joining up was no lark, Jarvis soon found. Addressing him and other recruits, General Taylor warned they must be ready to die. "He said that the British least expected to be met by militia at the point of a bayonet," the new sergeant confided to his journal. "When he said this, my belly trembled, but my heart was safe and in the right place, pretty high up. I was never anxious to meet an enemy at the point of the bayonet. . . . Upon the whole, this is a ticklish point."

Spring came without British attack, and Virginia's first hysteria subsided. Chesapeake ports now bulged with idle ships and seamen. In Portsmouth, innkeeper Edward Hansford felt safe enough to reschedule the ball he had cancelled after the British arrived. Again he advertised it to be held at his "commodious" tavern on London Street, "designated by the Sign of General Geo. Washington Commanding in the Field, and as a Planter on his Farm." Washington was the citizen-soldier incarnate.

Then the enemy again became threatening. "This morning," reported the *Norfolk Ledger* in a dispatch dated June 19,

three of the enemy frigates, two schooners, and the Baltimore cutter were at anchor off Hampton Bar, 12 or 14 enemy barges rowing about the Roads. . . . The uppermost frigate, being so far detached from her consorts, determined Captain Cassin to make an attack upon her with gunboats. On Sunday morning about 4 o'clock the attack was made by 14 boats at about three-quarters of a mile distance, under command of Capt. Tarbell. The attack was spirited, but a light wind springing up enabled the other two frigates to come to the assistance of their consort.

Captain John Cassin, USN, was in charge of all naval forces, while Captain Joseph Tarbell, USN, had command of the *Constellation* after Captain Stewart took command of the U.S.S. *Constitution*.

On June 21 the British force moved from Hampton Roads to the mouth of Nansemond River. It now consisted of 20 men-of-war, frigates, and transports. Its clear objective was Craney Island, a low fortified crescent near the mouth of the Elizabeth River, which an enemy must neutralize or capture if he were to enter Norfolk and Portsmouth by sea. Most of the island was surrounded by shoals, which at low tide merged with the marshy Nansemond shore. However, the east end extended into the channel. There the defenders had built a fort mounting two 24- pound and one 18-pound cannon.

"Our force has about 400 militia infantry," wrote Sergeant William P. Young at Craney Island,

one company of riflemen (from Winchester) and two companies of light artillery. . . . We saw by the movement of the enemy's boat in passing and repassing from their ships to the shore that they were landing troops, so that a fight was expected to come off, and we went to work. . . . The three cannons from the fort and four six-pounders belonging to the Artillery were taken to the west side of the Island. . . .

Early in the morning we were joined by order of Capt. Tarbell of the frigate *Constellation* (then lying in the harbor of Norfolk blockaded), by Lieuts. Niele, Shubrick, and Sanders, with about 150 sailors. Every arrangement being made to defend the fort, we waited the approach of the enemy. . . . As we had no flagstaffs, a long pole was got, to which the "Star Spangled Banner" was nailed. . . .

Whilst we were making our arrangements, the enemy was landing his Infantry and Marines, in all about 2,500. We could distinctly see them marching and countermarching on the beach, and after forming into columns, they took up the line of march. But such was the dense growth of trees and underwood between us that they were soon lost to our view. We knew not but their intention was to march to the town of Portsmouth, get possession of that place and Gosport, and destroy the Navy Yard. We were, however, soon undeceived. . . .

Congreve rockets now began arcing from the invaders on the mainland into the fort. Craney's battery on the western end of the island, which had thus far held its fire, opened up in reply. A barrage of grape and canister shot peppered the British, killing two officers and several men.

While the defenders fought off this feint, the main invasion force suddenly appeared on the seaward side. "The enemy was approaching the island with about 50 of their largest barges filled with sailors and marines, supposed to be from 1,200 to 2,500," one militiaman wrote. "They were advancing in column order, led on by Admiral Warren's barge, the Centipede, a boat about 50 feet long, rowing 24 oars, with a brass three-pounder in her bow."

The force of sailors, marines, and militia troops trained its guns and held its fire. The word soon came. "Now, boys," asked Captain Arthur Emmerson, an ex-merchant mariner who commanded the Portsmouth Artillery Company, "Are you ready?" On his next signal, "Fire," the first wave of invaders was hit. "So quick and galling was our fire that they were thrown into the greatest confusion and commenced a hasty retreat," noted the diarist. "Four or five of their boats were sunk, one of them the Admiral's barge. Many others were so shattered that it was with difficulty they were kept afloat."

Among British losses were Admiral Warren's handsome *Centipede* and two other landing boats. One contained 18 former troops of Napoleon's, captured by the British in war with the French in Spain and promised release after serving His Majesty's forces. These undisciplined 'Chasseurs Britanniques' were soon to prove an embarrassment to the British.

Wounded seriously in the attempted invasion was Captain Hanchett, commanding officer of the 102nd Regiment of Infantry, who was on board the *Centipede*. He was an illegitimate son of King George III and half brother to his successors, Kings George IV and William IV.

Some of the sharpest shooting at Craney Island was done by naval gunners, led by officers of the *Constellation*. "The sailors under Lieutenants Niele, Shubrick, and Sanders were brave fellows and rendered great assistance in the management of the 24- and 18-pounders," Sergeant Young wrote. "During the hottest of the fight, Lieut. Niele came to my gun and requested to have a fire at the boats. I granted his request with great pleasure, and his shot did its work. . . . The sailors waded to the Centipede and hauled her on shore. From the boat was taken a number of guns, pistols, and cullafors. She was made tight and sent to the Navy Yard, Gosport."

In the afternoon, British forces on the mainland returned to their ships, after shooting livestock and wreaking havoc on waterfront farms. But were they planning a new invasion after dark? As the defenders waited and rereadied their guns, a great explosion shook the island. It was the militia's reserve powder, which had been stored in a tent under care of a Quaker pacifist. "Many of us hurried to the place," the militiaman wrote, "but not a vestige of the tent was to be seen. We then went in search of the sentinel and found him on the beach, outside of the fort, completely stripped of his clothing, his left arm nearly torn off, and his whole person as black as powder could make him."

Hearing the blast in Norfolk, General Taylor supposed that Craney Island had been attacked again and had blown up its fort to prevent capture. He learned better when a rowboat reached the *Constellation* with an urgent request for gunpowder. The island was resupplied, but the British did not return. Then darkness enveloped the island. It had had its moment in history.

Was victory so easy? General Taylor reinforced his troops during the night, but the British did not attack again. "The enemy has been completely foiled in an enterprise of great importance," the *Norfolk Gazette and Public Ledger* exulted, "and without the loss of one man on our part, or even one wounded. . . ." But since the British force did not disperse, another attack seemed likely.

The answer came on June 24. "Accounts just received [are] that the enemy landed last night at New-Port-Neuse, at the entrance of James River," the *Norfolk Gazette* reported. "An attack upon Hampton is probably meditated." By sunup the landing force had come ashore at Celey's, Miles Cary's plantation bordering Hampton Roads at Newport News point and was marching toward Hampton, a town of 1,000 inhabitants. About the same time 40 British landing craft made a feint toward's Blackbeard's Point on Hampton River.

Hampton's incised shoreline made the town readily vulnerable to naval invasion. The defense force, commanded by Major Stapleton Crutchfield, was encamped at Little England plantation, close to Blackbeard's Point. As British barges approached the shore, they drew

the militia's attention for some time before the Virginians belatedly turned to meet the main force. After a lethal exchange, the militiamen were forced by superior British firepower to withdraw.

Crutchfield wrote to Governor Barbour three days later:

> The enemy landed and had drawn up in battle array at least 2,500 men. Their loss cannot be less than 200, but it is believed to be half as many more. Our little force was 349 infantrymen and riflemen, 62 artillery and 25 cavalry. The loss on our part is seven killed, 12 wounded, one prisoner, and 11 missing, who are believed to be in the neighborhood with their families.

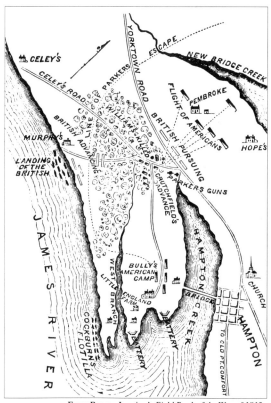

From Benson Lossing's *Field Book of the War of 1812*

The British navy in 1813 invaded Hampton and burned most of the town.

Hampton now became a scene of atrocities that would inflame the nation and make the name of Admiral George Cockburn, Warren's second-in-command, odious to Americans. In his diary, Lieutenant Colonel Charles James Napier, who led the British invaders, wrote that "Every horror was perpetrated with impunity—rape, murder, pillage—*and not a man was punished.*" Many atrocities far exceeded what Napier called "a necessary part of our job, viz., plundering and ruining the peasantry."

While Warren remained on his flagship, Cockburn and General Sir Sidney Beckwith, the commanding general, moved ashore into the handsome residence of Mr. and Mrs. John Westwood to command the occupation. The British took over the town, seized Point Comfort lighthouse and defenses, and commandeered food. Angered by their repulse at Craney Island, soldiers committed an orgy of looting and occasional rape. After months at sea in close quarters, the French Chasseurs ran wild.

Slaves were offered freedom if they went with the invaders, and some left their masters.

"The unfortunate females of Hampton who could not leave the town were suffered to be abused in the most shameful manner, not only by the venal, savage foe but by unfortunate and infuriated blacks, who were encouraged in their success," Major Crutchfield reported to the Governor. "They pillaged and encouraged every act of rapine and murder, killing a poor man by the name of Kirby, who had been lying in his bed at the point of death for more than six months, shooting his wife in the hip at the same time, and killing his faithful dog lying at his feet."

An anonymous writer to the *Richmond Enquirer*, later identified as Colonel Richard E. Parker of the Westmoreland County Militia, added other details:

> That the town and county adjacent was given up to indiscriminate plunder of a licentious soldiery—except perhaps the house where the headquarters was fixed—is an undeniable truth. Every article of valuable property was taken from it. In many cases not even a knife or fork or plate was left. British officers were seen by Doctor Colton in the act of plundering Mr. Jones' store. His house, although he remained in town, was rifled and his medicine thrown into the street.... The church was pillaged, and the plate belonging to it taken away, although inscribed with the donor's name. The windmills in the neighborhood were stripped of their sails. The closets, private drawers, and trunks of the inhabitants were broken open, and scarcely anything seemed too trifling an object to excite the cupidity of the robbers. . . . In fact Hampton exhibits a dreary and desolate appearance which no American can witness unmoved. . . . Men of Virginia! Will you permit all this? Fathers and Brothers and Husbands, will you fold your arms in apathy and only curse your despoilers? NO. You will fly with generous emulation to the unfurled standards of your country. . . .

General Taylor sent a protest to Admiral Warren expressing "great grief and astonishment" and asking that the offenders be punished. "We are, in this part of the country, merely in the novitiate of our warfare," he declared. "The character it will hereafter assume, whether of mildness or ferocity, will materially depend on the first operations of our arms and on the personal character and dispositions of the respective commanders."

Aboard H.M.S. *San Domingo*, Admiral Warren acknowledged the protest and referred it to Beckwith for reply. Sir Sidney informed Taylor that his troops were merely retaliating against Americans' cruelty. "At the recent attempt on Craney Island," he wrote, "the troops in a barge sunk by the fire of your guns clung to the wreck of the boat. Several Americans, I assure you most solemnly, waded off from the island and, in presence of all engaged, fired upon and shot these poor fellows. With a feeling natural to such a proceeding, the men of that corps landed at Hampton...."

Taylor was amazed and skeptical. He

Admiral Sir George Cockburn was blamed for burning Hampton in the War of 1812.

appointed a board of offers to investigate. Meanwhile, he wrote, "I have reason to think that you are mistaken in your impressions of the conduct of our troops at Craney Island. That they waded into the water on the sinking of your boat is true; but I learn it was for the purpose of rescuing their conquest and assisting the perishing. . . ." The next day, Taylor's aide, Captain John Myers, was rowed from Norfolk to H.M.S. *San Domingo* to deliver Virginia's formal protest. Admiral Warren received him "with civility," but General Beckwith was ashore and Myers waited for him till 8 at night.

When Beckwith read Taylor's complaint, he turned to Myers and repeated his belief that disorderly Americans at Craney Island had first been guilty of cruelty. Myers denied it. Finally, Beckwith said he had ordered re-embarkation of French troops as soon as he learned of their outrages. "Appealing to my knowledge of the nature of the war in Spain, in which these men had been trained," Myers wrote, "he told me they could not be restrained." As proof of his

sincerity, Beckwith said he had just been ashore to find a water source to which his troops could move from Hampton "to quiet the minds of the inhabitants."

The findings of General Taylor's inquiry were dispatched to the British and to U. S. Secretary of War John Armstrong in Washington. They concluded:

> It appears from the testimony adduced that, on the 22nd of last month, in the action of Craney Island, two of the enemy's boats . . . were sunk by the fire of our battery. The soldiers and sailors who were in those boats were consequently afloat and in danger of drowning. And being in front of the boats which were uninjured, to disable these, our guns were necessarily fired in the direction of the men in the water but with no intention whatever to do them further harm, but, on the contrary, orders were given to prevent this by ceasing to fire grape and only round shot. It is also substantiated that one of the enemy, who had apparently surrendered, advanced towards the shore about 100 yards when he suddenly turned to his right and endeavored to make his escape to a body of the enemy which had landed above the island and who were then in view. Then—and not till then—was he fired upon to bring him back, which had the desired effect, and he was taken unhurt to the island.

The Virginia militia board investigating the incident found no cruelty by its troops. "The character of the American soldier for humanity and magnaminity has not been committed, but, on the contrary, confirmed," concluded Lieutenant-Colonels Constant Freeman, Armistead Thomson Mason, Francis Boykin, and Thomas Reed, its members.

Beckwith acknowledged the report and assured Taylor that "Any infringements of the established usages of war will be instantly noticed and punished."

Thus began Britain's Chesapeake offensive in the War of 1812. Though the two engagements destroyed property and brought commerce to a halt, they took few lives. Indeed, they helped solidify American sentiment and hastened the end of the war. "Remember Hampton!" became a rallying cry.

The invasion also revealed the inadequacy of American naval and coastal defenses. As James Jarvis, the zealous sergeant, wrote in his journal, "In most of our defeats, we may trace them to want of men. Our force was altogether insufficient at Hampton. Had our people been equal or two-thirds the number of the enemy, the Hamptonians would not have been compelled to retreat. They fought like heroes . . . ."

Soon after Hampton's conquest the British withdrew, leaving ships to blockade the bay until the war ended. Admiral Warren returned to England. The main force sailed southward under Cockburn into the Carolinas, where it harassed the country by seizing goods and liberating slaves. Reuniting in 1814 in the Chesapeake, the ships proceeded up the Potomac to burn the White House and Capitol, forcing President Madison to flee for his life.

By that time, hostilities had ruined many American farmers and shippers. Since President Jefferson had imposed his embargo in 1807, overseas trade had virtually ceased. Peace found the United States determined to arm for the future. To better protect the Atlantic's largest harbor, President James Monroe's administration began building Fortress Monroe at Point Comfort, with Fort Calhoun on a built-up channel shoal nearby. The navy expanded beyond the handful of ships that had faced Britain.

Several survivors of Craney Island and Hampton marched on to fame. Although Cockburn went down in history as a ruthless pillager, his invasion of Washington was cheered in London. After successfully convoying the defeated Napoleon to St. Helena in 1815, he was made Admiral of the Fleet and then First Sea Lord of

the Admiralty. Beckwith became British commander-in-chief at Bombay. Sir Charles James Napier, promoted to general, conquered Sind and died one of Britain's celebrated warrior-statesmen.

On the American side, Robert Barraud Taylor ended his days as judge of Virginia's General Court, after declining an army commission as general. Captain Charles Stewart, USN, brought the *Constitution* triumphant through the war, winning for it the name "Old Ironsides" and for himself the thanks of Congress. William Branford Shubrick, a navy lieutenant at Craney Island, rose to commodore and led the navy's Pacific force in the Mexican War.

One man was marked for tragedy: Colonel Armistead Thomson Mason, who led the cavalry at Norfolk, was killed in a duel with his brother-in-law in 1819. The great-grandson of statesman George Mason, he had been elected a United States senator four years before.

As for Sergeant Jarvis of the Portsmouth Rifles, he spent his life reliving events of June 22, 1813. First as a Portsmouth boatbuilder and later as inspector for Gosport Navy Yard, he treasured the memory of that day. In 1846 he completed his "Reminiscences of Events Which Were Glorious to the American Cause" for the son of his dead hero, Arthur Emmerson. The Emmersons presented the manuscript in 1966 to the College of William and Mary.

Jarvis chose as his theme:

Let Glorious Acts more Glorious Acts
  inspire
And catch from breast to breast the Noble
  Fire.
On Valour's side the odds of combat lie.
The brave live Glorious or lamented die. . . .

Though warfare may change, he seemed to say, courage remains the one imperative for victory.

17. *A Visit by a French Botanist*

AN early nineteenth-century French botanist, who traveled on the James River and wrote interestingly about Virginia was August Plée. He sketched and collected specimens while traveling through North America and the Caribbean between 1821 and 1825.

Plée's manuscript notes, sketches of Virginia, and specimens are preserved at the Musée d'Histoire Naturelle in Paris, where they were discovered nearly a half-century ago by Professor Gilbert Chinard of Princeton. They tell us a lot about Hampton Roads and other Virginia ports. He came at a time when steamboats were just coming in. Virginia's largest towns—Norfolk and Richmond—then held only a few thousand people each. Along the shore of Hampton Roads stood windmills to grind corn and wheat.

Plée was appointed an explorer-naturalist by the Paris museum in 1819. He sailed first to the Caribbean island of Guadaloupe. Later he moved on to nearby Martinique, where he remained almost a year, cataloguing and shipping living and dried plants back to Paris. Next he moved on to Puerto Rico and then sailed to the United States on the French frigate *Juno*.

Reaching Hampton Roads in late March or early April 1821, Plée sketched the Virginia coast at Cape Henry, Old Point, Hampton Roads, the Elizabeth River and Craney Island at Norfolk, Gosport (Norfolk) Navy Yard, and Portsmouth.

Temporarily leaving the *Juno* at Norfolk, Plée went by passenger ship up the James to visit and sketch Jamestown, Richmond, the Richmond tobacco boat canal, and Mayo's wooden bridge which spanned the James at Richmond.

Then, venturing down the York, Plée took in Yorktown, Gloucester Point, and Queens Creek before returning to his ship.

The chief objective of Plée's American visit was Philadelphia, where Benjamin Franklin had founded the American Philosophical Society in 1743 and where such naturalists as Benjamin Rush and David Rittenhouse lived and worked.

Plée went by steamboat to explore northern New York state and Canada. He visited New York City, Albany, Buffalo, the villages of the Seneca Indians, Niagara Falls, and then the Canadian towns of Newark, York, Kingston, and Fort Caratacoui.

Like most Europeans, he was disappointed by the Indians. "These wretched Indians have

*The James flowed smoothly when Auguste Plée
first saw Richmond's skyline in 1821.*

taken on, along with our wine and strong liquors, all our faults and vices, without acquiring any of our virtues," he wrote. "Their number diminishes each day, and it is the English policy to take care to do nothing to arrest the causes of depopulation which promises them free possession of the lands [the Indians] inhabit."

After pressing on to Montreal and Quebec, Plée returned to Norfolk, where his luggage was still aboard the *Juno.* From there he returned to Martinique, whence he wrote to his museum that he was shipping 209 items of fruit and seeds in 80 crates.

So involved was the scientist in his studies that he seldom wrote his wife. Fearing her absent husband might be dead, Madame Plée wrote to French authorities to urge a search for him. Then, just as he was preparing to sail home, he sickened and died in Martinique on August 17, 1825. He was only 38 years old. His specimens were sent to France, along with seven books of journals and sketches.

After his death, Plée was memorialized by a botanist, Marcel Raymond, in *August Plée (1787–1825) and the American Flora.* In it he expressed belief that "Plée would doubtless have left an interesting body of works on natural history had he not died when his career was only beginning. His notes . . . show that he had in him the stuff of explorer-naturalist. While he examined men and things attentively, natural history never ceased to be the principal object of his study."

Through the work of such devoted naturalists, the flora and fauna of the New World was gradually found and catalogued. August Plée joined the company of others like Karl Linnaeus and Charles Darwin, who have unlocked nature's secrets for the world.

Virginia State Library

An early wooden bridge across the James was built at Richmond by John Mayo, replacing a ferry.

Nathaniel Harrison of Prince George imported the English thoroughbred Monkey in 1737.

18. *Upper Brandon and the Harrisons*

COUNTRY living is beset nowadays by the high cost of farm and household workers, but the James River plantations continue to exert fascination for wealthy families.

Recently the Prince George County estate of Upper Brandon has been bought by the James River Corporation of Richmond to serve as a demonstration tree farm, wildlife refuge, and training center for managers of the Richmond-based pulp and paper conglomerate.

Upper Brandon is one of four major James River seats of the prolific Harrison family. The first, Wakefield, in Surry county, was destroyed by Benedict Arnold's troops in the Revolution. The second is Berkeley in Charles City, seat of Benjamin Harrison of the Revolution and ancestral home of Presidents William Henry and Benjamin Harrison. It is owned by the Malcolm Jamiesons.

The two other Harrison seats are Brandon and Upper Brandon, both built in the nineteenth century on a Prince George County peninsula. You can see both easily from the James, not far across the river from Sherwood Forest and Weyanoke plantations in Charles City.

Once they were stops for James River steamboats halfway between Norfolk and Richmond, a river distance of about 120 miles, but few vessels transit the James nowadays.

Upper Brandon is 12 miles upriver from Jamestown, so the early Harrison owners in steamboat days frequently did business in Williamsburg. In the automobile era, however, the houses are more closely linked with Hopewell and Petersburg.

The north shore of the James was the hoity-toity side of the river in early times because of its closer proximity to the capital, first at Jamestown, then Williamsburg, and finally at Richmond. In colonial times, the north shore drew an array of first-class mansions that included Shirley, Westover, Berkeley, and Carter's Grove. The south shore came later and never has been as stylish.

John Martin, a Jamestown settler in 1616, acquired 5,000 valuable acres on a southside peninsula just west of the Chickahominy River's influx into the James. He called it Brandon for a place in England. Thus it began. By 1712, the land had been acquired by wealthy Benjamin Harrison II.

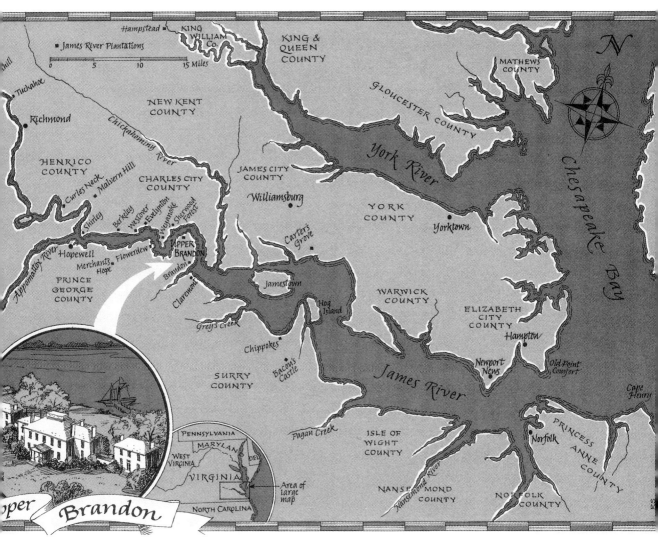

James River Corporation

The Harrison family built Upper Brandon on the James in the nineteenth century.

That peninsula remained as Brandon until Benjamin Harrison III died in 1807. His will divided it between two sons, which led to the confusing creation of two adjoining plantations, Brandon and Upper Brandon. The older house site is owned by ex-Congressman Robert Daniel.

The newer house, Upper Brandon, was built beginning in 1821 by William Byrd Harrison, whose Harrison and Byrd heirs lived there till 1948. Since then, it changed hands twice before the James River Corporation bought it in 1984.

The undeveloped shores of the James attract abundant wildlife. Brandon and Upper Brandon have long been famous for their extensive marshlands that attract thousands of migrating wild ducks and geese each winter. The James River Corporation has made a waterfowl refuge on Upper Brandon's 580 acres of marsh. It will continue to farm 750 other acres, demonstrating sound environmental practices.

The company has restored the 1821 mansion as it was in the life of its builder, William Byrd Harrison, to be used in conjunction with its Upper Brandon corporate training center. The manor house is a brick federal-style mansion with balancing hyphens and wings, the latter added in 1859. The house is architecturally related to Hampstead in New Kent and Horn Quarter in King William, and all three are thought to have been built by the same craftsmen. The exterior of the main house is so similar to Richmond's Wickham-Valentine House and the Governor's Mansion that it may have been designed by their architect, Alexander Parris, of Boston.

Upper Brandon felt the economic decline of all Tidewater plantations after the Revolution reduced Virginia's tobacco sales to England. Yet, one cannot fail to admire the optimism of William Byrd Harrison, who built the plantation, and his many descendants who farmed it until the family had to sell. They were devout and educated people, unfortunately victimized by slavery, by the Civil War, and by the decline of Southern life after 1865.

When William Byrd Harrison died in 1870, he was buried beneath a tombstone which reads:

> An eminent Agriculturist
> An intelligent Patriot
> An elegant Scholar
> A refined Gentlemen
> And above all an earnest
> and devoted Christian

A nineteenth-century Harrison guest thus described the elaborate hospitality of a James River plantation:

> There were 30 or 40 guests gathered at the house . . . with about two negroes to each white . . . for three hours or more the ladies talked among themselves, looked after their children, sewed, knitted, embroidered. The gentlemen generally kept apart, smoking, chewing, drinking whiskey, talking politics, anecdotes, facetious and frequently coarse. At four dinner was announced. . . . The dinner was rich, varied and in quantity and continued until seven or eight.

Scholarly Francis Otway Byrd was the last Harrison descendant to live at Upper Brandon. It was a sad day for the Harrison kin when he sold it in 1948. But the James River Corporation will restore Upper Brandon's 1,809 acres as well as anyone possibly could.

The manor house of Upper Brandon plantation faces the James River in Prince George County, 12 miles above Jamestown.

Colonial Williamsburg

19. *Lafayette Sails the River*

GLIMPSES of two Revolutionary figures, John Marshall and the Marquis de Lafayette, emerge from valuable nineteenth-century letters owned by John Marshall, Jr., of Newport News.

One was written by Chief Justice Marshall's granddaughter, Agnes, describing her meeting with General Lafayette.

Lafayette's return from France to America in 1824 was a romantic moment of American history. Then 67 and stout, the one-time Revolutionary leader drew huge crowds as he toured Virginia, New York, and other states where he had fought in 1777–81. He visited the Yorktown battlefield and was honored at banquets in Williamsburg, Norfolk, and Richmond.

Young Agnes Marshall met Lafayette when he came down the James River from Richmond in February 1825 to visit at Westover and at Weyanoke plantations. It was at Weyanoke, where Agnes was staying with her Douthat relatives, that she met the Frenchman.

"Papa and Mama [Mr. and Mrs. Thomas Marshall] went to Richmond on purpose to see General Lafayette." Agnes wrote to her brother John at the University of Virginia. "Well, they came down in the steamboat with the General as far as Westover. When they got out, they persuaded him to come on shore with them, which . . . surprised us very much."

Agnes shook hands with Lafayette, his son George Washington Lafayette, and his secretary. Then she wrote, "After the General

Colonial Williamsburg

Lafayette in old age returned to America and sailed up the James to Weyanoke and Richmond.

A nineteenth-century Norfolk newspaper carried advertisements of available ship services.

returned to the boat, I went to a window and waved a handkerchief." Lafayette responded by waving his hat. He asked one of the Marshalls who was waving, and "the answer was 'I believe it is Pocahontas.' And then it was that he waved."

Another letter in Marshall's possession, from the chief justice's son Thomas to his son John at the University of Virginia, was written at Philadelphia on October 24, 1831. There John Marshall had just undergone a history-making operation by the famous Dr. Physick.

Thomas had good news for his son: John Marshall was recovering from surgery and "your grandfather's prospects of returning health are as favourable as the most sanguine wishes could have anticipated. He bore an operation of unusual severity and duration with a firmness that could not have been surpassed."

The family was relieved, for John Marshall was 76, though in good health. He died four years later.

"At present he suffers but little pain," Thomas Marshall wrote, "and feels no other inconvenience than what results from wearisome confinement to his bed and separation from all the world."

The only people admitted to Marshall's sickroom were his sons Jacquelin and Thomas, plus the doctors and nurse. "This requires a high degree of passive fortitude, to bear without a murmur as he does," Thomas Marshall wrote his son. "You cannot imagine the extent of the veneration with which he is regarded by the citizens of this place."

From his sickbed John Marshall sent word to his grandson at the University that he should gain experience by writing. He "remarked that you ought to employ yourself as often as possible in composition—writing theses, for example—and asked if you could not contribute in that way to the Gazette published at the University. Early habit makes composition in every branch easy and agreeable."

An 1832 letter by Agnes Marshall to her brother John describes her recent visit from her father's Oak Hill plantation in Fauquier County to the city of Washington. There she went to the Senate and talked with Senators John Tyler, Henry Clay, and John C. Calhoun. Later Agnes met President Andrew Jackson. The president passed his snuff around for his visitors, but Agnes politely declined.

The Douthats and the Marshalls spent most of their lives around the James River. In their lifetime it was Virginia's Main Street from Hampton Roads to Richmond.

Lawrence Lewis Jr.

Weyanoke on the James near Williamsburg was threatened in the Revolution and the Civil War.

*U.S. Navy warships gathered off Berkeley plantation in July 1862
when McClellan's army camped there.*

II

The Age
of Steam

20. *Exploring the Seven Seas*

AN unusual event occurred at the mouth of the James in 1838. It was the departure of a U. S. naval fleet on a four-year, round-the-world scientific expedition. Authorized by President Andrew Jackson and Congress, the voyage was a sequel to President Monroe's 1824 assertion of American interests in the New World, known since as the Monroe Doctrine.

In 1987, the Smithsonian's Museum of Natural History in Washington exhibited a year-long panorama titled "Magnificent Voyagers: the U.S. Exploring Expedition, 1838–1842."

I'd never heard of Lieutenant Charles Wilkes, USN, or of his expedition until I read of it recently. Yet it gave our infant nation knowledge in the 1840s of unexplored regions, especially the Antarctic and the South Seas. The Smithsonian contains its findings: 50,000 plant and 4,000 zoological specimens, 3,000 anthropological artifacts, scientific paintings, and 19 volumes of reports and maps. A few were in the exhibit.

Wilkes, who was chosen by the secretary of war to head the expedition after several senior naval officers had declined, was a severe skipper. His crewmen disliked him, but he made the exploring expedition a success. Even so, it cost the United States $928,183 instead of the $300,000 Congress had first allotted.

The six sailing vessels of Wilkes's squadron sailed from Hampton Roads on August 18, 1838. Wilkes commanded from the USS *Vincennes*, his flagship. Four years later only four ships returned, for one had been lost near Cape Horn and another—the supply ship—had left the squadron early and returned to the United States. It was too slow.

Wilkes's expedition was this nation's first venture at "showing the flag," displaying naval strength. In 1838 the United States was trying to build up foreign trade. Its tiny navy was also developing charts of world waterways, which were largely uncharted then except for Europe and North America.

Wilkes sailed south from Hampton Roads first to South America, around Cape Horn, and then to the Antarctic. After charting the Antarctic land mass, Wilkes led his ships to the South Pacific, where they visited Australia, the Fiji Islands, and Hawaii. He came back via the West Coast, collecting many anthropological specimens on the shoreline of the later states of Washington and Oregon.

Lt. Charles Wilkes, USN, led a four-year round-the-world expedition from Hampton Roads.

President Jackson may have been influenced to send the expedition by Thomas Jefferson, who as president in 1804 had sent the Lewis and Clark expedition from St. Louis to explore the west. "American fishermen and whalers needed more accurate maps of the South Seas," explains a Smithsonian press release, "and merchants sought new sources of commodities for the China trade."

Unfortunately, Wilkes was too hard on his crew, and "broils and contentions" filled the voyage. He was a strict disciplinarian and carefully inspected his crew each morning. "That third man, his legs are dirty, sir," Wilkes would bark to the inspecting officer. "The next man's head has not been combed! Stand up, you rascals!"

Even so, his officers admired Wilkes's knowledge and dedication. The *Vincennes*'s surgeon noted that, "The number of hours Captain Wilkes spent without sleep was extraordinary."

Artists assigned to the voyage painted pictures of tribesmen, exotic animals, and other strange sights. They made up the most interesting part of the exploring expedition's records in the Smithsonian.

After exploring the Pacific Coast, Wilkes's ships sailed back around Cape Horn again to New York. By this time Presidents Van Buren, William Henry Harrison, and John Tyler had succeeded Jackson. The Smithsonian notes that "Instead of a hero's welcome, the explorers returned to New York on June 10, 1842, to find a new president, an unfriendly Congress, a seemingly disinterested public, and even a series of courts-martial" involving Wilkes and his officers.

The Wilkes expedition's departure from Hampton Roads is one of many little-known voyages to have taken place from Virginia since Christopher Newport's three ships crossed the Atlantic in 1607. Truly, ours is one of the world's greatest ports.

Tobacco producers sent hogsheads to waiting James River ships by horse-drawn rig.

21. *From Richmond in the Gold Rush*

THE James River played a tiny part in California's 1849 Gold Rush, for at least two boats sailed out of it in that exciting year, bearing hopeful Virginia men and boys to the far Pacific.

It all began when a woodsman setting up a sawmill near Coloma, California, discovered gold. When the word got out, America went wild. Soldiers deserted, crews walked off ships, and farmers left their plows to heed the siren's song of riches.

In Atlantic seaports like Richmond, ships were bought and fitted out to take venturers west to the gold fields. Two water routes were favored by easterners over the long wagon trek overland. One led south to the Isthmus of Panama and overland to the coast and another voyage north to California. The longer voyage was around South America to Cape Horn and thence to California.

The *Marianna*, a 379-ton sailing vessel, was bought by 117 men from Virginia and sailed from Richmond on March 16, 1849. She chose the long route. One of the youngest men to sign up was Alexander Breckenridge Heiskell, 17, a native of Augusta County, Virginia, who made the trip with his uncle, John Blair Richardson of Hanover. Both were from Scotch-Irish and English families, reared as farmers and unversed in sailing.

Heiskell, a courageous lad, paid $300 for his share in the joint stock company which bought the *Marianna* and provisioned her for two years. That was in hopes the venturers would find gold immediately and return. Elsewhere along the Chesapeake and in other Atlantic ports, other hopeful men were hastily packing and embarking, for every ship was anxious to reach California ahead of others to stake out the best claims.

Young Alex kept a diary of his journey, offering a typical view of venturers to those faraway gold fields. The trip began with elation. Heiskell writes gleefully of the *Marianna's* departure, waved off by "our friends and the large crowd who had assembled on the wharf." There were "loud cheers and hearty wishes for a safe voyage and a great success in our enterprise," which had been incorporated under the title The Pacific Trading and Mining Company.

The first day out the inexperienced *Marianna* grounded on a bar in the James, just below Richmond, and had to pay a towboat $25 to get her off. Once underway, the voyagers passed

Richmond's harbor was much like this when Alex Heiskell
sailed for California in 1849.

the town of City Point, now Hopewell, where another company of Virginians was thronging aboard the *Glenmore*, another ship heading for the gold fields. To expedite the *Marianna's* sail down the James, a steamboat was engaged to tow her to Hampton Roads, where she anchored off the Rip Raps near Fort Monroe—now the route of the bridge-tunnel connecting Hampton with Norfolk.

Once in Hampton Roads, many of the company went ashore to Norfolk to enjoy their last port of call before the voyage. The *Marianna's* captain fortunately enlisted two more trained sailors at Norfolk to round out his crew. Then at last, after several days' delay because of bad weather, the ship boarded her pilot and proceeded through Capes Charles and Henry, headed into the Atlantic. "And now," Heiskell penned, "with strange feelings many of us for the first time view the mighty ocean and look at the prospect of a six-month voyage with great curiosity and some dread. Even now, as the land fades from view, some of the company are seasick and look as if they had rather be at home."

Only a day at sea, most of the company were seasick. The vessel labored and pitched badly in heavy squalls. Once she shipped a wave that bashed in her water casks and set others adrift. "Washed off part of the bulwarks and hatch house, some potatoes, onions, and other loose things," Heiskell noted. While the youth stood on the quarterdeck with the captain, the helmsman roared, "The wheel rope is broke." Heiskell reports that "the ship went round like a top" but rode out the storm.

During the blow the *Marianna* encountered a ship throwing cattle overboard. "Some of our company very anxious to go back, willing to give up their interest in ship," he reported, but it was too late. Then Heiskell caught cold and became so ill he stayed in his bunk for several weeks.

In mid-May, as the storm-tossed *Marianna* approached her first stop at Rio de Janeiro, a strange craft, with "felluca sails at night and muddy lug sails in day," created fears that a pirate was about to attack. "All hands getting out guns, pistols, knives, etc. preparing for fight tonight with the pirates," Heiskell wrote, but the strange ship disappeared.

Docking at Rio de Janeiro was a heaven-sent pleasure to the exhausted mariners. "The entrance to the harbor is grand," wrote the youth. "We came in between the Sugar Loaf, towering high towards the sky on one side, and the Fort of San Juan, bristling with cannon, on the other. The shores of the harbor are covered with beautiful green shrubs and grass, and we are now lying among hundreds of ships of different nations, with boats passing over the smooth waters of the harbor in every direction. . . . It is one of the most beautiful spots I ever beheld and among all the flags that are floating from the different ships I like our own Stars and Stripes the best."

On Sunday Alex Heiskell went ashore to find the Episcopal church, but he ended up in the Catholic cathedral. "I could not understand their jargon, though their chants were very sweet," he recorded. "I hear the Glenmore has arrived." One of its passengers brought the boy a letter from home, which assuaged his homesickness, and he spent a pleasant afternoon in the Brazilian emperor's garden overlooking the harbor. Already two investors had had enough and left the ship to return to Virginia.

The ship tossed badly for most of the next month as the *Marianna* made her way in the stormy seas approaching Cape Horn. Once the ship seemed about to sink, but "after a struggle she righted, and we are now scudding before the wind at a rapid rate." Heiskell joined an "antiswearing society for the purpose of putting a stop to profanity." Temperatures dropped and snow fell as the *Marianna* rounded Cape Horn and stopped at Tulcuhuano. Life grew bleaker, and the ship's sailing was delayed when 19 drunken shipmates tarried ashore.

Then, in September, the *Marianna* was becalmed in the Pacific. Two hungry sailors caught a rat and ate it.

On October 1—seven and a half months after leaving Richmond—the *Marianna* sailed into the harbor of San Francisco, the closest port to the Gold Rush area. "We were soon surrounded by the boats of the place," Heiskell recorded, "which bring us fine news. Gold is plenty, provisions cheap. . . . I worked for an hour and a half at a dollar per hour. Found things cheap and money plenty, so much so that I cannot as yet realize it. Want to go to the mines as soon as possible."

The *Marianna* docked close to Telegraph Hill among 400 vessels from all ports. Going ashore, Heiskell saw a dead man lying against a fence, where he lay 48 hours. "A number die so from disease, and the coroner said as many as eight in a day sometimes. . . . They come for gold and die in the streets without anyone to take care of them."

But the boisterous life of the frontier town

excited the 17-year-old. "It is situated on elevated ground and laid off very well, with broad streets," he noted, "though most of the houses are nothing but small huts and tents. Everyone is peaceable, and we have no use for our guns, pistols, and knives. . . . The laws are very strict, and persons leave all kinds of goods and even money on the side of the street and they are never stolen. If they catch a man thieving, they cut his ears off and make him leave the place.... Everything is bustle, coming and going to the mines."

The first Sunday after Alex arrived he went ashore to attend services in the Presbyterians' tent, then to the dedication of a Methodist chapel. He was glad to see Virginia friends who had just arrived on the *Glenmore*. "They are a good deal cut at our beating them in," he wrote.

Those were the last words Alexander Heiskell entered in his diary. Next day his fever suddenly recurred, and soon he was dead. He was buried by his shipmates in San Francisco, and his trunk containing his diary was returned to his mother in Virginia.

Many of Heiskell's fellow Virginians who sailed from the Chesapeake died at sea or soon after reaching the West Coast. Some were victims, like him, of mysterious fevers, probably from impure water or food. Others soon grew discouraged at failing to find gold and returned east. A few made their way as miners or found other jobs in the flourishing boom that accompanied California's entry into the union in 1850—the first West Coast state to be admitted.

Today few records survive of Chesapeake Bay vessels which sailed, like the *Marianna* and the *Glenmore*, in the great '49 gold rush. Do other families have inherited mementoes of Chesapeake area venturers, as descendants of Alexander Heiskell do? If so, their records might make up a colorful chapter of Virginia maritime history that has largely perished.

Daily Press

*Steamers provided Norfolk-to-Richmond service until the 1930s,
carrying much cargo and few passengers.*

*James River's scheduled
freight ships connected
at Hampton Roads with
coastal service.*

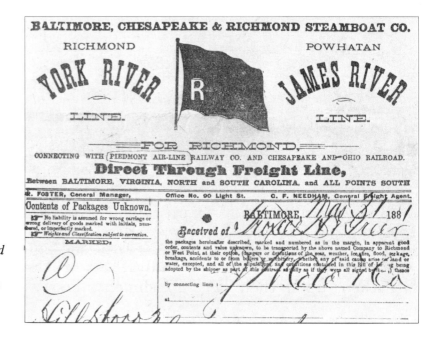

22. *Steamboats Linked Planters' World*

THE lower James River in the steamboat days of the nineteenth century was very much like that bigger midwestern river that Mark Twain made famous in *Life on the Mississippi*. Daily routine along each waterway centered on the scheduled arrivals of the big, white riverboats that every day or so brought passengers and cargo to enliven the backwoods river communities.

You can read about the James River's boats in *Plantation on the James*, by Ransom B. True, a history of Weyanoke, which we already know as an eighteenth-century plantation in Charles City County owned by generations of the Lewis, Douthat, and Harwood families.

Like all James River plantations, Weyanoke depended greatly on its wharf on the James. There those Norfolk-to-Richmond boats stopped to bring mail to the tiny Weyanoke post office. It was one of about a dozen stops that riverboats made on their two-day progress up the James. For years there was a "day boat" and a "night boat," lasting to the 1920s.

"The steamboats were the main attraction at the Weyanoke wharf," True writes. "During their heyday on the river—the years from 1815 to 1920—perhaps one hundred or more different steamers called at Weyanoke Wharf."

The earliest James River steamboats, based on Robert Fulton's first successful *Clermont* operation in 1807, were side-wheelers. These picturesque ships abound in Civil War photos of Tidewater, but the wooden sidewheels proved fragile and were eventually replaced by one or more metal propellers at the stern.

By the beginning of the twentieth century, nearly all James River steamboats were propeller-driven. I remember the ones that called at Pier A in Newport News when I was a boy, both on their upriver and downriver voyages. In the 1920s, when I roamed the shore at North End, the "night boat" to Richmond chugged up the James past our house nightly about 7 o'clock.

Besides stopping at Newport News, the boats visited Mulberry Island (now Fort Eustis), Carter's Grove, Jamestown, Scotland Wharf, Claremont, Ferguson's Wharf, Brandon, Westover, and Harrison's Landing, or Berkeley. Some stops were automatic and others were signalled from shore by a flag, run up on a halyard.

Sometimes to save time, passengers boarded the ship in mid-stream from a rowboat. An English visitor to Weyanoke once wrote, "I then

The James River steamer Mobjack *docked at Shirley plantation on its way upriver in 1900.*

crossed to the north side of the James River, being rowed out at sunrise far from shore to wait for a steamer. The hour of her arrival being somewhat uncertain, we remained for some time in the cold. . . . At length we gladly hailed a large steamer as she came down rapidly toward us, and my baggage was immediately taken care of by two of the crew."

A famous James steamer was the *Ariel*, owned by the Virginia Steamboat Company, which served off and on from 1878 to 1904. Built in Wilmington, Delaware, in 1858, she was one of the first iron-hulled passenger ships of her time.

The best-remembered James River tripper was the *Pocahontas*, known as "Poky," which operated from Richmond to Norfolk from 1893 till 1919. Once she partly burned at Richmond but was rebuilt. Then an engineers' strike ended her river run. She was sold to a New Jersey firm and served in the New York area until scrapped about 1935.

James River steamers called at many plantations on the James to serve passengers and shippers.

A *Pocahontas* passenger paid $1.50 to travel the river, with meals costing 60 cents more. She sailed from Richmond on Monday, Wednesday, and Friday at 6 A.M. and arrived at Norfolk at 7:30 P.M. She left Norfolk at 6 A.M. on Tuesday, Thursday, and Saturday to go back to Richmond.

Describing Poky's arrival at Weyanoke plantation, Ransom True writes, "When she approached Weyanoke, Captain Graves or any of the innumerable small boys to whom he gave permission would pull the *Pocahontas's* unique three-note whistle. Sounding across the river, the notes formed a chord long remembered by river dwellers. She would pull up to the wharf. Then she would embark or debark passengers and all types of freight."

The *Pocahontas* boasted an electric organ plus bridal chambers, card parlors, and staterooms. When the Old Dominion Line sold her in 1919, several successors tried steamboats, but the advent of automobiles doomed them all by 1924.

Today the James sees little shipping except for oilers, timber and gravel barges, duck-hunters' bateaux, and summer pleasure craft. The dock at Weyanoke today is dismantled, like those of all other one-time stops of the *Ariel* and the *Pocahontas*. We can only imagine what James River steamboat travel once was like.

The Confederate ship Virginia, *formerly the* Merrimack, *attacked the USS* Cumberland *at Newport News in 1862, sinking the vessel.*

The CSS Virginia *fought the Union ship* Monitor *to a standoff in Hampton Roads.*

23. *The James in the Civil War*

WHEN Virginia voted in 1861 to secede from the Union, it doomed itself to become a major battleground of a war between North and South. It had not long to wait. On May 27 farmers living at Newport News Point, at the junction of Hampton Roads and the James River, saw troop-laden vessels approach their shore. The Yankees had come! The peaceful farmlands of Virginia would be red with blood before peace finally came at Appomattox four years later.

As the border line of the Confederacy, Virginia hoped for a quick war. Like other Southerners, Virginians had an absurd faith in the skill of the South's sharpshooters. With South Carolina's Wade Hampton, they believed "Southern hot-headed dash, reckless gallantry, and spirit of adventure" would quickly overwhelm the North. Only a few realists like Robert E. Lee understood what odds the South faced.

Lee, who had declined the Federal government's command of Union forces, resigned his army commission to become the defender of Virginia. "Trusting in almighty God, an approving conscience, and the aid of my fellow citizens," he said, "I devote myself to the service of my native State, in whose behalf alone will I ever again draw my sword."

Lee's sentiments were shared by most eastern Virginians, but in the state's far western counties, slavery and secession were anathema. At a meeting in Wheeling a few months after the war began, Appalachian Virginia "seceded" from Virginia and became the state of West Vir-

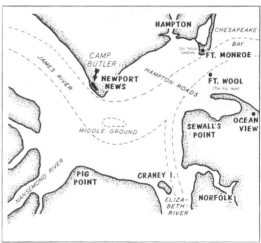

Chester D. Bradley

The James and Hampton Roads were crucial in Civil War naval campaigning.

95

Daily Press

For four years Federal strategy sought to unseat Jefferson Davis's Confederacy in Richmond.

ginia. In that act the proud Old Dominion lost one-third of her territory and her citizens.

Once Jefferson Davis and his cabinet were installed in Richmond in 1861, the Confederates hoped to carry the war to the North in blitzkrieg fashion. However, Lincoln and his generals had other ideas. They saw the South's weak navy as an invitation to take control of Hampton Roads and then to march up the Peninsula to Richmond, supported by Federal gunboats on the James and York. The result was General McClellan's Peninsula campaign of 1862, which was defeated at last by Lee's heroic defense of Richmond in the Seven Days' battles of June and July of that year.

The Union navy's superiority was challenged at Hampton Roads in 1862 by the Confederate ironclad *Virginia*, (originally the Federal frigate *Merrimack*), which battled the Union's *Monitor* to a stand-off while spectators watched from Norfolk, Hampton, and Newport

Harper's Weekly from Virginia State Library

Confederates shipped war supplies over the James River canal till Federal forces took it.

*Armament fires set by Confederates in downtown Richmond
spread as troops fled south across the James.*

News. Neither ship seriously hurt the other, but the battle introduced the age of iron ships.

Thanks to its strong navy, the Union soon took control of the James and all other of Virginia's tidal rivers during the war. It used the James and the York during the Peninsula campaign to supply McClellan's army. After the brief resistance of the CSS *Virginia* in Hampton Roads, the Confederacy could do little to oppose McClellan's invaders.

Like the Revolution, the Civil War reached its climax in Virginia, close to the James. After choosing a succession of hapless commanders, Lincoln in 1864 named Ulysses S. Grant, who at first suffered heavy losses in the Wilderness Campaign. Grant then moved more successfully against Lee at Petersburg, an important railhead and supply center.

Grant's siege of Richmond and Petersburg in 1864 led at last to Lee's evacuation of Richmond in April 1865. Jefferson Davis and his cabinet meanwhile fled across the James southward to Danville and then on to Greensboro, North Carolina, before their government dissolved. Pursued by Grant to Appomattox, Lee surrendered his Army of Northern Virginia on April 9, 1865. Other Confederate surrenders followed until Davis was captured in Georgia and brought back to Fort Monroe. At last the tragedy was ending.

Visitors in search of the Civil War will find a wealth of it along the James River as well as in Virginia's many war sites. Although a century has dimmed a nation's memories, the men who fought and died are enshrined on the battleground named Virginia.

24. *When Peanuts Came to America*

ALONG the James River in the Civil War, Union soldiers for the first time discovered a Southern edible called goobers or ground nuts. Originally a slave food, they became commercially traded as "peanuts" in the 1840s. A highway marker on Route 480 near Waverly notes the farm on which Dr. Mathew Harris in 1844 first produced peanuts for public sale in Virginia.

Virginia's sandy counties on the southside of the James River were the peanut's first home in America, leading to early peanut markets in Smithfield, Suffolk, and Norfolk. Today Suffolk is "Peanut Capital of the World," though other Southern states now exceed Virginia in quantity, though not in quality. By the time of the Civil War, farmers in seven other states were growing and selling them.

Peanuts came to Virginia with slaves from Africa soon after the settlement of Jamestown. Africans in turn had got them from the Spanish and Portuguese, who had discovered them in South America after Columbus opened up the New World. The Incas of South America called peanuts "ynchic" and put them in tombs with the dead as food for their voyage to the hereafter. In sacrifices to the Sun God, Incas offered peanuts with the incantation, "Eat this, Lord Sun, and acknowledge thy children."

From Africa the "nguba" or "goober" as Africans called the nut, was brought by blacks and planted in slave gardens on Virginia plantations. The familiar folk song, "Eating Goober Peas," dates from those times.

Early in the 1900s, an Italian immigrant in Wilkes-Barre, Pennsylvania, foresaw the demand for peanut products and created Planters Peanuts. He was Amedeo Obici, and he soon moved his business and his family to the source and built his main plant at Suffolk. Today Planters Nut and Chocolate Company is a huge worldwide network.

My grandmother as a girl in Surry County in the 1870s enjoyed autumn "pea-parchings" in her father's peanut fields, after the crop was dug. A shock of peanut vines, reserved for the children, would be burned and the children allowed to recoup the roasted peanuts from the embers.

In those days in peanut-growing areas, hogs were turned into the fields after the harvest to root up any goobers left in the ground. That created the celebrated peanut-fed ham, but the big commercial Smithfield hamcurers now say it makes the meat too greasy. Hogs are no longer fattened on leftover peanuts.

When I was growing up, peanuts were laboriously harvested, largely by hand. The mature plants were plowed up in mid-October and raked into shocks to dry in the weather. Then the dried plants were fed into a big four-wheeled peanut picker, which dropped the run-of-mill peanuts into burlap bags and left the vines as livestock feed. The bagged nuts were then taken to Smithfield and sold to buyers. So far as I remember, there was then no government inspection or grading.

Many peanut-picking machines were invented in Virginia after the Civil War, some by the Gwaltneys of Smithfield, and others by the Ben-

thalls of Suffolk. Pembroke Decatur Gwaltney, Sr., who had been a gunsmith in the Civil War, went to Smithfield in 1870 and developed cleaning methods which made him rich. His Gwaltney-Bunkley Company made Smithfield "the Peanut Capital of the World" before a Smithfield fire in 1920 left Mr. Obici in Suffolk as "Mister Peanut."

Peanuts now take less hand labor but more elaborate equipment. Like hams and tobacco, their curing is speeded up by the use of circulating hot-air dryers. Today harvested peanuts stay only five days in the field after plowing. Then they're sucked into a machine which separates nuts from chaff. The nuts are dumped into a drying bin, where hot air is blown over them till their moisture content is almost nil.

Painting by Sydney King, Colonial Williamsburg

The first blacks arrived from the Caribbean to the James River in 1619, brought by a Dutch trading vessel.

The ornate stove from the Governor's Palace in Williamsburg roasted peanuts in Richmond's nineteenth-century state capitol.

Then, after two or three days, they're dry enough to be hauled to market, inspected, graded, and sold to buyers.

That happens each fall at the Farmers' Union in Smithfield and at other buying stations through the Peanut Belt. My Smithfield cousins sold their crop to the Birdsongs of Suffolk, but buyers in the region include Whitleys, Ponds, Hancocks, and the Columbia, Sedley, and Planters Peanut companies. You'll eat their products as roasted or salted nuts, peanut butter, peanut oil, or candy. Some of the best goobers are saved for seed.

The promotion which Obici's Planters Peanuts about 1915 began giving "Mister Peanut" helped to build a huge market. By the 1920s peanuts were being planted not only in Virginia and North Carolina, but in the Deep South, Southwest, and California, where Japanese immigrants grew them. The Depression of the 1930s increased demand for the "nickel lunch," as Planters called its five-cent salted peanut bags.

George Washington Carver of Tuskegee Institute in Alabama also helped expand the market. The black scientist, a graduate of Hampton University, demonstrated 105 ways of cooking "pindars," as Alabamians called them: as flour for bread, as a substitute for coffee, and in peanut soup, among many other ways. Dietitians say peanuts are one of the best all-around foods known.

Georgia is today the top peanut-grower in the nation. However, the Georgia product is the tiny "runner" peanut which Virginia growers disparage as a poor second to Virginia's pearl-shaped "ballparks." Even smaller is the Spanish or "redskin," grown in Texas, Oklahoma, and New Mexico.

The onetime slave food even penetrated the Virginia General Assembly in 1902, when the *Richmond Dispatch* teased the South Carolina legislature for its "abnormal fondness for pindars during business hours." Then the *Dispatch* admitted that Virginia solons loved peanuts too, roasting them in the shell on the surface of Lord Botetourt's iron stove, which then heated the hall of the Capitol in Richmond. Now the old stove is back in the ballroom of the reconstructed Palace in Williamsburg, as it was after Governor Botetourt brought it from Europe, before the Revolution.

In a world threatened someday by food shortage, the peanut may save us.

25. *Billy Mahone's Years of Glory*

T HE James River rapidly lost its importance as Virginia's major water artery when railroads replaced ships as the principal carriers of passengers and goods. The two main figures in the railroads' rise in the Old Dominion were Billy Mahone, a tiny Petersburg civil engineer, and Collis Potter Huntington, a giant New York millionaire.

Mahone stretched his Petersburg to Norfolk railway along the south side of the James in 1858, to become the first link in the Norfolk and Western, now the huge Norfolk-Southern rail system, third largest in the nation. It provided needed shipment for the abundant timber and produce of Southside, and it eventually carried immense coal shipments from the Ohio Valley that continue to pour through Hampton Roads today.

During the Civil War Mahone's railway was badly damaged, and when peace returned it soon gained a strong rival. In 1870, Collis Huntington, of Pacific railway fame, gained control of the tiny Chesapeake and Ohio in Richmond and extended it on the opposite shore of the James from Richmond to Newport News. It was a first step in his design to build a transcontinental line to bind more closely the recently fractured Union.

The N & W and the C & O together ate rapidly into the riverboat traffic of the James and Hampton Roads. And in the 1920s, after highways were built for Henry Ford's new Model Ts, James River shipping declined still further, dropping to almost nothing by the 1950s.

Today the somnolent James below Richmond is travelled by few ships except oil tankers and newsprint freighters, plus a sprinkling of gravel and timber barges. At a few tiny ports on the tidal lower river, like Menchville and Battery Park, a few dozen determined fishermen and oystermen still work the James. Gone are the slim white passenger ships and the rusty iron freighters of the nineteenth century.

Tidewater's phenomenal railroad era owes more to Billy Mahone than to any other man. His imprint is still on the 80 miles of track he laid down in the 1850s—just a few years out of VMI—through the pine forest of Prince George, Sussex, Southampton, and the scraggly towns of Portsmouth and Norfolk. It gave unity and purpose to Virginia's Tobacco Belt, with its thousands of newly-freed farm slaves needing jobs.

Billy Mahone was one of Virginia's rare rebels, the son of a tavern keeper who grew up to resent the planters' unconcern for public education or individual opportunity. In his lifetime he helped to engineer two of Virginia's pioneer short-haul railroads, to become a hero and overnight general in the Confederacy, and after the war to lead proletarian "Readjusters" to demand a better life for Virginia's underclass of blacks and middle class whites. For a brief time in the 1870s and 1880s, he and his cohorts broke the power of the old line planter Democrats, who had governed Virginia through its Democratic office holders, but Mahone's triumph was brief.

Billy Mahone wasn't all good. As a self-made political boss, he introduced some features of machine politics into easy-going Virginia. The twentieth-century conservative Democratic organization of Senators Martin, Glass, and Harry Byrd, Sr. owed something to his example. But for a while he beat the big boys at their own game.

Mahone was a bantam who measured five feet five and weighed no more than 100 pounds. Though president of the Norfolk and Petersburg when Virginia seceded from the Union, Billy became a lieutenant colonel under General William Booth Taliaferro, CSA, and was put in command of the defense of Norfolk. By the time of the second battle of Manassas, he was serving as a brigadier general and was badly wounded.

Recovered, he led demoralized Confederates to a dramatic Civil War victory at Petersburg in 1864. Almost single handedly, Billy Mahone turned defeat into victory in the bloody Battle of the Crater. He inflicted Union losses of 4,400 men compared to his own 1,400, briefly delayed Grant's capture of Petersburg, and became a revered southern hero.

Conscious of Virginia's lack of pubic education throughout its first 250 years, Mahone as a Reconstruction politician organized the Readjusters to write off part of Virginia's Civil War debt and leave enough money to revive the

Virginia State Library

General William Mahone, CSA, was a Civil War hero and postwar politician.

prostrate state. He gained control of the General Assembly, put his candidate in the Governor's mansion, and was himself elected to the United States Senate from 1881 to 1887. In those years he was Virginia's strongest voice.

Born in Southside near the present Franklin, Mahone grew up in Jerusalem, now Courtland, when Nat Turner's insurrection there was still vivid. His father ran Mahone's Tavern at Southampton's courthouse, where the little boy early observed life and developed ambition. Earning money carrying county mail on horseback, he entered Sussex County's Littletown Academy at 15, showed genius in mathematics, and was accepted by VMI as a state cadet, receiving free tuition in return for teaching in public school.

Billy was a good cadet, graduating eighth in a class of 27. After discharging his teaching obligation, he became a railroad surveyor and then an engineer. In the 1850s, when Virginia cities were building short-haul railroads to ship their produce, he perceived the need to connect these into rail systems long enough to move the timber, farm products, and eventually coal from the western frontier to Hampton Roads.

It was a timely move, for Virginia's ports were losing coastal trade to New York and Baltimore, which were reaping fantastic benefits from new internal improvements. The Erie Canal in 1824 had created a boom in New York City. Maryland businessmen had countered in 1830 by building the Baltimore and Ohio Railway to bring Ohio River products from Wheeling across Virginia and Maryland to Baltimore. Most Atlantic ports were outgrowing Hampton, Norfolk, and Portsmouth.

Ever since 1785, Virginia had pinned her trade hopes to the concept of a James River-Kanawha Canal, originally advocated by George Washington. At first it had looked easy. Besides, river shipment was cheaper than rail, and the tidal James offered a fairly straight shot from Richmond to the sea. But by 1850 it was clear to most Virginians that dredging channels on the lower James and maintaining canals on the upper river were endlessly expensive, thanks to constant flooding and shoaling. After the Civil War, Virginia wisely shifted from canals to railways.

Billy Mahone in his twenties married the strong-minded Otelia Butler, daughter of Dr. and Mrs. Robert Butler of Smithfield. Along the N & W Southside tracks today, legend credits Otelia's passion for Scott's novels for her naming early N & W stops such novelistic names as Waverly, Wakefield, Sedley, and Ivor. Another stop—Disputanta—was said to reflect Otelia's disagreement with Billy.

One of Billy's railroads, the Atlantic, Mississippi and Ohio, or A M & O, was known in Billy's lifetime as "All Mine and Otelia's."

Billy remained thin and wiry all his life. When Governor John Letcher brought Otelia Mahone word of her husband's injury at Manas-

Malcolm Jamieson

Lincoln and his staff, on horseback, review McClellan's army at Berkeley, facing the James.

Norfolk-Southern

Billy Mahone built much of the Norfolk and Southern Railway south of the James.

Though it was only 20 miles south of the James River's principal city of Richmond, Petersburg was Virginia's boom town in the 1850s, its farm prosperity dwarfing that of the earlier Peninsula and Tidewater tobacco counties. It was discovering wealth in cotton, timber, barrel staves, naval stores, and peanuts. Accordingly, Petersburg's ambitious Scottish traders in 1851 decided to extend their railroad eastward to the deepwater port of Norfolk. They chose Billy Mahone, then 27, to engineer it. His combined salaries then reached $25,000 yearly, at a time when Robert E. Lee was heading Washington College at Lexington for less than $5,000 yearly. Billy was a foretaste of the twentieth-century American tycoon.

To reach Norfolk, the railroad had to penetrate the Great Dismal Swamp, whose marshy terrain posed huge construction problems. But ingenious Billy was equal to the task. The 52-mile straightaway track Billy drove through the Nansemond County swamp is still very much in use today for Norfolk-Southern's booming coal business, terminating in docks at Norfolk which ship Ohio Valley coal to nations around the world.

A yellow fever epidemic struck Norfolk in 1855, while Mahone was directing the Dismal Swamp track laying. For a while all progress ceased. Wrote a survivor, "It was painful to walk the street; there was a sense of loneliness and melancholy never before known. On streets that had been crowded, not a human being or living creature of any kind was seen. The only sound that was heard was once a day when a heavy wagon came tumbling along, stopping at one house and then another until it had gathered its load of dead bodies and proceeded to the cemetery."

In appreciation for his skill, Billy was made president of the line, which now stretched from Norfolk to Bristol on the Tennessee line, 408 miles away. After the Civil War's interruption, he was elected in 1867 as president of the enlarged Atlantic, Mississippi, and Ohio. He was now at the height of his power and famous

sas, he consoled her with the news it was "only a flesh wound." "Flesh wound?" demanded Otelia. "Billy hasn't got any flesh."

The Norfolk and Western had got its start in Petersburg in 1833, when 41 businessmen sought a railroad to link that town with the nearby James River port of City Point, now Hopewell. The resulting City Point railroad was joined in 1856 by the Virginia and Tennessee and later by the South Side Railroad between Petersburg and Lynchburg. Billy's celebrity helped him to persuade stockholders of the three short Virginia lines to merge their interest and eventually become the Norfolk and Western.

for his big salary and his direct, imperious manner. In these years he travelled on his own railway car, accompanied by his own cook, his own cow, and his own chickens to cater to his queasy digestion. A show-off, he dressed eccentrically and talked in a high voice. To all the world he was "Billy."

Billy's rail days ended in 1881, when the N & W was sold to Philadelphia owners after going belly up in the financial upheavals of the times. That same year he was elected senator from Virginia and played a major role in populist efforts to create Virginia public schools and to provide vocational and scientific education for blacks and whites. One contemporary called him "the most influential political figure Virginia has produced since the days of Thomas Jefferson."

Billy's Readjuster triumphs, alas, were short lived. In 1885 ex-General Fitzhugh Lee, nephew of Marse Robert, became Democratic governor of Virginia to succeed Mahone's man, William E. Cameron. In 1887, when Billy finished his Senate term, he retired and died in 1895 in Washington.

Virginia State Library

Petersburg was the center of Billy Mahone's railways and of his Readjuster party.

Tobacco, early Virginia's mainstay, was shipped from James River ports to Europe.

Colonial Williamsburg

26. *Tobacco's Mighty Empire*

VIRGINIA was the center of tobacco culture in America from the time John Rolfe planted his first crop at Jamestown in 1612. After the Civil War Richmond had more than 100 leaf-tobacco firms plus many small manufacturers of chews and smokes.

Then, alas, in 1889 one James Buchanan "Buck" Duke formed his huge American Tobacco Company. Operating in Durham, North Carolina, and in New York, Buck Duke took the lead in cigarette making away from Virginia. Since then North Carolina has become the leading tobacco state, but Richmond is still a tobacco center, making one out of every three packs of cigarettes sold in America. Several major brands are made there and export houses send U. S. leaf to Europe.

The men who made Richmond tobacco-rich in the 1870s and '80s were John Allen and Lewis Ginter, both emigrants from the North. They started with a cigarette called Richmond Gems that was promoted across the land from 1875 till Allen and Ginter sold out to Duke 14 years later. The sale made them millionaires. Their names and civic deeds are remembered in Richmond.

Cigarettes were little known in America till the 1870s. When the first were introduced from Egypt and Russia, they became popular as a quick and easy smoke. They were milder than cigars, which till the 1870s vied with pipes and chewing tobacco in popularity. The first cigarette maker in the U. S. was F. S. McKinney, who in 1868 brought workers from Russia to his New York tobacco shop to make cigarettes. The new product was a hit, though exotic and expensive.

That news was brought to Richmond by Lewis Ginter, who had moved there from New York in 1874 to work as a traveling tobacco salesman for John F. Allen, then Virginia's most successful cigar and snuff maker. Ginter, the enterprising son of Germanic emigrants named Guenther, got Allen to start making Richmond Gems in 1875.

Allen and Ginter's cigarettes were made by hand by women. They became so popular the two men expanded their original force of 20 girls to 120. The firm produced 1,500,000 cigarettes a month. In 1876 the Richmond company displayed its Gems to big crowds at the Philadelphia Centennial. Gems were sold in colorful packages, designed by Ginter.

The successful company of Allen and Ginter opened offices in London, Paris, and Berlin. New brands, all using mixtures of Virginia and foreign tobaccos, were added. They were variously called Virginia Pets, Napoleons, Dandies, Dubecs, Virginia Brights, and Old Dominions.

In 1887 *Harper's Weekly* magazine devoted an article and many illustrations to Allen and Ginter's big Richmond factory. One picture showed women seated at counters rolling ground tobacco into cigarettes.

But change was coming. Machinery was invented in the 1870s by a Virginian named James Bonsack to roll cigarettes, speeding up the process. Allen and Ginter tried the device, but they unwisely discarded it as less effective than hand labor.

Then Bonsack offered his machine to Buck Duke in Durham. Duke liked it, improved it, and contracted with Bonsack to sell him more cigarette rollers. The new machine made cigarettes much cheaper, enabling Duke to undersell Richmond Gems. Duke became the number one cigarette maker and his cigarettes and Bull Durham smoking tobacco made him a fortune, later used to endow Duke University.

By the time Allen and Ginter began mechanizing their factory in 1887, Duke's tobacco company was outselling all other cigarette makers. In 1889 Duke began buying out and merging his competitors into the giant American Tobacco Company. Allen and Ginter fought him for a while, but eventually Duke got control of them and three other leading American cigarette firms which produced 90 percent of all domestic cigarettes. That's how the American Tobacco Company was born. Duke, age 33, became president.

Duke's American Tobacco Company was a monopoly, and press and politicians opposed it. That was the beginning of "trust-busting" and of the Sherman Antitrust Act, passed by an

Harper's Weekly

Women rolled cigarettes by hand in Allen and Ginter's Richmond factory in 1887, before mechanization.

aroused Congress. The Virginia General Assembly refused to grant a charter for the American Tobacco Company in Virginia, but Duke got a charter in New Jersey and moved his company headquarters to New York. With his advertising genius George Washington Hill, Duke built cigarettes into a national craze. Other firms like Pierre Lorillard, Liggett and Myers, R. J. Reynolds, and Philip Morris launched brands, creating big sales and hot rivalries.

Allen and Ginter held $7,500,000 of the $25 million stock in the original American Tobacco Company. The aging Allen sold his stock in 1884 to Ginter, who was then the wealthiest man in the South. After Allen died in 1890 at 75, Ginter became Richmond's leading citizen. He developed the northside residential area called Ginter Park, gave land in Ginter Park as the site of the Presbyterians' Union Seminary,

Daily Press

South of the James today, the tobacco auction belt spreads into the Carolinas.

and donated to many civic causes. The Lewis Ginter Community House is one of his benefactions. He remained unmarried.

Before Ginter died in 1897, he was Richmond's best-known figure. His big brownstone house on Franklin Street, now part of Virginia Commonwealth University, was a Richmond showplace. He was a friend of such men as Joseph Bryan, Major James Dooley, Thomas Fortune Ryan, Thomas Branch, Frederic Scott, and other Richmond industrialists. It was an age of new industry in the South.

Tobacco today continues to be a major Richmond industry, but no leading cigarette firm is now headquartered in Richmond. However, the city serves as a market for tobacco raised throughout southside Virginia. Cigarette factories along Richmond's waterfront and Petersburg Pike also produce other tobacco products. These include plug tobacco for chewing, leaf tobacco for cigars, and granulated or flaked tobacco for pipe smoking.

The leading Richmond-headquartered tobacco handler nowadays is Universal Leaf, which buys tobacco around the world for U. S. and foreign tobacco manufacturers. These firms combine domestic and foreign tobacco into saleable blends.

Lewis Ginter's last achievement was the building of his beautiful and luxurious Hotel Jefferson on Franklin Street a few blocks from his house. Designed by the celebrated New York architects Carrere and Hastings, it was a Virginia showplace until it was closed in the 1970s as unprofitable. Now it has been bought by the Sheraton chain and, rebuilt for more than $30 million, reopened to the public.

Even though the tobacco economy has largely moved southward since its start at Jamestown, the industry remains important in Virginia from Richmond southward to Petersburg, South Boston, Martinsville, and Danville. But its Virginia heyday was clearly in the 1870s and '80s, when John Allen and Lewis Ginter made cigarettes into an American habit. They deserve the credit—or the blame—for that.

27. *A Connecticut Yankee on the James*

THE industrial age entered Chesapeake Bay on the heels of the Civil War. Coal-burning steamships gradually replaced the schooners which hauled America's commerce, and railroads slashed their way through worn-out tobacco fields to create ports at Norfolk, Newport News, and Baltimore.

All this was symbolized in a hulking, six-foot-two-inch titan of finance who as early as 1837 recognized Chesapeake Bay as a coming giant of industry. He was Collis P. Huntington.

Little except farmland surrounded the Chesapeake when Huntington sailed into Newport News Point as a 16-year-old boy, peddling watches and hardware for New England manufacturers. Pine trees fringed the blue waters, and "buy boats" moved lazily from one wharf to another, loading wheat, corn, and tobacco. But the ambitious Connecticut youth recognized the area as "ideal for enterprise," he wrote later.

The vision of the Chesapeake stuck in Huntington's mind throughout the years of the California Gold Rush, when he went west and made a fortune selling mining gear in Sacramento. Then, becoming a railroad builder after the Civil War, he turned his eyes again toward the riches which he had seen in the James River hinterland.

Huntington recognized the need for railroads linking the growing west to the ports of the Great Lakes and Chesapeake Bay. In the troubled years of Reconstruction, he laid his plans. To the railway which the "Big Four"—Leland Stanford, Mark Hopkins, Charles Crocker, and he—cut from the Pacific to Chicago, he would attach an eastern railroad extending to Chesapeake Bay and the Atlantic.

Because the Baltimore and Ohio Railway already served the upper bay area, Huntington decided to confine his search to Newport News and four other lower bay sites fronting on deep water: Norfolk, Yorktown, West Point, and the mouth of the Piankatank River. Secretly choosing Newport News at last, he had his agent quietly buy up acreage down the Virginia Peninsula as right-of-way for the Chesapeake and Ohio.

When he revealed his plan in 1872, Huntington expressed belief that the Peninsula, "so designed and adapted by nature" for man's use, would become a metropolis. Applauding his choice, *Scribner's Monthly* for December 1872 declared that "Nowhere on the four continents is there a more magnificent expanse of land-locked water than this Hampton Roads in which the navies of the world might ride at their moorings."

As the 100th anniversary of Washington's victory at Yorktown approached, the C & O's main line stretched westward from Newport News. In Williamsburg it ran down the middle of Duke of Gloucester Street. On the centennial of Cornwallis's surrender, October 19, 1881, Collis Huntington played host to senators and congressmen who came to Yorktown to dedicate the Victory Monument.

But Huntington had only begun to stir up the lower Chesapeake. Steamships were by that time replacing sails, and he saw the need for a modern shipyard to repair the steel ships which were flocking to the C & O's Newport News coal piers. In the depression year of 1886, he chartered his Chesapeake Dry Dock and Construction Company, built on the James near his railway terminal. Its name was soon changed to Newport News Shipbuilding and Dry Dock Company.

Though he lived in New York, Huntington frequently rolled into Newport News on his private car to check on his empire. When his shipyard opened in 1889 with the drydocking of the United States Navy's *Puritan*—one of the new ironclad monitors—Huntington brought with him a wild haired poet, Joaquin Miller, whose verse he admired. Miller recorded his impres-

Author's collection

USS Puritan *was drydocked at Newport News for the shipyard's opening in 1889.*

sions in a poem titled "Newport News":

> The huge sea monster, the *Merrimac*
> The mad sea monster, the *Monitor*,
> You may sweep the sea, peer forward and
>   back,
> But never a sign or a sound of war
> A vulture or two in the heaven's blue;
> A sweet town building, a boatman's call;
> The far sea-song of a pleasure crew;
> The sound of hammers. And that is all.
>
> And where are the monsters that tore this
>   Main?
> And where are the monsters that shook this
>   shore?
> The sea grew mad! And the shore shot
>   flame!
> The mad sea monsters they are no more.
> The palm, and the pine, and the sea sands
>   brown;
> The far sea songs of the pleasure crews;
> The air like balm in this building town—
> And that is the picture of Newport News.

The Newport News enterprises attracted thousands of men from Virginia and North Carolina, seeking jobs. Many were victims of the panic and depression which had followed the postwar boom. Others were Negroes, who had been encouraged by Lincoln's Emancipation Proclamation to leave their masters and seek refuge behind Union lines in the last years of the Civil War.

Collis Huntington's capital attracted other business to Newport News, just as the Norfolk and Western was doing in Norfolk across the water. The area drew an endless procession of ex-farmers for the next 100 years from former "black belt" counties south of the James and in eastern North Carolina. The yard also attracted skilled British shipbuilders from Clydebank, Glasgow, and Plymouth. In place of "The palm, and the pine, and the sea sands brown," Hampton Roads became a melting pot of races and nationalities.

Powerful as he was, Collis Huntington was bitterly fought by rival financiers who saw the commerce of New York and Boston threatened by the rise of the Chesapeake region. He was assailed as a "robber baron," who used his wealth to achieve selfish gains. While this was true, it was also true that he possessed unusual vision. He had brought the industrial age to the Chesapeake region and given jobs to thousands.

C & O Historical Society, Inc.

A C & O steam locomotive built in 1873 was used along the James River tracks in the railway's early days.

To induce more ocean trade to come into Hampton Roads, Huntington signed agreements with European and British shipping lines. In the same years, coastwise steamboat services operated to connect Chesapeake Bay ports with the Atlantic and gulf coasts. Not until highways blossomed after World War I did the graceful white passenger boats disappear from the Chesapeake. Rotting docks today testify to their passing.

By the time Collis Huntington died in 1900, the character of Chesapeake Bay was changing. Poet Joaquin Miller hymned him as "first to lead the steel-shod cavalry of conquest through the Sierras to the Sea of Seas . . . who has done

Collis Huntington utilized the lower James for the C & O terminus and shipbuilding yards.

the Greater West and South more enduring good than any other living man." The heyday of laissez faire ended a year later, when Congress introduced the first antitrust laws.

The outgrowth of Huntington's enterprises is familiar. Although he never spanned the continent with his railroad, he lived to see Hampton Roads grow into the port he had visualized. His shipyard a few years after his death became the largest privately-owned yard in the world, building the greatest passenger liners and warships ever to fly the American flag.

The growth of the city which he built up illustrates the change which industrialization brought in the 100 years after the Civil War to towns which line the Chesapeake. Once they looked to the water for livelihood. Today, the Chesapeake plays a less visible but still important part in the urban life which surrounds it.

So war-torn is the twentieth century that a

ring of military bases has encircled the Chesa-peake, detracting from its native charm. But despite the hum of jets and the clatter of coal trains, the smell of saltwater still rises from creeks and rivers which feed the bay.

Can these be kept unspoiled? Most people who live along the rural reaches of the bay are determined that they shall be. They cherish Joaquin Miller's vision of the old Newport News terrain:

A vulture or two in the heaven's blue;
A sweet town building, a boatman's call;
The far sea-song of a pleasure crew;
The sound of hammers. And that is all.

Collis Huntington has left his legacy, but Joaquin Miller's vision is worth remembering, too.

The C & O Railroad vitalized the Peninsula in 1881 by running the first passenger train to the Yorktown Centennial.

28. *Towards an Atlantic Canal System*

NINETEENTH-CENTURY America built many canals. Ships were small then, and they voyaged much more safely on protected waterways than on the ocean itself.

That's why Marshall Parks, who ran the early Hygeia Hotel at Old Point Comfort in the 1820s and 30s, conceived the present Intracoastal Waterway, which conveys small vessels on a corridor of rivers and bays paralleling the Atlantic from New Jersey to Texas. The system, adopted by the United States about 1915, is today maintained by the U.S. Corps of Engineers, chiefly for the benefit of pleasure craft and small work boats.

Parks was an engineer and land developer, born in Massachusetts in 1786, who moved to Norfolk in 1814. His first big job was building the Dismal Swamp Canal from Norfolk through the swamp in upper North Carolina. While at work on this in 1820, he received a contract from the War Department to provide masonry and fill to build Fort Calhoun, a built-up island fortification in the Hampton Roads channel off Fort Monroe. The joint forts had been authorized by Congress and President Monroe to protect Virginia against a recurrence of Britain's

invasion in the War of 1812, but Fort Calhoun was never a success.

While directing his men at the Rip-Raps, Parks in 1821 bought an interest in the Hygeia Hotel that William Armistead of Buckroe had just built to house Army officers and engineers building Fort Monroe. Parks continued to serve as superintendent and design engineer of the Dismal Swamp project, which had been advocated earlier by George Washington.

Parks married Martha Boush, great-granddaughter of Norfolk's first mayor, Samuel Boush. Martha was a descendant of George Wythe's sister, Anne, who had grown up at the Wythe plantation near Hampton, in the present Langley Air Force Base.

Living at the Hygeia, Marshall and Martha Parks reared a talented son, Marshall Parks, Jr. The elder Parks died at 54 in 1840, when his namesake son was only 19. However, the young man worked with his father's executors to sell off part of his father's large estate. He became a well-known constructor along the coast.

Young Parks also inherited his father's enthusiasm for an Atlantic intracoastal waterway. When he grew up he conceived the sea-level Albemarle and Chesapeake Canal, to run from Norfolk through Dismal Swamp to North Carolina's Albemarle Sound. Soon he sold his interest in the Hygeia and moved to South Mills, North Carolina, to run his father's sawmill and succeed his father as engineer of the Dismal Swamp Canal.

When the Civil War burst in 1861, young Parks volunteered for the Confederate navy and was commissioned a commodore. In the style of his day, he remained "Commodore Parks" till he died in Norfolk at 79 in 1900.

Parks's design of the sea level Albemarle and Chesapeake Canal in the 1850s attracted the attention of the French engineer Ferdinand de Lesseps, who was then designing the Suez Canal in Egypt. De Lesseps sent an associate to Virginia to observe Parks's canal.

Parks's project had first been proposed in 1728 by William Byrd II, when he wrote his *Journey to the Dividing Line*, between Virginia and North Carolina, but it had to await invention of steam shovels before it could be realized. Even so, cutting through the marshy forests of Virginia and North Carolina proved a huge job.

Governor Henry A. Wise, a progressive who headed Virginia in the years 1856–1860, persuaded the General Assembly to invest state funds in the larger, newer canal to expedite Hampton Roads trade with North Carolina. The huge project was finished in 1858, with federal and state investment, quickly surpassing the trade and traffic of the earlier Dismal Swamp Canal.

Editor James Barron Hope wrote in his *Norfolk Landmark*, later to be merged into the *Virginian Pilot*, "Commodore Parks was a man widely known perhaps as any man in Virginia. . . . He is the father of internal waterways."

Parks's concept of the Intracoastal Waterway was finally adopted by Congress in the early twentieth century, when the United States bought out other investors. Depredations of the British navy in the War of 1812 had convinced legislators of the desirability of a protected

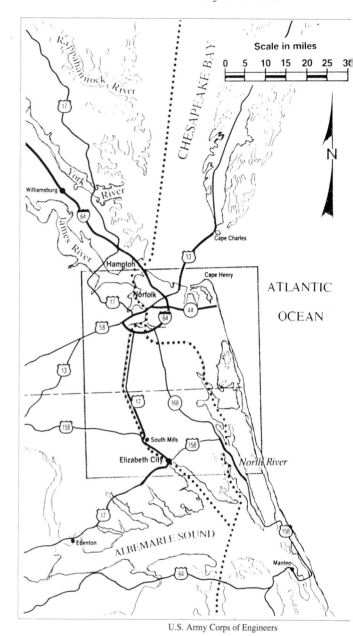

U.S. Army Corps of Engineers

The lower James connects at Norfolk with the Intracoastal Waterway's two canals through North Carolina.

inner waterway that could be used during war and peace. Over succeeding years, the U. S. Corps of Engineers has expanded the intracoastal system to extend from Trenton, New

Jersey, to the mouth of the Rio Grande River at Brownsville, Texas, on the Gulf of Mexico.

Many miles of navigable rivers, including the James, connect with the waterway. Other links are the Hudson River, the Erie Canal, and the New Jersey Intracoastal Waterway.

Describing canal life, onetime Dismal Swamp resident Charles E. Stewart wrote in *American Neptune* magazine in July 1947:

> I remember the flat-bottomed and square-headed "lighters" loaded with cords of six-foot juniper logs, pushed along by Negro boatmen, their breasts leaning against a stout long pole, reaching over to the tow path, one at the stem and one at the stern. It was always a mystery to me how such a heavily laden craft could be slowly but steadily pushed along by the shoulder of only one man at each pole.
>
> Then there were the neat little sloops and two-masted schooners that carried corn or fish or watermelons from the Carolina country to the (for me) far North. . . .
>
> The captains of the canal steamers were profane and they would hurry up the Negro deck hands taking on freight by a sound "cussing." We boys thought this profanity was a part of the game and necessary to keep the boats running properly. But when the handsome and gentlemanly Captain Conkling of Staten Island, N.Y., came to command the steamer *Thomas Jefferson*, he used no swear words but directed the work of loading cargoes in a mild conversational manner. . . .

For many years the little steamers navigating the canal, plying between Norfolk and Elizabeth City, carried the mail between those two

Author's collection

Marshall Parks, Jr. promoted the Intracoastal Waterway and built the Dismal Swamp canal.

points. The intermediate post offices, Deep Creek, Lake Drummond (later Wallaceton), Lilly (Cross Canal), and South Mills were served on this route.

Parks tried to raise capital in Tidewater Virginia in the 1890s to build a third canal, this one extending through Lynnhaven and Back Bay to connect with the Albemarle and Chesapeake. However, railways had become the vogue. It was never built.

When Commodore Parks died in 1900, he had lived to see Tidewater Virginia become a network of interconnecting rivers, canals, and railroads. The old man must have died happy.

29. *The Story of Newport News*

THE birth of Newport News as a settlement in 1881 forecast the emergence of the United States as the world's greatest power. Together the nation, the city, and Newport News Shipbuilding helped make the twentieth century a triumph of American enterprise, technology, and leadership.

It began on January 28, 1886, when the Virginia General Assembly in Richmond approved a charter for a $2 million dry dock backed by Collis P. Huntington, the railroad millionaire. Today that tiny Chesapeake Dry Dock and Construction Company has grown into the largest corporate shipyard in the world. In the intervening century the city that grew up with the yard has also become renowned, and interaction between them has helped both.

Consider the Peninsula in 1886, when the yard was chartered. Virginia was digging out of the rubble of the Civil War. Five years earlier, the rural Virginia Peninsula had suddenly become accessible to the rest of the nation for the first time by railway—Huntington's Chesapeake and Ohio. The C & O and its coal and freight docks offered jobs to hundreds of unemployed men in the area.

The village of Newport News started life when the C & O's builders cleared trees, graded fields, and laid off rights-of-way for streets and utilities. The C & O's trackage was soon paralleled by five infant avenues—West, Washington, Lafayette (later renamed Huntington), Virginia (later Warwick Boulevard), and Jefferson—all running east and west down the tip end of the Peninsula. Intersecting these were numbered streets, beginning at Hampton Roads and extending west. The most important at first was 18th Street, where the town's first commerce was centered. Soon Huntington chose 24th Street as the site of his Hotel Warwick; a year or so later 25th Street became the site of the relocated Warwick County Courthouse, plus a marble Federal Building.

The Hotel Warwick was the scene of the first meeting of the board of Chesapeake Dry Dock and Construction Company stockholders in June 1886, five months after the company was chartered. In the interim, $600,000 in stock had been subscribed and $600,000 in bonds issued. Huntington himself owned most of the enterprise. His tall, bearded presence dominated both his shipyard and his rail operations until he died in 1900.

*Collis Huntington's Hotel Warwick in 1889 had boathouses
and a pier on the James River.*

At the company's organization in Newport News the board was authorized to choose a site for the yard and to start building it in 1887. The Act of Incorporation called for the yard to be placed either in Newport News, Norfolk, Portsmouth, or Berkley. However, Huntington already had his eye on the ideal site. Soon after the meeting he ordered the driving of test piles in shoal waters along the James, just west of his Casino recreational area. The results showed the land well suited. Clearly a local shipyard would serve many vessels needing overhaul or repair after handling cargo at the C & O docks.

To no one's surprise, then, the Newport News site was recommended by Huntington when the company's board met on December 1, 1886, in New York City. It was quickly approved, and plans were made to start work in the spring. Huntington agents had bought the land in 1866 from the Lee family, who had farmed it. The original corporate plans called for a 425-foot Chesapeake company frontage on Washington Avenue. Down a steep bluff from the high plain traversed by Washington Avenue, the shipyard land dropped away to a wide waterfront shoal projecting into the James River channel. On this shoal the first shipyard dry dock was built in the years 1887–1889.

Of this site, Huntington later wrote: "It was my original intention to start a shipyard and plant in the best location in the world, and I have succeeded in my purpose. It is right at the gateway of the sea. There is never any ice in winter, and it is never so cold but you can hammer metal out of doors."

From this first site the yard grew in all directions over the next 100 years. Today it extends from below 24th Street westward beyond 70th Street. Similarly, its original northern boundary on Washington Avenue has pushed nearly a half mile across Huntington Avenue and Warwick Boulevard to the C & O right-of-way, providing extensive space for a foundry, office buildings, and employee parking.

The beginning of yard construction in 1887 spurred the westward growth of Newport News, especially in the unbuilt area north of 25th Street. Blocks were gradually laid off between the river and the C & O as far westward as 64th Street. Encouraged by the yard's start, workers moved in from surrounding areas of Virginia and North Carolina.

The 1880s not only brought the C & O and the shipyard to Newport News, but also the civilizing effects of churches and schools. Several denominations met for the first time in the Union Chapel which Huntington built for the town, forming early churches that survive. In the same years public and private schools took root. The 1880s also brought many stores, row houses, and apartments.

In 1888 the seat of Warwick County was moved from rural Denbigh to 25th Street in response to the new population; later the county seat was returned to Denbigh in 1896 after the General Assembly declared Newport News a city of the first class, with its own mayor and council.

In 1891 came the first banks, the Huntington-backed First National and the locally-owned Citizens Marine. In 1900 a $100,000 Academy of Music gave new lustre to Washington Avenue, the main business street. Newport News was growing.

One of the few native-born original residents was George Ben West, whose family had owned about 400 acres of farmland on Newport News Point, where Federal fortifications were built in the Civil War. After the area became piers and marshaling yards for the C & O in the

Apr. 1897

Daily Press

The new shipyard in 1897 overhauled wooden and steel ships at docks on the James.

Schooners like the five-masted Edna Hoyt *hauled coal before the 1940s from C & O Newport News piers.*

1800s, West became a local banker and founder of what grew into Riverside Hospital, the Peninsula's largest.

Another pioneer businessman was Colonel Carter Braxton, president of the Newport News Street Railway when it was founded in 1890. The horse-drawn trolleys were later electrified, and the line was merged with the Hampton–Old Point system.

Calvin Orcutt, the yard's first on-the-scene president, was typical of the energetic men the yard has brought to Newport News. He took over the helm in 1889 after having first worked for Huntington as New York agent for his Old Dominion Land Company, the holding corporation which had laid out Newport News and which brought in water and gas services. John Swinerton, who managed Huntington's Hotel Warwick, called Orcutt "jolly and chock full of optimism" and said he often regaled hotel visitors with talk of "the great possibilities of Newport News."

To provide the yard and the town in 1889 with water and electricity, Huntington interests organized the Newport News Light and Water Company. The engineering for these was directed by another Huntington mainstay, the youthful Walter Post. Post's waterworks created a reservoir at Lee Hall and piped water 18 miles to town, at first through wooden conduits. In 1925 the City of Newport News bought the waterworks and expanded it to supply water to most of the Peninsula east of Williamsburg.

Post proved a highly effective force in Newport News. After directing the engineering of the C & O trackage and terminals in the early 1880s, he was involved in other Huntington innovations. He was a founder of the First National Bank in 1891 and served as president of both the Old Dominion Land Company and its subsidiary Light and Water Company. From the 1890s onward he worked his way upward as a shipyard executive, dying of a heart attack at age 55 in 1912 while serving as president.

Post served at a time of fast growth for both the shipyard and the city. When war over Cuba threatened between the United Sates and Spain, the navy in 1894 awarded contracts to the shipyard for its first two major ships: the battleships *Kearsarge* and *Kentucky.* The proud people of Newport News immediately petitioned the General Assembly to incorporate their town as a city of the first class. When the Assembly obliged on January 16, 1896, Walter Post was named in the charter as mayor until the first election could be held. Post was also elected mayor from 1896 to 1898, but he declined further service in 1898 to become general manager of the yard.

The best known figure in the first century of Newport News, however, was Homer Lenoir Ferguson. A shrewd and colorful Scotch-Irishman in background, Ferguson led the yard for 38 years, through the Great Depression of 1929 and two World Wars. He was president from 1915 to 1946, and chairman from 1940 until 1953.

Although he achieved many accomplishments while at the yard's helm, perhaps Ferguson's most noteworthy achievement was his ability to adapt to changes in the marketplace.

When faced with the demands of a massive shipbuilding war effort during World War I, housing yard employees became a critical issue. Ferguson took action by initiating negotiations to develop what would become Hilton Village, the nation's first war-housing project.

Later, when the wartime surge subsided, Ferguson began an ambitious diversification that adapted builders of ships to builders of yachts, boxcars, hydraulic turbines, traffic lights, trans-

mission towers, aqueducts, and even a 20-story office building.

It was during this time that the Mariners' Museum was founded. It was Collis P. Huntington's son, Archer, and his wife, sculptress Anna Hyatt, who enabled Ferguson to realize his ambition to create the facility in recognition of the Huntington role in Newport News.

After Henry E. Huntington's death in 1927, Archer became the yard's principal owner and chairman. But like his cousin, Archer rarely

Daily Press

Giant aircraft carrier and SS United States, *foreground, were built on the James River.*

visited the yard and left its management to Ferguson and the directors. As the childless Archer and his wife began to disperse their art and their fortune, Ferguson began to build the Mariners' Museum at a time when Newport News and its unemployed would especially benefit from its stimulus.

The museum opened in 1930 after Huntington had bought many acres of woodland along Waters Creek in Warwick County as its site. The creek was dammed near the James River shoreline to create Lake Maury. Today the Mariners' is one of the world's top maritime museums.

Archer Huntington also gave a golf museum to the James River Country Club when it opened in 1931 near the museum. Both projects lent impetus to the development of suburban Warwick County, contributing to the growth which led eventually to the Newport News–Warwick County merger in 1958, creating the third largest municipality in acreage in Virginia. A similar merger of Hampton and Elizabeth City County followed.

In 1940 Archer Huntington sold his family's controlling interest in the shipyard to a group of New York investment bankers. Thus the yard became for the first time a widely-held pubic company, with stock traded on the New York Stock Exchange. President Homer Ferguson and his management remained in office throughout the sale.

In Homer Ferguson's long tenure, the yard became one of the world's foremost shipyards. To offset the instability of shipbuilding, the yard developed its foundry, pioneered in building turbines for waterpower dams, and opened its apprentice school under G. Guy Via, Sr.

A genial North Carolinian, Ferguson was a familiar sight to workers as he periodically toured the yard and kept in touch with his workers. In his career he became one of shipbuilding's premier spokesmen, serving as president of the United Sates Chamber of Commerce and in other industrial roles.

In the years following Ferguson's leadership, the yard adjusted to the cold war and the rapid growth of Peninsula population and business. Traffic growth necessitated new bridges and freeways. The Hampton Roads Bridge-Tunnel, Yorktown Bridge, and a new four-lane James River Bridge eased commuting to the yard. The creation of Interstate 64 down the Peninsula and across Hampton Roads reshaped and unified the area.

The outflow of residents from downtown regions to Peninsula suburbs, plus Gloucester-Mathews and the Southside, continued to alter Newport News and Hampton. As a result, the two original business districts have been challenged by several dozen shopping centers on major arteries.

Industrial and technological change has also affected the area. In 1963 the Chesapeake and Ohio—Collis P. Huntington's first Virginia undertaking—merged with the Baltimore and Ohio to form CSX, headquartered in Richmond. Five years later, in 1968, Tenneco Inc., a gas and oil corporation, acquired Newport News Shipbuilding.

The yard's new management made many changes, but its major thrust—construction of nuclear-powered warships for the navy— continued. With the mid-century decline of America's merchant marine and the rise of subsidized foreign shipbuilding, Newport News Shipbuilding is one of only four U. S. shipyards handling 80 percent of the navy's work.

The yard has fared well under Tenneco's aegis. It has achieved a stability rare in shipbuilding, with steady profits. A strong backlog of navy contracts promises to keep the yard busy through the 1990s.

Looking back to the yard's start, it is hard to imagine the single dry dock that was planned in 1886. But from that little beginning, Newport News and its proud shipyard have grown to make twentieth-century history.

*British beginnings at Jamestown
are recalled by the tower of the
settlers' 1639 church.*

30. *Saving the Past*

THE blight of slavery that had sapped the economy of the James River in the nineteenth century began to disappear in the decades after Appomattox. Railroads were run, banks chartered, cities were built, and public schools started.

Fortunately, in the rush to modernize, Virginia did not turn its back on its heritage at Jamestown, Williamsburg, and Yorktown. In fact, the Yorktown Centennial in 1881 marked a revival of interest in those first years.

After a seven-year closure, the College of William and Mary opened anew in 1888. And in 1889 Virginia women started a movement for restoration through their Association for the Preservation of Virginia Antiquities that later helped the National Park Service and John D. Rockefeller, Jr., to save much else of English America's first years along the James, from Carter's Grove westward to the mountains.

Appropriately enough, two Williamsburg-born women took the lead in alerting Americans to the decline of ancient sites, overlooked in the years of Civil War and Reconstruction. The two—Miss Mary Galt of Norfolk and Mrs. Cynthia Coleman of Williamsburg—organized the first state preservation society. Today the

APVA is restoring and preserving some 40 sites across Virginia, most of them along the James.

Mary Galt's family had run the Williamsburg asylum in its youth. Cynthia Tucker Coleman was the great-granddaughter of St. George Tucker. Both were energetic ladies who inspired their impoverished state to scrimp and save to keep cherished sites standing. Many others joined in.

It's hard to realize how miserably poor most Virginians were 100 years ago. Wages for laborers were $1 a day. Professors taught for $1,000 a year. Meals were 25 cents and up.

How could the APVA hope to save Jamestown and Williamsburg without money?

Fortunately, businessmen and legislators agreed to help. The Commonwealth of Virginia deeded to the APVA the Jamestown church and churchyard. Thereupon Mr. and Mrs. Edward E. Barney, who owned Jamestown Island, gave the APVA 22 additional acres surrounding the church.

Mary Galt's Norfolk branch of the APVA raised most of the $400 to buy the colonial Powder Magazine in Williamsburg. Wealthy New Yorkers gave money to repair Bruton Parish Church. And the Old Dominion Land

Company of Newport News gave the APVA the Williamsburg acres surrounding the ruined colonial Capitol.

Dues charged by the APVA have been kept low to encourage many people to take part —and wisely so. In early years, dues were $1 a year, but a few big spenders came to the ladies' aid. Major James Dooley, CSA, gave $50 and "Officers of the C & O" gave $25. President Calvin Orcutt of the Newport News shipyard gave $25, and Charles "Broadway" Rouss, a New York merchant born in Winchester, gave $5.

Feisty little Cynthia Coleman, the twice widowed co-founder and for the first 10 years director of the Williamsburg branch of the APVA, arranged "silver teas," bringing in donations of silver money. Other APVA chapters raised money by holding costume balls in colonial getup.

Fortunately the APVA found many friends. One was Mrs. Fitzhugh Lee, its first president, whose husband was then Virginia's governor. Another was Lyon Gardiner Tyler, William and Mary's president.

In 1902 the APVA gained its best friend of all. He was the minister of Bruton Parish Church, William A. R. Goodwin. Invited to the church's ministry to heal a bitter division, he saw the need to preserve what was left of the structure as well as all that still stood of colonial Williamsburg.

Many years later, after Dr. Goodwin had helped J. A. C. Chandler expand William and Mary and had persuaded John D. Rockefeller, Jr., to save Williamsburg, he tipped his hat to the handful of ladies who had met in Williamsburg to start the APVA. He wrote: "These devoted ladies bent like priestesses over the dying embers of ancient times and breathed

Virginia State Library

Thousands of militiamen camped at Jamestown in 1857
to mark the 250th anniversary of English settlement there.

Sidewheelers brought celebrants to Jamestown's 250th anniversary ceremony.

upon them and made them glow again."

Reading the history of the APVA tells us a lot about Tidewater in the 1880s. In those days Virginians called frequently on wealthy Northerners to help save decrepit buildings, as Dr. Chandler and Dr. Goodwin were to do at William and Mary in the 1920s and '30s. From its 25 cents admission to the Powder Magazine, the APVA was able to hire a guide and to shore up the old building.

After Jamestown's brick church was rebuilt by the Colonial Dames in the early 1900s, the APVA's momentum was speeded up by the Jamestown Exposition of 1907. Branches sprang up around Virginia, and landmarks, such as Mary Washington's Fredericksburg home, were acquired. Similar movements in other states awakened Americans, and restoration projects were born. Williamsburg's revival after 1926 and the start of the Colonial National Historical Park in the 1930s were evidence of preservationist zeal.

The APVA was a ladies' organization for its first 50 years but men lent a hand. Today its good works are visible up and down the James River.

31. *Tourists Came by Boat*

THE James was a busy place in steamboat days. Freight and passenger steamers every other day connected Norfolk and Newport News with Richmond, traveling the 90 miles in a little over 12 hours. The river boats—a "day steamer" and a "night steamer"—stopped along the James at any of two dozen docks that happened to have passengers or freight. Autos were few, and train service limited. Boats like the *Ariel* and the *Pocahontas* provided Norfolk-to-Richmond service, hauling produce, livestock and passengers. I can remember seeing them dock at Pier A in Newport News during voyages in the 1920s and 1930s.

Among the steamboat stops was Jamestown, whose pier also received excursion steamers loaded with day trippers from Richmond or Hampton Roads. Jamestown was a favorite landing, for its 1639 brick church had recently been restored for the Jamestown Exposition of 1907, and statues of John Smith and Pocahontas had been erected on the waterfront. The 1907 Federal obelisk today seems a regrettable intrusion amid Jamestown's ruins, but it's here to stay.

To enlighten 1911 visitors, historian William G. Stanard wrote a pamphlet, "Notes For a Journey on the James." It listed the plantations and docks along the James and included a fold-out map of the river. It was sold at the Jamestown post office and souvenir stand, operated by the Association for the Preservation of Virginia Antiquities.

Having sailed the lower James often, I can appreciate Stanard's advice to Jamestown viewers: "As the steamer approaches Jamestown," he writes, "the tourist's eye is caught by . . . the massive sea wall erected by the United States Government which will forever protect the Island." Alas, the wall had to be replaced in the 1950s, but it has saved the shore.

Stanard extolled the work of Colonel Samuel Yonge, the U.S. Army engineer who had directed the army's sea wall construction. Yonge had discovered the early statehouse foundations in the course of his work. Fascinated by Jamestown's archaeology, he stayed on to excavate more of the 22 ½ acres of the island surrounding the brick church, which a wealthy Ohio owner, Edward E. Barney, had given to the APVA in 1893.

Stanard urged readers to buy Yonge's book, *The Site of Olde James Towne, 1607–1698*. It's Yonge's story of his findings, complete with diagrams.

The river steamer Pocahontas *lands commemorative excursioners at Jamestown dock in 1907.*

Stanard described for passengers sights other than Jamestown to be seen along the river: Mulberry Island, now part of Fort Eustis, Burwell's Bay on the Isle of Wight shore; Carter's Grove, Hog Island, Kingsmill, Archer's Hope, Swan's Point in Surry County, Gray's Creek in Surry County, Four Mile Tree, the Chickahominy River, and Sandy Point in Charles City County.

Stanard also wrote of the surviving plantations between Jamestown and Richmond: Brandon, Weyanoke, Westover, Berkeley, Appomattox Manor, Shirley, Wilton, and Ampthill. The last two—Wilton and Ampthill—were later moved to Richmond and now adjoin each other in the Westhampton suburbs, overlooking the James.

The guidebook warned that pilfering old brick and other mementoes was forbidden by the APVA. A custodian "will rigidly suppress all disorder and arrest any person guilty of disorderly conduct . . . or injuring buildings, tombs, fences, monuments, ruins, etc.," it warned.

Daily Press

*The earliest auto ferries were double-end
vessels of limited capacity.*

Stanard explained that until Edward Barney
bought the 1,550-acre island in the Reconstruction era to raise fruits, "the tombs and tower had
been constantly subject to the vandalism of visitors." He declared that many acres of shoreline
had eroded before the federal government built
its revetments.

Sightseeing boats on the James have
declined to nothing since 1911. Jamestown no
longer even has a dock to receive passengers.
But the James remains very much a visitor
attraction, thanks to the attention of the federal
and state governments. As a result of the
APVA's initiative, Americans are now learning
that English-speaking America began on the
James River.

Daily Press

Ferries linked Newport News with the Norfolk Naval Base from 1907 till the tunnel opened in 1957.

32. *"Hell's Half Acre" on the James*

THE disillusioned decades after the Civil War led to a lot of hard drinking in Virginia, eventually bringing abolition of saloons by state law in 1916. But even after Congress passed the Eighteenth Amendment and the Volstead Act three years later, whiskey flowed freely in waterfront towns like Hampton and Newport News, catering to sailors. Bootleg whiskey was easily available, and houses of prostitution flourished, subject only to requirements that practitioners subject themselves periodically to health inspection.

As in most port towns, Newport News's saloons huddled close to the dockside around 18th and 25th Streets. The bordellos were mostly on Warwick Avenue, a short thoroughfare now called Terminal Boulevard.

Not until Virginia got its ABC system did it reach an effective middle ground between wide open and tightly closed liquor control.

Industrial America grew fast after the Spanish-American War. American commerce was expanding over the world, which brought us into competition with European industry. We needed a bigger navy and a standing army so that we could "walk softly and carry a big stick," as Teddy Roosevelt put it. Big business rode high, unhampered by income taxes till the Sixteenth Amendment made it constitutionally acceptable for Congress to impose one in 1913.

That was the era in which lower Newport News was a sailors' delight, a situation that grew from the rugged enterprise that Collis Huntington brought here in 1881, when he built his C & O terminals and started a town where Civil War guns had just been silenced. Large numbers of freed blacks, attracted to the Peninsula by federal military bases in the Civil War, congregated in areas like Hell's Half Acre, near 18th Street and Bloodfield, on lower Jefferson Avenue.

Hampton, Phoebus, and Yorktown had their shanty towns in those days, too.

The C & O and the yard lured the ships to Newport News. The ships brought the sailors. And the sailors attracted saloons and honky-tonks. Actor James Barton worked in one bar on 24th Street before he became Jeeter Lester in *Tobacco Road* on Broadway. The Irish mimic Walter Kelly had a bar on 25th where he developed his "Virginian Judge" routine for vaudeville. Saturday nights downtown were riotous.

Those were violent years on the James. Seamen were robbed while ashore and drunk. Some were even shanghaied: carried unconscious to a ship to become a crew member, soon to be far out to sea.

Knifings were common, for pistols were few then. The old-fashioned straight razor was the weapon, aimed at the heart, throat, or carotid artery. Weekends were busy for the police and hospitals. The *Daily Press* each Sunday would describe Saturday night's bloodbath.

Gradually, public opinion began to change. Churches and citizens began to try to improve things. One man who did a lot was Charles C. Berkeley, known as "Captain Charlie." He was a lawyer who served as commonwealth's attorney in Newport News from 1908 till 1926.

He died in 1949 at the Kecoughtan Veterans Facility.

Born in Staunton and educated at VMI, he went to Lincoln, Nebraska to read law in William Jennings Bryan's law office. Like the "Great Commoner," Mr. Berkeley was always a friend of the underdog. After he served in the Spanish-American War, he came back to town and hung out his shingle.

Lawyers like William E. Carleton of Newport News and Judge Robert Armistead, who got their start in Captain Berkeley's law office, remembered him well. He was hot-tempered, often vitriolic, and unconventional. But he had courage, and he never hesitated. He often rode a motorcycle. He was an ex-soldier, and he never forgot it.

Daily Press

Newport News in World War I overflowed with servicemen who frequented "Hell's Half Acre."

The Newport News dock area attracted many saloons and bordellos before World War II.

To help get himself elected commonwealth's attorney, he had to post two or three friends at each city ballot box to keep the opposition from stuffing it. The opposition even brought over boatloads of men (women couldn't vote) from Norfolk and Portsmouth to vote against Captain Berkeley, but he won.

Berkeley believed in discipline. He made his children sleep with open windows. He loved military life and VMI. When a fellow lawyer remarked that VMI was "just a prep school," Captain Charlie nearly exploded. He had played on the VMI football team, though slight, and was a track star.

Once he and another attorney became so incensed with each other in Newport News Corporation Court that they jumped onto a table and mixed it up. It took four policemen to part them. Judge T. J. Barham fined each man $50 for contempt of court and proceeded with the case.

When Berkeley became commonwealth's attorney, he found the city exercised little control over the health of prostitutes in its licensed bordellos, so he had city council push through a requirement that they be examined by the city health office on 25th Street each week. One resident remembers seeing the gaily-dressed floozies walking to their examination and waving happily to passers-by. They didn't mind publicity.

Newport News changed from a horse-and-wagon village to an automobile town in Berkeley's 18 years as commonwealth's attorney.

Runaway horses were frequent when cars first began to travel city streets. A few businesses continued to make horse-and-wagon deliveries in the 1930s.

The adoption of the Eighteenth Amendment created huge law enforcement problems in Newport News. The profits in liquor attracted normally lawful people to become distillers, bootleggers, and rum runners. Makeshift stills operated around the city. As a boy in the North End, I often found stills along Briarfield Road and in the Newmarket area, whose woods attracted boys with BB guns, like my brothers and me.

Commonwealth's Attorney Berkeley once had to call on the Coast Guard to prevent Newport News tugboats from patronizing rum runners off the Virginia Capes, beyond the three mile limit, to sneak bootleg liquor back to town. Berkeley learned of one such mission just before Christmas. He called the Coast Guard and the jig was soon up.

Prohibition gradually tamed Newport News, as it did other American towns, especially those serving sailors. By the time the 1930s came, the saloons were gone and houses of prostitution were dying out. The enfranchisement of women undoubtedly had a lot to do with the improved public morality.

Newport News wasn't unique in this, for America in the '30s was giving up its old free and easy ways. Governor Harry Byrd had imposed severe fiscal morality on the state of Virginia, and Bishop James Cannon, a Methodist prelate, and a host of revivalists were denouncing liquor, beer, wine, card playing, and ballroom dancing. A few diehards even refused to read Sunday newspapers because they felt them a violation of the Bible's "day of rest."

I'm glad Captain Charlie Berkeley and his generation helped clean up Newport News, but I still enjoy hearing about the town's wicked days. It was sinful, all right, but it was full of the primal juices of life.

33. *Bennett Green and His "Word-Book"*

THE speech habits of the denizens of the James River shores are interesting and revealing. Like Professor Henry Higgins in Bernard Shaw's *Pygmalion*, the knowing listener can often determine a stranger's origin by the way he slurs his rs or drops his gs. Yet the original regional differences in American speech are clearly disappearing with the spread of television, radio, and family mobility. In another generation or two even the Southern drawl—that delight of raconteurs and butt of Thespian humorists—may give way with other peculiarities to a colorless uniform nationwide usage.

How greatly Virginia speech has already changed is shown by a perusal of the *Word-Book of Virginia Folk-Speech*, printed in Richmond in 1899 by William Ellis Jones. Compiled over many years by Dr. Bennett Wood Green, a scholarly physician, it was hailed on publication by J. Lesslie Hall, professor of English at William and Mary, as "the harbinger of a new day" in linguistic studies in the South. So well was it received that a new edition was warranted in 1912. Though long out of print until reissued in 1971, it is known and referred to by antiquarians and philologists.

Dr. Green's thesis was that the English spoken by Virginians of his day reflected the speech of the English settlers of Virginia, this oral language—rich in Elizabethan and medieval words, pronunciations, colloquialisms, aphorisms, and figures of speech—having been passed down from the indistinct Anglo-Saxon past. "The sounds tell of a race," he wrote. "Language is really made of sounds, and not of written signs." Though Virginia folk speech might not conform to the dictionary norm, he implied, it had the sanction of precedent and wide use.

Though critics chided the author for failing to discriminate between the current and the archaic and for not indicating whether certain usages were common to all Virginians or only to Southside field hands, they justly applauded Dr. Green's industry. And well they might have, for in its 580 pages the *Word-Book* offers an unsurpassed view of the speech of James River Virginians in the nineteenth century, when the influence of English folk speech was very much in evidence.

"There is no more fruitful and less cultivated soil for the philologist than the 'folk-speech' of some parts of the United States," wrote Prof.

Hall in his review of the book in the *Virginia Magazine of History and Biography*. He welcomed it as

> the modest contribution to scholarship of an unassuming man of scholarly tastes, of a man who loves learning for its own sake; and we believe that the book, in spite of faults not easy to overlook, entitles the author to a position in the Virginia School of English scholarship which began with Thos. Jefferson, bloomed with new vigor in Thomas R. Price, and has, in more recent years, made several Virginia institutions recognized as centres of illumination in the study of the mother-tongue.

Bennett Wood Green was born in 1835 at the family home, Shelly, on Mulberry Island in the James River, which since 1618 had been the site of one or more farms. The island's waterways and its accessibility to deep water made it eminently suitable for settlement. There and along the adjoining Warwick River lived such early settlers as the Carys, the Harwoods, the Wills, the Scervants, the Joneses, and the Pierces, whose daughter Jane had married Mulberry's most celebrated resident, John Rolfe, after the death of Pocahontas.

Green's lineage is not available to the author beyond the last several generations. However, a Green family and eight families of the name Wood are listed in the 1850 United States Census for Warwick County. By the marriage of his sisters, Bennett Green was connected with the Youngs and the Garrows of Warwick, both of whom are identified with its nineteenth-century history.

Describing his birthplace, Dr. Green in 1906 wrote of Mulberry Island: "When the tides are high, it is an island, formed by the water from Butler's Gut, on the James river side. . . . Butler's Gut was the dividing line between my father's land, and 'Sweet Spring,' owned by Mr. Horrod." He referred to the well-to-do Humphrey Harwood, whom he called "Mr. Big

Humphrey Horrod," proprietor of Martin's Hundred and other James City lands which have in modern times become the site of the Dow-Badische and Anheuser-Busch companies. (It might be noted that Green and many other early Virginians followed the English practice of dropping the internal w in such names as Warwick, Berwick, Chiswick, Burwell, and Harwood.)

Young Bennett occasionally ascended from Mulberry Island to nearby Grove Wharf, at Carter's Grove, to board riverboats which were then the chief link between Norfolk and Richmond. Occasionally he ventured to Williamsburg, then a scraggly market town of fewer than a thousand people. "I used to put up at the 'Raleigh Tavern' when I staid over night in Williamsburg," he reminisced in 1906. "That was not often, as I lived only 18 miles off, and I did not think that anything as I had a good buggy mare, and have left Williamsburg at 11 o'clock at night and at 12:30 would be in my yard at home."

In his mid-teens, Bennett Green entered the University of Virginia, graduating in 1855 with a degree in medicine. After practicing four years in Virginia, he accepted appointment as an assistant surgeon in the navy and embarked at New York for the Pacific on October 21, 1859, sailing on board the *North Star.* When the vessel stranded for a week on the Plana Cayos off the Isthmus of Panama, he and the other passengers were reported in the press as lost. However, the physician safely made his way to the navy's sloop-of-war *Saranac*, whereon he received word in 1861 of Virginia's secession from the Union.

A traditionalist and a states' rights Virginian, Bennett Green promptly resigned his commission and was put ashore by the *Saranac*'s captain without pay or belongings. Only a loan from the purser enabled him to return to New York and thence, via the Confederate underground, to Richmond. There Green served as assistant surgeon in the Confederate naval hospital before being ordered abroad in 1864 to be

Fort Eustis

Bennett Green grew up on Mulberry Island, which became Fort Eustis.
Note the idle fleet in the river.

chief surgeon aboard the CSS *Stonewall*, built at Laird's shipyards at Birkenhead, England. Her commanding officer was Thomas Jefferson Page of Gloucester County.

Green's career aboard a Confederate ship was even briefer than it had been aboard a Federal vessel. When the *Stonewall* reached Havana five months after Green came aboard, news of Lee's surrender at Appomattox was awaiting her. Captain Page observed the surrender terms and quit the ship with the rest of the ship's company. To evade the charge of piracy which awaited them in the United States,

many of the company, among them Bennett Green, sailed for England.

Though normally of mild disposition, the physician was too angered by Federal conduct of the war to want to return to his native land. "He was a man of great modesty," recalled President W. Gordon McCabe in his eulogy of his fellow Confederate before the Virginia Historical Society in 1914,

yet, on occasion [he] had a sharp tongue and never hesitated to 'speak his mind' with vigorous bluntness and epigrammatic terseness,

The Matthew Jones house is the only survival of many colonial plantation houses in present Fort Eustis.

whenever he deemed it his duty to do so. Thus it was that in those tragic days of '65, full of the bitterness of defeat (as indeed were most of us), he declared in his downright fashion that he 'would not live in the same country with the Yankees.'

Then ensued the exotic phase of Bennett Green's career. With Lieutenant William H. Murdaugh, another Virginian, he set out from England for Argentina to begin a new life. Like Captain Page and other disillusioned Confederates, he hoped to establish a group of Southern emigres in South America. Green and Mur-

daugh settled at Cordoba, a trading center between Buenos Aires and the upper Argentina provinces, where the physician practiced his profession and Murdaugh engaged in sheep farming. When a cholera epidemic broke out in Buenos Aires, the two and a Catholic priest volunteered to go there and help treat the stricken populace. For their part in quelling the outbreak they won public gratitude.

When Murdaugh relented at last and returned to Virginia, Green went to live with the priest and became United States vice consul and later consul at Cordoba. As a consequence of his medical practice, his shrewd investments, and frugality (McCabe wrote of his "most abstemious habits, never touching spirits or tobacco"), he amassed a substantial estate.

Inevitably, however, ties of blood and kinship which bound him to Virginia proved too strong to deny, and at last he returned to the Old Dominion. At first he practiced medicine in Norfolk, to be close to family and old friends; he visited frequently at Mulberry Island and at nearby Denbigh, the erstwhile seventeenth-century seat of Colonel Samuel Mathews and of Samuel Mathews, Jr., governor of Virginia from 1656 to 1660, at the confluence of the Warwick and James. Denbigh was the home of his sister, Ann Benson Green Young, and of her husband, William Garrow Young. As the Greens' house on Mulberry Island had been destroyed, Denbigh plantation became his adopted home.

Testifying to his attachment to his home county, Bennett Green signed the introduction to his *Word-Book*: "B. W. Green, Warwick, Virginia," dedicating the volume "To Virginia People, by One of Them." When in 1906 he contributed recollections of his youth to the *William and Mary Quarterly*, they were bylined "By a Warwicker." (The editor erroneously credited the contribution to "Benjamin H. Green," perhaps misled by his nickname, "Ben.") The doctor insisted on the British pronunciation of his county's name, "Warick," and called his birthplace "Mulbriland."

The completion of the Chesapeake and Ohio Railway to Newport News in 1881 made the Peninsula more accessible to Richmond than it was to Norfolk, and Dr. Green moved shortly thereafter to the capital city. There he frequented the Westmoreland Club with other ex-Confederates, telling and retelling the Homeric chronicles of the Lost Cause, and serving on the executive committee of the Virginia Historical Society. Colonel McCabe depicted him thus:

He was, in truth, what was called in Virginia fifty years ago 'a character'—alas! in these days of telephones and aeroplanes, there are no longer any 'characters' left—

just 'the dead level of mediocrity,' as Tocqueville says. He was full of the most delightful prejudices and not a few eccentricities, which made him irresistibly attractive to his intimates. What was regarded here in Richmond as one of these marked eccentricities (though some may think it deserves a nobler name) was his custom, every day of the year, and year after year, no matter what the weather, rain, sleet, or torrid sun, to walk out punctually at 4 o'clock P.M. to the Lee Monument, gravely uncover and salute the 'presentment' in bronze of our great captain, and then walk back, 'with sedate step, to his rooms or to his corner of the Westmoreland Club.'

About 1901 Dr. Green moved from Richmond to the University of Virginia, drawn thither by his recollection of happy student years and by the prospective companionship of books and scholars. There he became a familiar figure during the last two decades of his life, walking the Lawn in high silk hat and cutaway coat or reading in the library, wearing the black skull cap then resorted to by balding men, before central heating. A portrait of him in those years records his patrician features and luxuriant mustache and beard.

In return for the University's permission to reside on the grounds (he occupied the quarters on the East Range which Jefferson had designated as Hotel D), he promised the University on his death nearly all his books and five-sixths of his estate, which totalled about $175,000. In his lifetime he also gave $24,000 to endow two scholarships for medical students, preferably from the South. "When I say a Southern boy," the old man told Dean William Mynn Thornton, "I mean a boy from south of Jeams's River!"

Although Dr. Green corresponded widely, he wrote only one other published work besides the *Word-Book*. This was a 142-page pamphlet, "How Newport's News Got Its Name," published in 1907 on the 300th anniversary of the settlement of Jamestown. It was intended to

Fort Eustis

Fort Eustis, begun in 1918 on the James, is now Army Transportation Corps headquarters.

refute Hugh Blair Grigsby's surmise that the name honored Christopher Newport and Sir William Newce, marshal of early Virginia—a theory which Green pronounced erroneous. He held the view, now generally accepted, that Newport News (or "Newport's News," as it was often called then) commemorated the arrival in the James of Newport's four voyages after 1607 to resupply the Jamestown settlement.

Except for his *Word-Book*, Bennett Green would be merely another casualty of the Civil War—a man whose predestined life of staid convention was twisted into unexpected shape by a conflict which smote a whole generation. However, the *Word-Book* reveals the physician to have been a man of discernment, with an ear for language and an eye for the interrelationship between history and linguistics. To him, as to Shaw in *Pygmalion*, how a man spoke told as much about him as what he said. Southern speech habits became the consuming interest of his old age.

As dated and imperfect as it is, the *Word-Book* offers an insight into the character of the English yeomanry which largely peopled Virginia for its first 200 years. Compiled just before the automobile and two world wars changed the face of the Old Dominion, it mirrors an insular society in the gathering twilight of an agrarian age. Bennett Green saw this doomed neo-feudal order as the proud survival of the medieval world of Camelot and Kenilworth. He was a WASP among WASPs.

In Virginia, [he wrote in his foreword],

essentially the whole of the white blood is English, that has been on the soil for over two hundred years. It is not believed that there is any body of folk of as purely English stock as the white population of Virginia, and the States descended from her. . . . Nothing in their history shows the least falling off from the qualities that have always distinguished their race in all times and all places. The Virginian has a good opinion of himself, is calm, well-balanced, is self-reliant and has the English quality of not being afraid to take responsibility.

This enthusiastic judgment recalls Henry Adams's that "Nowhere in America existed better human material than in the middle and lower classes of Virginia."

Green declared that Virginia's earliest English settlers had chiefly come from England's West Country, bringing with them speech habits which King Alfred and his successors of the kingdom of Wessex had planted during their overlordship of Britain from the ninth century onward.

The language of Alfred, [he submitted], is to be found in the present rustic speech of Wiltshire, Somersetshire, Dorset, Gloucester, and western Hampshire; and these, with the Devonshire dialect beyond them to the westward, are the descendants of the early southern English, which at one time was the literary or classical form of speech. From the time of Alfred or earlier, until after the Norman conquest, for a period of some two hundred and fifty years, the West-Saxon English was the only written or literary form of the speech of the country and it is in the main to the writings of that period that we must look for the groundwork on which our modern English has been built up. Virginia English is the southwestern.

Green's conclusions as to the geographic origins of the early Virginia settlers were not wholly accurate, for many came from London and other areas as well as from the West Country. Also questionable was his assertion that the West Saxon dialect of early English was the only literary dialect of the Anglo-Saxon peoples. This work was more useful as a record than as analysis.

Based on his research in rural England and his acquaintance with Virginia, Green was impressed with what he took to be Middle English pronunciations dating from the years 1100 to 1500, which he found in Virginia speech. Among these he cited "tribbet" for trivet, "holt" for hold, "rench" for rinse, "gearden" for garden, "warnut" for walnut, "sebm" for seven, "churm" for churn, "mossel" for morsel, "gearl" for girl, "foller" for follow, "cotch" for caught, "fur" for far, "drean" for drain, "gret" for great, "brek" for break, "git" for get, "wrastle" for wrestle, "sarvant" for servant, "varmint" for vermin, "heerd" for heard, "peart" for pert, "yeea" for ear, "blate" for bleat, "yoe" for ewe, "pet" for pith, "sut" for soot, "jine" for join, "kiver" for cover, and others which still persist.

Some linguists questioned Green's identification of many of these locutions as Middle English. Indeed, they would seem to be simply the errors of illiterates, in some cases. Clearly, the *Word-Book* falls short of professional philological study.

"Virginia English seems to resemble the standard English of the time that the first immigrants came to the country, and there has been no foreign mixture, as the comers were English, and few or none have come from other parts of the United States. . . ," Green wrote in conclusion. "Virginia English is not a development of the American soil, but a survival of archaic English forms that have been lost in England." Like much else in the book, however, this was too broad a generalization; for one thing, it overlooked the many ill-effects of illiteracy on the language of rural Virginia. In linguistics as in other subjects, the truth often lies in very small distinctions.

Green was also mistaken in attributing greater effect to Indian than to Negro influence on the oral English of Virginia. Though there is no doubt that more words of Indian than of African origin were introduced into Virginia speech, the role of the blacks was much greater in shaping rural speech habits. As to Indian influence, he cited the many place-names and 17 common nouns, (chinkapen, chipmunk, hominy, moccasin, moonack [in some areas, the woodchuck], opossum, persimmon, hickory, pone, poquoson, raccoon, skunk, squaw, tomahawk, tuckahoe, wampum, and wigwam) which had come from the red men. He overlooked other examples.

Eccentric pronunciation of family names, such as "Tolliver" for Taliaferro, was even more common in Green's time than today, judging from his "Some Virginia Names Spelt One Way and Called Another." Here are such familiar surnames as Burwell, Chiswell, Jordan, Seawell, and Sandys as well as the now archaic "Boler" for Boulware, "Chaumberlin" for Chamberlain, "Fernall" for Farinholt, "Goin" for Gawin, "Jimmerson" for Jamieson, "Parrot" for Perrott, and "Sarmple" for Semple. Of course, the classic English example is "Chumley" for Cholmondeley.

Among "Some Virginia Folk-Sayings," Green listed various saws and superstitions, many of them still current. His most useful compilation was of familiar words having a special regional connotation which seemed to indicate survival from a simpler age. Here again the author failed to indicate the incidence,

currency, or propriety of each special use. "The author has drawn no distinction as to time, as to place, or as to class of speakers," complained Prof. Hall in his generally favorable five-page review in the *Virginia Magazine of History and Biography*—a criticism also voiced later by Lyon G. Tyler in an unsigned review in the *William and Mary Quarterly*. "Colonial, post-revolutionary and modern words are put together with no dates to guide us," Hall objected. "Negro jargon, low-white or illiterate corruptions, and interesting provincialisms of the educated classes—all are crowded promiscuously together, with no signs by which the outside student can classify them. . . . We hope that he will soon publish a new and revised edition. Of misrepresenting the speech of Virginians, he is unintentionally guilty."

Thirteen years after the *Word-Book* appeared, its author issued a new edition, but he made little effort to mollify Hall, Tyler, or other reviewers. Indeed, he actually baited them. "It may not be amiss that some mistakes should be allowed to remain for the consolation of the critics," he observed saucily. "An author is one who knows how to do things; a critic is one who knows how things ought to be done. Few of us realize what an artificial and abnormal thing a literary language is. A literary language does not represent exactly the speech of any one, and the speech of the many it ignores altogether."

A year after the new edition appeared, Dr. Green died at the age of 78. As he had requested, the old Warwicker was buried in a plot with other members of his family at Denbigh Baptist Church, originally the site of the Anglican Lower Church of Warwick Parish, the original wooden structure of which had been built in 1638 near the present Oyster Point in Newport News. With the march of industry up the Peninsula, however, little evidence now remains of the Mulberry Island or the Denbigh plantation which Ben Green knew. Nevertheless, the author of the *Word-Book of Virginia Folk-Speech* is not apt to be soon forgot. The "unassuming man of scholarly tastes" left his modest mark.

34. *A Year to Celebrate*

WHEN I grew up, nearly every adult in Tidewater talked about "the exposition." They meant the Jamestown Exposition of 1907, a six-month celebration of Jamestown's 300th anniversary. It had centered around an elaborate waterfront fairground on the Norfolk shore of Hampton Roads where the naval base now stands. History records the exposition as a fiasco; it was never completed and was dogged by crises.

From Hampton Roads at the exposition, Teddy Roosevelt sent our fleet around the world. The fleet was assembled offshore from the exposition site, built on what we used to call Sewells Point, near the docks of the ferries that crossed Hampton Roads from Newport News's Boat Harbor. On April 26, 1907, the air resounded with a salute of 100 guns, touched off by Norfolk's Light Artillery Blues.

Roosevelt came down from Washington on the *Mayflower*. As he arrived, 16 U.S. battleships and five cruisers fired salutes of 21 guns. The expo anchorage also harbored four British warships, three Brazilian, two German, two Austrian, one Chilean, and one Argentinean.

Representatives of 35 foreign nations gathered near Raleigh Lagoon, looking out from the Norfolk shore toward Hampton. There Roosevelt reviewed a parade described as "the

The Exposition in 1907 centered around the auditorium at center, later used by Norfolk Navy Base.

greatest military pageant witnessed in the South since the War Between the States."

Sightseers from all along the East Coast thronged to Norfolk by train and boat for the occasion. Trolleys and wagons conveyed travelers to the exposition, which spread over 450 acres. Visitors trooped through pseudo-colonial exposition buildings.

Dorothy Draper, and is now a naval museum.

Adjacent to Pennsylvania's was Virginia House, the quarters of the Fifth Naval District commandant. In Missouri House many Atlantic fleet commanders have lived. Nearby are houses built for Maryland, North Carolina, New York, and states as far west as North Dakota.

The exposition was chiefly the brainchild of

The Jamestown Exposition created a lagoon facing Hampton Roads, now the site of Norfolk Naval Base docks.

The event was chiefly Virginia's but it had the support of the federal government and other states. Twenty states opened hospitality houses fronting the water, many of them preserved to house admirals and generals today.

The most elaborate was Pennsylvania's, a replica of Independence Hall. It long served as the navy officer's club, redecorated once by

U.S. Representative Henry St. George Tucker of Lexington. Alas, the project was badly delayed by a political brawl over its location (Norfolk, Richmond, or Williamsburg). Despite round-the-clock construction in 1906, its buildings were unfinished on opening day. The grounds were muddy.

Tucker and other sponsors were humiliated.

The delay cut into attendance, resulting in a big deficit when the exposition closed.

Even so, Virginians loved the exposition and kept its souvenir postcards, plates, and arrowheads. Many households still have these keepsakes, which came to light in 1957, on the 350th Jamestown anniversary.

After the exposition closed, its buildings lay idle and unused nearly 10 years, while creditors sought their money. When World War I loomed in 1916, the navy bought the exposition site for its Atlantic fleet headquarters. The Hampton Roads Naval Operations Base was commissioned in October 1917. The exposition auditorium was converted to NOB headquarters, and Raleigh Lagoon was filled in.

The original 450 acres have since been increased by the navy tenfold by purchase and by filling in the shorefront. Since World War I, a naval supply center and a naval air station have been added.

When I sailed into Norfolk in World War II, the exposition buildings were very evident, but time has erased many. The wooden Pine Beach Hotel was demolished on the naval supply center site, and the Friendship Arch given by Japan in 1907 for the Raleigh Lagoon was torn down after Pearl Harbor was attacked in 1941.

Even so, the 1907 Jamestown Exposition left many memories—and several big benefits—to the James River region.

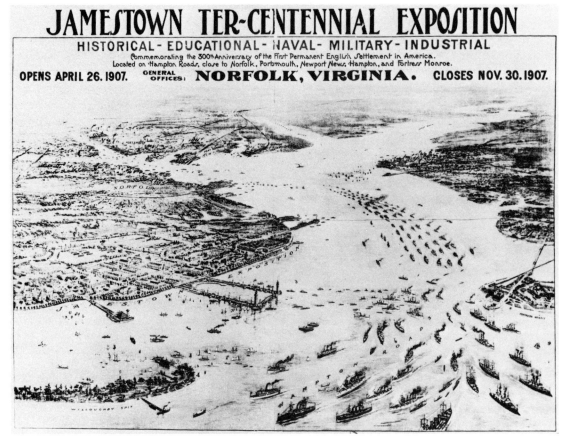

Ship lines and railroads brought visitors to Virginia in 1907 for the Jamestown Exposition.

35. *From New York to Jamestown*

IT was cheap and easy to get from New York to the James River in 1907—just $10 for a round trip on the Old Dominion Line, plus another $1 or so for meals.

An ad by the shipping line for the Jamestown Exposition that year shows ships of all nations gathered in Hampton Roads. It offered to depart Pier 26 in New York's North River any weekday at 3 P.M., reaching Norfolk at 10 next morning. There you could catch a James River steamer to take you anywhere up to Richmond.

The ad is one of many at the Mariners' Museum in Newport News that illustrates the breadth of Atlantic coastal shipping in steamboat days. Coastal Virginia was beginning to emerge as an area of shipbuilding, military bases, and summer resorts.

Even Newport News went after tourists. Collis Huntington had built his big wooden Hotel Warwick in the 1880s, and the Old Dominion Land Company had created a waterside park on West Avenue as its front yard, with a casino building. The original hotel has been razed, but a later brick one is standing today.

"In the early days, Newport News was considered not only an industrial center, but also a pleasure resort," wrote Harold Sniffen, of the Mariners' Museum, 40 years ago in the book, *Newport News' 325 Years*. "The Hotel Warwick attracted vacationists and advertised a casino, refreshment pavilion, bowling alley, as many as sixty bath houses, and a 'Pleasure pier.'"

Among ship lines serving Hampton Roads in 1907 the Old Dominion was foremost. The company operated seagoing ships connecting with Atlantic ports plus a network of Chesapeake inlet "feeder" lines. The feeders brought freight and passengers to the two Hampton Roads transshipment points, Old Point and Norfolk. Old Point's pier was a busy hub.

According to Sniffen, "These feeders ran south from Norfolk through the Albemarle-Chesapeake Canal into North Carolina; across the mouth of Chesapeake Bay to Cherrystone (north of Cape Charles); up the Chesapeake to Mobjack Bay; to Old Point and Hampton; up the James River to Richmond; to Newport News and thence across the James to Smithfield; and up the Nansemond to Suffolk."

He lists among Old Dominion steamboats serving early Newport News such long-gone vessels as the *Hampton, Pamlico, Northampton, Luray, Accomack, Isle of Wight, Enola, Hamp-*

ton Roads, *Okracoke*, *Mobjack*, *Berkley*, *Brandon*, and *Pocahontas*.

A 1907 advertisement of New York ship service to the Jamestown Exposition shows that

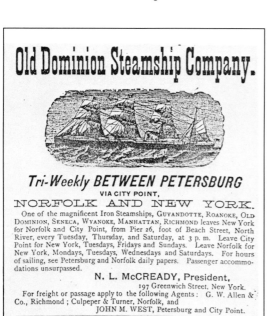

Old Dominion Steamship Company.

Tri-Weekly BETWEEN PETERSBURG
VIA CITY POINT,
NORFOLK AND NEW YORK.

One of the magnificent Iron Steamships, GUYANDOTTE, ROANOKE, OLD DOMINION, SENECA, WYANOKE, MANHATTAN, RICHMOND leaves New York for Norfolk and City Point, from Pier 26, foot of Beach Street, North River, every Tuesday, Thursday, and Saturday, at 3 p. m. Leave City Point for New York, Tuesdays, Fridays and Sundays. Leave Norfolk for New York, Mondays, Tuesdays, Wednesdays and Saturdays. For hours of sailing, see Petersburg and Norfolk daily papers. Passenger accommodations unsurpassed.

N. L. McCREADY, President,
197 Greenwich Street, New York.

For freight or passage apply to the following Agents : G. W. Allen & Co., Richmond ; Culpeper & Turner, Norfolk, and
JOHN M. WEST, Petersburg and City Point.

Virginia Steamboat Company's

JAMES RIVER LINE FOR

Newport News, Norfolk and James River Landings.

Passengers from Petersburg take the 8 a. m. train every Tuesday, Thursday and Saturday, connecting closely at City Point for above named places. Fare to Newport News or Norfolk, $1.40. Fare to Baltimore $4.40.

Close connection at Norfolk same afternoon for Baltimore and points North and West. Splendid Steamers. No transfers. No dust. Beautiful and Historical Scenery.

L. B. TATUM, Superintendent, Richmond, Va.
CHARLES H. SHELTON, Agent, Petersburg, Va.

Downtown Petersburg Inc.

Passenger ships linked James River ports in the nineteenth century with Norfolk and New York.

Old Dominion's New York-to-Norfolk line was served by five vessels: the steamships *Monroe*, *Hamilton*, *Jefferson*, *Princess Anne*, and *Jamestown*—all of 3,000 or 4,000 tons. Many smaller passenger ships operated inside the Chesapeake Bay.

My acquaintance with the Old Dominion Line was through its feeder line that operated from Newport News to Smithfield. Before I was born it had begun weekday sailings from Norfolk to Newport News, Battery Park, and Smithfield, at first using the ships *Accomack* and *Pamlico*. In 1909 it renamed its steamer called *Hampton* in honor of Smithfield and sailed it alternately with the *Okracoke*. "Each made a daily run," writes Sniffen, "the one lying overnight at Norfolk and the other at Smithfield."

Sniffen mentions one of the Old Dominion's competitors, the tiny mail boat *Oneita*, which plied daily from Newport News to Smithfield. "The late United States Senator Thomas Martin, feeling it advantageous that a regular midday mail leave Smithfield, secured a contract for Captain A. F. Jester to carry mail, passengers, and freight. This service was inaugurated about 1917 and continued until about 1931. . . . When the James River Bridge was built in 1928 . . . the knell of the boat service across the James was rung." Captain Jester, who lived in Smithfield, also operated ferries at Jamestown and at Chuckatuck.

Mementoes of America's steamship days now fill the Mariners Museum, reminding us of a pleasant way of life.

36. *The Great White Fleet Returns*

MANY excursion boats came down the James from Richmond and other ports on February 22, 1909, to see the return of the Great White Fleet. When President Teddy Roosevelt had come to Hampton Roads in 1907 to start the Jamestown Exposition, he had dispatched a fleet of navy ships painted white for peace to make a two year round-the-world trip and show the world how mighty Uncle Sam had become.

Teddy came back to Virginia to receive the fleet in an inspiring review at Old Point. A photograph of the fleet's arrival was taken from the old Chamberlin Hotel (it burned in 1920). It shows the Old Point dock surrounded by sightseeing boats with larger ships anchored offshore.

Teddy Roosevelt believed America needed a big navy. When he became president in 1901, he planned to "walk softly and carry a big stick." So he enlarged the navy, which had just fought and defeated the Spanish in 1898.

Teddy tried to disguise the navy's show of force by calling the voyage a "cruise around the world" and having the ships stop at Trinidad, Rio de Janeiro, Punta Arenas, Valparaiso, the Philippines, and the Suez Canal.

Newport News was involved in the voyage, for the shipyard had built two of the 16 battleships—*Kearsarge* and *Kentucky*—which made the cruise. Also in the fleet were six destroyers and several auxiliaries.

To greet the returning ships, Teddy sailed down from Washington on his presidential yacht, the *Mayflower*. With him were his wife, two sons, and two daughters, one of them Alice Roosevelt Longworth and her husband, House Speaker Nicholas Longworth. The *Mayflower* stood off the shore of Fort Monroe in order that the president could receive the 21-gun salute of the arriving ships. Shore guns at Monroe then fired to return the salute to each passing ship.

A witness that day was William Breslow, a 15-year-old New Yorker who had come to Old Point with two teenage friends to work on bumboats that would supply incoming ships with newspapers, ice cream, and other items the sailors had lacked at sea. Breslow later became a New York dentist. In 1971, when an old man, he wrote his memories of the event in a book call *Bumboater*.

"The *Mayflower* stood in and anchored at the entrance of Hampton Roads," Breslow recalled in his book, "while the guns of Fortress Monroe boomed out a 21-gun salute to the President. At last the moment arrived, and from the massed crowds ashore, the shout, 'Here they come!' burst from thousands of throats. A few moments later the masts of the leading battleship came into view."

Steaming in a single file, 400 yards apart, the ships slowed to ten knots as they neared Fort Monroe. "I could see that the rails were

The ships, after their salute to the President, formed a double column and swung around till their bows faced the Fort Monroe shoreline. There they anchored.

The young salesman remembered that Old Point had been full of people that day. "The wharf at Old Point was a beehive of activity," he wrote. "Some 2,000 New York newspapers would arrive at the Fort Monroe Post Office to be

Authors collection

Excursion boats crowded Old Point Dock in 1909 for the return of the Great White Fleet.

manned by officers and men in dress blues," Breslow wrote. "The thousands lining the shores were cheering and shouting, but I stood silently near my bumboat. . . . As each of the ships came abreast of the *Mayflower,* it boomed out a 21-gun salute to the President, who stood at attention on the quarterdeck."

carted down to the Wharf, where the local agent would distribute them to the bumboaters. . . . When local bakers could no longer supply the necessary pies, they had to be delivered daily from Norfolk."

After Teddy had greeted the fleet and congratulated officers and crews, he rushed back to

Daily Press

*The original Chamberlain Hotel at Old Point, later burned, was the site
of Great White Fleet parties.*

Washington. However, the fleet remained anchored near Fort Monroe for two weeks, enjoying shore duty and leave. Then all ships dispersed.

During the fleet's Hampton Roads visit, wives and sweethearts of officers and enlisted men stayed at the Chamberlin and the Hygeia, which were the center of social life. The navy had not yet established its Norfolk base, which began with America's entry into World War I in 1917.

Two weeks after Teddy welcomed the fleet, he left office, succeeded as president by Taft. Although Teddy was a Republican and Virginia was a heavily Democratic state, he remained highly popular in Tidewater. A lot of people liked to talk about the time "when I saw Teddy Roosevelt at the Jamestown Exposition" or "when I saw Teddy with the Great White Fleet."

37. *Bright Lights of Baltimore*

YOU'D have thought the commercial hub of maritime Virginia would have been Norfolk or Alexandria. But throughout the steamboat era Baltimore manufactories and wholesale houses sold most of the goods that were retailed in Tidewater's stores.

A chronicler of bay trade is A. T. "Lon" Dill of West Point, who wrote of it recently in *Virginia Cavalcade*. He describes a two-tier trade, whereby bay steamers brought Baltimore's cargo to centers like Old Point Comfort and Norfolk, and smaller river vessels delivered it to towns and plantations on Virginia waterways.

"Going to Baltimore" was a lifetime thrill of small town Virginians in the steamboat age. Its markets, Germanic restaurants, and its night spots—including burlesque—were an attraction to generations of Virginia merchants and buyers. Often they took families along to ogle the city.

"It was Baltimore—not Richmond—that served as a trading hub and enjoyed a virtual monopoly over the commerce of 15 or more Virginia counties," Dill writes in *Cavalcade*. "Served by the Maryland port city's pervasive steamboat fleet, the trade area by 1900 included the Eastern Shore, Northern Neck, Middle Peninsula, and a part of the Peninsula extending almost to Richmond."

After the South's surrender at Appomattox, while Virginia was bogged down in poverty, Baltimore investors virtually took over the Chesapeake region of Virginia. Since shipping by water was cheaper than by railroad, Maryland steamboats were welcomed by the river towns. "Separated from the railroads and cities . . . by miles of wretched country roads," Dill writes, "the small Tidewater towns had little choice: struggling inland with heavily laden wagons or shipping produce and seafood to Baltimore, at the head of the bay."

In lower Virginia, Old Point and Norfolk were the two key shipping points. Both were served by steamships of the Old Bay Line (officially, the Baltimore Steam Packet Company) and the competing Chesapeake Steamship Company. Many smaller lines traversed the James, York, Rappahannock, and Dismal Swamp Canal to bring passengers and freight to Old Point and Norfolk.

How glorious were the stops of those bay steamers at Old Point! They came in at a fast clip, tying their lines to the dock smoothly and

Ferries served most East Coast cities until bridges replaced them after World War I.

rapidly transferring passengers, crates of seafood, bulk newspapers, automobiles, and other freight. Then, in a flash, they blew their horns and were on their way again.

Peninsulans often went to Old Point until after World War II to see the ships. I remember the huge black crewmen rushing freight on board. Once I saw them handle three or four huge sea turtles, shipped live but on their backs, on their way to Baltimore restaurants.

Baltimore's Adams Express Company originally handled most Old Point freight. That company had brought Harrison Phoebus of Maryland to work at Old Point, where he took over the Hygeia Hotel after a few years and made it famous. Many Marylanders bought houses in Gloucester after first visiting coastal Virginia.

Lon Dill's article describes Baltimore residents' efforts to penetrate Tidewater after the Civil War by railways as well as ships. He recites little-known stories of many unsuccess-

ful short-haul railroads that were started in coastal Virginia. But Baltimore's shipping lines were its great pride.

How did Baltimore manufacturers get such a jump on Norfolk and Richmond in those years? Mostly because the Marylanders were more industry and trade minded, thanks to their mix of Germans, Italians, and middle Europeans. And they had suffered no Reconstruction. An 1887 Baltimore directory listed 400 firms doing business on Chesapeake Bay.

Dill writes, "The steamers sent down to Virginia coffee, sugar, vinegar, and molasses in barrels; hardware of all sorts; paints, linseed oil, firearms, and shells; farm implements of many kinds; household goods such as furniture and stoves; boots, shoes, and clothing; canned goods and beverages; marine supplies; and even rolls of brown wrapping paper."

Today many Tidewater households contain Maryland products of that era. In return, farmers around Old Point and other ports shipped to

Baltimore livestock, poultry, watermelons and cantaloupes, eggs, potatoes, and grain. The farms around the village of Newport News were particularly known for sweet potatoes. Hampton was a heavy shipper of crabs and crabmeat, fish, oysters, and other seafood. Those were the days of the McMenamin crab factory and J. S. Darling's oystering enterprise.

With Virginia's building of railroads and highways, Baltimore's domination of Tidewater Virginia declined, and Norfolk, Richmond, and Newport News grew.

Several Chesapeake lines linked Baltimore to the retail stores of Tidewater Virginia.

38. *Fortifying Mulberry Island*

THE nineteenth-century James was bounded by dozens of farm villages, whose residents found a good livelihood tilling the fields and fishing the waters near their homes. One such village was Mulberry Island on the lower James, which housed a number of prosperous farms till the army in 1918 bought the island as a bombing range.

In World Wars I and II, many tracts along the James and Hampton Roads became army and navy bases. Most are still in use but some are dormant.

Mulberry Island in 1918 became the army's Balloon Observation School and Coast Artillery Center. Though it had been named by John Smith for its mulberry trees, it was renamed by the army for General Abram Eustis, a Virginian who had set up the coast artillery school at Fort Monroe in 1824.

Fort Eustis has expanded greatly since 1918. Ironically, most of Mulberry Island, which was at first important to the fort, is now merely a gunnery range, little used for fear of civilian injury.

Might not the army have spared the island in 1918 and just built Fort Eustis on the adjoining

mainland? Alas, it's too late. The church and eighteenth-century houses once on Mulberry are long gone. Their memory is kept alive only by historians, who are impressed by the number of important Virginia families going back to Mulberry Island.

The most important Mulberry Islanders were William Peirce, a settler whose daughter Jane became John Rolfe's second wife after Pocahontas died in England, and Miles Cary, who came to Mulberry Island from England in 1645 and generated one of Virginia's First Families. Most of the public and college buildings in eighteenth-century Williamsburg were built by two of Cary's descendants, Henry Cary, Sr., and Henry Cary, Jr.

Mulberry Island isn't big, but it once had an Anglican church (James Blair came from Jamestown to preach) and several dozen farmhouses. Residents of the Denbigh area of Newport News get a good view of the 2,000 acre island from across narrow Warwick River, which with Skiffe's Creek separates it from the mainland.

Dorothy Vollertsen of Williamsburg wrote interestingly about early Mulberry Island and about William Peirce and Miles Cary in a booklet she put together with her late husband, Colonel Arthur Vollertsen, in 1983. Titled *The Carys and the Peirces: Mulberry Island Families,* it was published by the Fort Eustis Historical and Archaeological Association.

Skiffe's Creek and Warwick River gave Mulberry Island the protected harbor that early settlers sought, just as Jamestown, Archer's Hope, Hampton, and Poquoson did.

William Peirce lived there as a sea captain and sailed to England several times. After John Rolfe died in 1622—perhaps on Mulberry Island in the Indian massacre—Peirce, his father-in-law, was his executor. Peirce became captain of the Jamestown Fort in 1623 and then lieutenant governor of the colony. He also became a burgess, a member of the general court, and then a member of the Virginia Council until he died in 1647, probably at Mulberry Island, near which he acquired over 2,000 acres.

Daily Press

GIs based at Fort Eustis in World War I swam and dived in the James near Williamsburg.

Miles Cary, the Mulberry Islander best known to history, came to Virginia from England at age 22 in 1645. He married well and soon owned many thousands of acres in Warwick County on Warwick River. Cary became the militia colonel of Warwick and died fighting off an attack by Dutch ships at Old Point in 1667. His eroded gravestone bearing his coat-of-arms is the oldest in onetime Warwick County.

He left four Warwick plantations, including Windmill Point, the Forest, and Magpie Swamp. His descendants, including councilors and governors, spread to Hampton, Williamsburg, Richmond, and elsewhere, marrying other colonial families.

The Confederates in 1861 built Fort Crafford on Mulberry Island to deter Union ships on the James, but it was abandoned in 1862 when the Union army under General George McClellan invaded the Peninsula. Union forces pillaged the island's farms, which never regained their prewar prosperity. Few people were left on Mulberry by 1918 when the army created Fort Eustis.

One colonial house from the age of William Peirce and Miles Cary survives in Fort Eustis, close to Warwick River. It is the Matthew Jones house, begun in the 1600s and enlarged about 1770.

In World War II Fort Eustis grew huge as the home of the Army Transportation Command. As the base spreads, archaeologists try to see that important colonial sites underground are investigated and preserved. Unfortunately, the burning of Warwick County records in the Civil

Fort Eustis

The fort was named for General Abram Eustis, a Virginian who served in the Mexican War.

War has destroyed nearly all of the area's records.

An early map of Mulberry Island and the adjoining Warwick River shore shows many picturesque local names that have disappeared: Joyle's Neck, Jail Creek, Saxon's Gaol, and my favorite, Butler's Gut. A "gut," in case you didn't know, can be a narrow channel. It's still there at Mulberry Island.

39. *When World War I Came Along*

WORLD War I always seemed to me more romantic and colorful than World War II. Do other people feel that way?

Perhaps that's because I was an impressionable kid when General John "Blackjack" Pershing led the American Expeditionary Force to France. And I felt a child's delight when I saw doughboys marching back through Newport News after the Armistice was signed on November 11, 1918.

The recent removal of the C & O passenger ship dock at 23rd Street and the James River brings memories of navy transports docking there in 1919 to land the returning forces. The troops marched through the Victory Arch and up Washington Avenue, while Newport News went wild. The city also remembers the later return of Richmond's Blues from a commemorative visit to the battlefields in the 1920s.

Why does the first war so warmly stir American pride? Is it because that war elevated the U.S. to a fuller consciousness of its potential power in a world grown interdependent and increasingly imperilled? Or because it produced a rich harvest of slang, soldier songs, jazz, and literature that livened the world.

World War I's songs still haunt you. "Over There," "It's a Long Way to Tipperary," "There's a Long, Long Trail," "Look for a Silver Lining," and "Oh, How I Hate to Get Up in the Morning"—one of Irving Berlin's hits. It also spawned off-color ditties like "Mademoiselle from Armentieres."

Most Americans in 1918 lived on farms, so "How Ya Gonna Keep 'em Down on the Farm?" hit home to Smithfieldians. You remember the rest of the phrase—"After they've seen Paree." Matter of fact, lots of farm boys who saw Paree never did go back to the boondocks. Wars have a way of transplanting people to cities, as happened in each of America's earlier conflicts.

The novels and poems of World War I have a vividness that those of the next war never achieved. We loved a funny 1918 classic of soldiers' letters, *Dere Mable* and I read the ensuing *The Big Parade* and *All Quiet on the Western Front*—novels that made great movies. The war also produced Rupert Brooke's unforgettable poem, "In Flanders Fields."

Many surviving James River landmarks recall the war. Foremost is the Victory Arch, built in 1918 and restored in stone in 1962.

The shipyard in 1916 launched many ships at "Liberty Launching Day"
ceremonies at Newport News.

Fort Eustis and Langley Field were also spawned by the war, as were army warehouses along Warwick Boulevard in North End. Among surviving army names are Morrison, once Camp Morrison, and Stuart Gardens, built on the site of the first war's Camp Stuart. And, of course, there's Hilton Village, built in 1917–18 to house wartime shipyard workers.

That war also gave rise to a museum started in 1923 by the Braxton-Perkins Post of the American Legion. It's now the War Memorial Museum of Virginia and covers all American wars since the Revolution.

Compared to the idealism evoked by President Wilson's 1917 "War to end war," its successor was a dull replay. By 1941 most people except Hitler knew war doesn't solve anything. Americans lacked the optimism they'd had ear-

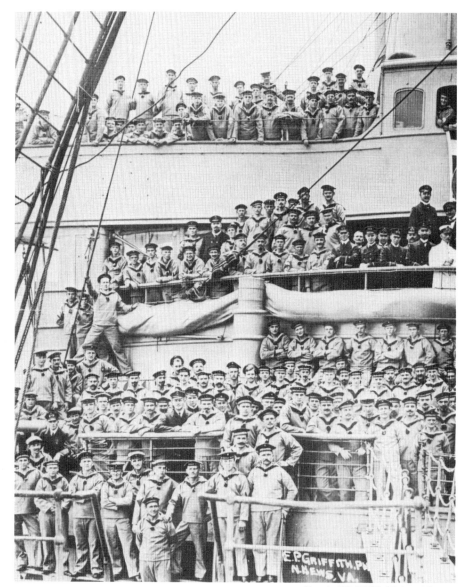

Photo by E.P. Griffith, Mariners Museum

Part of the crew of the German sea raider Prinz Eitel Friedrich
posed on arrival in Newport News in 1915.

lier, though they finally saw that the Axis had to be crushed.

World War II brought many more soldiers to Hampton Roads than the first war, but few of its place names have stuck. True, the Peninsula airport kept the name Patrick Henry from the 1940s embarkation camp it replaced, but some now think that name should be changed. World War II's Military Highway from Old Point to the James River Bridge was later renamed Mercury Boulevard, honoring the first astronauts at Langley Field.

Even the literature of World War II thrilled us less than its predecessor's. Oh, we liked

Michener's *Tales of the South Pacific,* and the novels of Norman Mailer and John Hersey, and *From Here to Eternity,* but little else comes to mind. Thrilling movies like Noel Coward's *In Which We Serve* and the aircraft carrier documentary, *Fighting Lady*, were produced, but I can't think of many others until *Tora! Tora! Tora!* and *Patton* came along much later.

If you were a World War II service man, your war memories undoubtedly include ribald barracks songs, jokes, and stories. Everybody laughed at "Kilroy was here" and the endless "Knock. Knock. Who's there?" jokes. And each war theater had sinister characters of its own, like the "Dirty Gertie" of soldiers' doggerel in North Africa. In the Pacific, we irreverent Navy types spent a lot of time vilifying Douglas MacArthur. We sang a song about him to the tune of "Bless 'em All," an old barracks ditty, with this felicitous verse:

> They sent for MacArthur to come to Tulagi,
> But General MacArthur said no.
> He gave as his reason "It isn't the season,
> And besides, there is no USO."

War has become too terrible for nostalgia. To me that's one of the lessons of World War II.

World War I Victory Arch was built on the James in Newport News to welcome returning troops.

Railroads made Richmond a transport center by the Civil War, when Confederate forces were sketched south of the James, near a railroad bridge across the river.

III

The Age of Rails and Roads

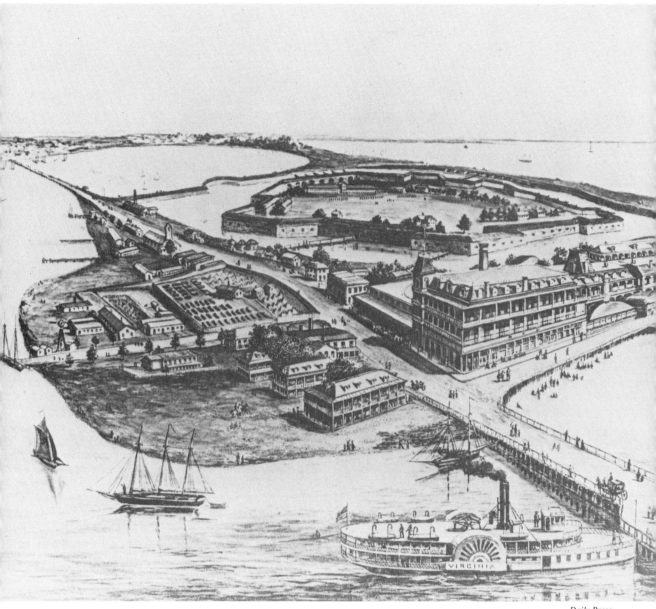

*Ships in Hampton Roads passed close to the Fort Monroe shoreline,
shown here with hotels and a government pier.*

40. *The Ship That Disappeared*

IN the days before radio, many ships were lost at sea without trace. Nowadays, though, most distressed vessels send an SOS—called a "mayday" in international usage—before they sink.

But old sailors are still mystified by the disappearance in 1918 of a ship which had sailed from the James River. She was USS *Cyclops*, a navy collier assigned to deliver a cargo of coal to Brazil and to bring back a cargo of manganese. She had radio, but no one heard distress signals before she disappeared. She left no clues, so far as the world knew. Down with her went 304 sailors—the biggest loss the U.S. Navy suffered in World War I. No floating debris or sunken hulk has ever been found to explain the loss. It's a mystery that may never be solved.

Our country had joined the Allies to fight Germany in 1917, and German submarines were roaming the Atlantic. For a while, many people thought the *Cyclops*'s captain, who had been born in Germany, may have taken his ship to some German port and betrayed the United States. He was Johann Frederik George Wichmann, from Bremen. After coming to the United States as a boy, he had changed his name to

Worley and become an officer of the U.S. Naval Auxiliary Service. In 1910 Worley had been made master of the 10,000 ton *Cyclops*.

The ex-German was still fond of Germany and its kaiser. When World War I broke out, he made no secret of his sympathies. Before the United States entered the war, Worley entertained officers of German ships calling at then neutral U.S. ports, including those from the German raider *Prinz Eitel Friedrich,* which had been interned in the James River at Newport News.

Once Worley was accused by the navy of showing lights aboard his ship at night, presumably to signal German U-boats. He was also accused of having threatened to run his ship into Rotterdam and deliver her to the Germans. However, he was cleared after an investigation. He was merely eccentric.

Such was the skipper who was at the helm of the *Cyclops* as she pushed her way through heavy ice of Hampton Roads in January 1918— the coldest winter in Virginia's history—en route to South America.

The ship was loaded to her plimsoll mark with coal and stores for the navy's South American patrol fleet. The day was overcast and bitterly cold. Snow was falling.

Painting by Sydney King for Newport News Historical Commission

The James was crowded in 1918 when USS Cyclops
departed on a voyage, never to return.

As she plowed through ice floes past Old
Point, *Cyclops* narrowly avoided a collision
with USS *Survey*, which was headed out for
anti-submarine patrol. As *Cyclops* neared the
capes, one of her watch officers heard a sound
like metal plates scraped together. He reported
later that the ship was twisting and bending so
badly that her hull seemed to be coming apart.

Captain Worley was unfazed. "Son," he told
the young officer, "she'll last as long as we do."

Reaching Bahia, Brazil, after a week at sea,
Cyclops supplied coals to the USS *Raleigh*, a

veteran of the battle of Manila Bay 20 years
earlier. Then she continued south to Rio de
Janeiro to distribute her cargo. She loaded up
with manganese ore and left South America on
February 21.

The collier then notified the navy that she
expected to arrive in Baltimore on March 7 and
made a brief stop at the island of Barbados.
Twenty-four hours later, she exchanged radio
messages with a passing liner in the Atlantic.

That was the last ever heard from *Cyclops*.
Nobody saw the ship or any of her 304 officers

and men again. It is one of the mysteries of American naval history.

For a while, nobody noticed. Then, on March 13, an officer at U.S. Atlantic Fleet Headquarters in Norfolk noticed that *Cyclops* was overdue reaching the United States. He sent out a radio message asking her to report her estimated arrival. No answer.

Life was casual in those days. The navy didn't try to reach *Cyclops* again for a week. Still no answer.

Finally, the navy in Charleston, South Carolina, began sending radio messages to rouse *Cyclops*. When she still didn't answer, the navy sent patrol vessels from Guantanamo, Cuba, to search for her. All navy radio stations from Norfolk southward continued trying to radio the ship, without success.

Then the navy began to investigate Worley's record. Had the German-born captain taken his ship over to the enemy? Could *Cyclops* have sailed to Germany?

All sorts of lurid details came to light. Worley was depicted as a psychopath. Some of his crew were suspected of having mutinied. Naval intelligence officers suggested the ship may have sunk after a magazine explosion. If a German sub had sunk her, it was reasoned, the Germans would have told the world.

When the ship was a month overdue, the *New York Herald* carried a front page story, "Big War Supply Ship Vanishes Without Trace." Since then a lot of people have searched for the *Cyclops*.

The navy gave up its intensive search in 1918. It had begun to believe *Cyclops* had sunk because of her heavy cargo, without having opportunity to send an SOS. Some experts thought the manganese in the hull may have shifted to cause the ship to list and turn over. Naval intelligence investigated a dozen theories.

In 1956, an officer who had once served aboard *Cyclops* before her last voyage came forward with the theory that the ship had broken in two.

In 1968 a wreck was discovered in two pieces at the bottom of the Atlantic, 70 miles off Cape Henry. Thought for a while to have been *Cyclops*, it was later found to be a freighter lost in 1960.

The likeliest explanation was suggested in 1970 by Rear Admiral George van Deurs, who had served aboard a sister ship of *Cyclops*, the *Jason*, before the war and was aware of her serious structural defects. Van Deurs concluded that corroded I-strengtheners had snapped aboard *Cyclops* and that the weakened hull had broken in two in a storm, accounting for her disappearance without radio SOS.

The navy is still hoping to learn what happened. Perhaps deep-sea exploration for minerals will turn up the *Cyclops'* hull. Unless that happens, though, believers in the mystic demons of the Bermuda Triangle will continue to hold that the ship is resting on the bottom somewhere between the James River and Bermuda. I suspect the sea will never give up the secret of the *Cyclops*.

41. *Smithfield Was the Peanut City*

WHEN the Norfolk and Western chose its route through Southside Virginia before the Civil War, it bypassed the counties that fronted the James River; they already had steamboat service. That's how Smithfield, on the Pagan River in Isle of Wight County, came to depend on its daily Old Dominion steamer service to Newport News and Norfolk. Smithfield was a typical steamboat town.

What's more, tiny Smithfield seemed destined to become Virginia's peanut metropolis until disaster struck. That was the terrible fire of August 17, 1921.

After that, Suffolk took over as "Peanutville." But Smithfield managed to survive anyway as producer of the world-famous Smithfield ham. Though still a small and isolated town, it ships its product around the globe—fit food for kings and commoners. In fact, Smithfield has been sending hams to Europe and other faraway places since the eighteenth century, when the town began.

I remember Smithfield's old P. D. Gwaltney peanut factories and warehouses, for they were among the few structures in the low-lying bottomland along the Pagan River when I summered in Smithfield in the 1920s and 1930s.

The Gwaltney firm was started on a shoestring in 1871 by Pembroke Decatur Gwaltney of Surry County, who had served the Confederacy as a gunsmith. After the Civil War, P. D. and his wife, Martha Harris Gwaltney, moved to Smithfield and started a general store, with Captain O. G. Delk as a partner. In addition, Gwaltney and Delk owned a schooner, the *Three Sisters,* which transported Smithfield's produce to market.

"Old Man P. D.," as folks in Smithfield called him, used his gunsmith's skill in the 1800s to develop peanut picking machines. Along with Augustus Bunkley, he organized the Gwaltney-Bunkley Peanut Co., which bought peanuts from farmers in Isle of Wight and shipped them to Norfolk and other markets. The demand for peanuts had boomed after the Civil War, when Yankee soldiers tasted the South's "goober peas."

When I was a child, the Smithfield peanut factories of Gwaltney-Bunkley and of Colonel Charles Fenton Day enlivened Smithfield's wharf area. Then, suddenly, they caught fire that early August morning. Dry peanuts burned fiercely, and soon the warehouses, meat smoke-

*Pembroke Decatur Gwaltney made
Smithfield "Peanut City"*

houses, and docks were aflame. The passenger steamer *Smithfield,* which was just getting up steam for her run to Newport News, hastily cast off and backed out into the Pagan River, training her fire hoses on the burning dockside.

Smithfield people still talk of that hellish fire. Lard stored in the meat houses melted and ran across the wharf roads staining firemen's shoes.

That fire changed Smithfield's history. The Gwaltney-Bunkley and C. F. Day peanut factories lost their market to nearby Suffolk, where Amedeo Obici began his Planters Nut and Chocolate operation. But fortunately Smithfield held on to its ham business.

"Old man P.D." had added hams to his peanut business and was already known for his Gwaltney Genuine brand. His son, P. D. Gwaltney, Jr.,

*Smithfield was a flourishing Pagan River port town in the 1920s,
when its Main Street was lined with wagons.*

Until the 1950s, peanuts were dried in stacks, then picked by machine and bagged in the field.

Picking machines separated peanuts from the vines, in the old days.

Leftover peanut vines were stored in Southside barns to feed to livestock after the peanut crop was in.

in the 1920s and '30s expanded Gwaltney's into a big business, incorporating in 1929 with his son, Howard, as vice president and his son, P. D. III, as secretary-treasurer.

Gwaltney's continued to operate until 1937 in its rebuilt wharf headquarters. Then it moved to a new and larger plant on Wright's Point, where Jim Sprigg's Smithfield Ham and Products Company had already located. Gwaltney's new slaughtering and processing plant was the second U. S. meat-inspected plant built in Virginia. When P. D. Junior died, his son Howard became president with his brother Julius as vice president and brother P. D. III as secretary-treasurer.

By the 1930s the fame of Virginia cured ham and bacon attracted other firms—V. W. Joyner in Smithfield, Todd's in Richmond, Pruden's in Suffolk, and Edwards's in Surry. The competition grew more heated after Joseph Luter left Gwaltney's to start his own firm. Now the Gwaltney operation is part of the worldwide Smithfield Foods Corporation, headed by Joe Luter, Jr., with headquarters not far from my grandparents' old farm.

Recently Smithfield's meat curers have been accused of dumping chemicals into the Pagan River, contrary to law. Under state pressure, they are trying to correct the problem and to continue their expanding industry, so vital to the Smithfield economy.

Today, Smithfield Foods stock is traded nationally, but its meats are still cured in Smithfield. And the wharf, which once smelled

Author's collection

Smithfield's prosperity was built on peanut factories, like this one started by Pembroke Decatur Gwaltney.

of hams and peanuts, is now the scene of expensive condos facing the picturesque Pagan River.

Yes, Smithfield has lost its peanuts, but still has its hams.

42. *When Sealanes Were Crowded*

WHEN I sailed on the James River on the passenger liner *Canada Star*, I stood on deck and thought how empty the harbor looked. Except for ships loading coal at Point Breeze, I could see few big ships in the waterways of the Peninsula. I miss them.

How different from my youth! The James then was one of the busiest rivers of the United States, recalling those pungent lines from John Masefield's "Cargoes":

Dirty British coaster with a salt-caked
  smokestack.
Butting through the Channel in the mad
  March days.
With a cargo of Tyne coal, road-rails,
  piglead,
Firewood, iron ware, and cheap tin trays.

The James in the 1920s was a romantic harbor. A lot of ships anchored there, waiting their turn at the coal docks or the shipyard. We also had many tramp steamers seeking enough cargo to get on with their voyage. From the Casino shore in downtown Newport News you could see flags of many nations, flying from ships at anchor. Jitney boats kept busy ferrying crewmen and ship chandlers from ship to shore.

Hampton Roads and the James have designated anchorages for navy and commercial ships. In the James anchorage, above and below the shipyard, I could see as many as 30 ships at anchor. The colors and insignia of their smokestacks told what line owned each. Old-time shippers knew them all.

What glamorous home ports they listed on their fantails: Rotterdam, Gothenburg, Oslo, Panama, Singapore, Liverpool, Vancouver. When their crews came ashore, the tough seamen stood out in the crowds on Washington Avenue. Before Prohibition came, crewmen hung out in bars along River Road, fronting the C & O piers. Those were the days when 18th Street and "Hell's Half Acre" reeked with whiskey, bawdy houses, and fist fights. Some sailors were shanghaied into serving on crews after being hauled aboard a ship while drunk.

Walter Kelly, a Philadelphia Irishman, ran a saloon on lower Washington Avenue and broke up many a fight between sailors. The uncle of actress Grace Kelly, he later became a vaudeville comedian, famous for the "Virginian judge" routine he developed after listening to

Early drydock at Portsmouth's navy shipyard built and overhauled men-of-war of the sail era.

Newport News police Judge J. D. G. Brown dispense justice in the raw seaport.

I encountered the Newport News dock area about 1925, when I walked with my father along 18th Street—part of "Hell's Half Acre"—to collect rents from tenants of his. A few years later, I began working for the C & O as summer help, checking freight on the merchandise piers between 18th and 23rd streets. There I glimpsed the lives of crewmen whose ships brought cargo to the C & O docks. Theirs was a rough life, but to my eyes it seemed glamourous. It reminded me of books by Joseph Conrad, Somerset Maugham, and John Masefield.

In those between-war days, many shipping lines—Merchants and Miners, Eastern Steamship, Baltimore Mail—brought cargo to Newport News. Unloaded on the piers, it was shipped by train to cities along the C & O—Richmond, Charleston, West Virginia, Huntington, Toledo, St. Louis—and westward.

The docks are now controlled by CSX and the Virginia Port Authority.

Newport News in my days was a handler of grain, manganese, tobacco, raw rubber, and other commodities. But fires long ago destroyed the C & O's grain elevators and other ports took away its tobacco exports. It was slow getting around to containerized cargo handling, so lots of that trade went to Baltimore and Norfolk. Today coal is Newport News's major cargo.

As a reporter in the 1930s, my daily beat started from the *Times-Herald* office on 25th Street and went down to the waterfront. In those days the office of the Virginia Pilots Association stood on West Avenue, near the Virginia Commission of Fisheries. There I visited such ships' agents as T. Parker Host, and Allan Hoffman. Harry Keitz bossed the stevedores and Harry Reyner was a ship chandler, supplying crews with provisions.

Many ships then put into the James River for

*C & O passenger depot at Newport News before the 1950s handled passengers
arriving by train and steamboat.*

repairs or overhaul at the shipyard. Lem
Robertson, then vice president for repairs,
answered my daily queries about arriving and
departing vessels.

The popular hit, "I Cover the Waterfront,"
echoing the title of a 1930s novel, heightened
my youthful infatuation with the sea. I learned in the navy that life at sea isn't all that
Masefield and Joseph Conrad made it out to
be, but that's another story.

Even so, I miss those busy tugboats, rusting
tramp ships, and the raffish crewmen who once
enlivened the James River. I hope someday the
United States will rebuild its merchant marine.
Then the James will come fully alive again, as it
was in the days of bartender Walter Kelly and
those other characters of our maritime past.

43. *A Virginia Farm Christmas*

THE white James River boat rounds the bend of Pagan River, blows for a landing, and then slows as she approaches the dock. On the wharf, against a warehouse stored with Smithfield hams and peanuts, wharf hands stand by to catch the mooring lines.

With a great churning of creek water, the *Smithfield* reverses her engines and slows her sidewise crawl toward the dock. Then, in a flash, mooring lines are thrown from ship to shore. From the dockside, friends and kinsmen peer alertly at the river boat's passengers in search of city cousins, coming to spend Christmas in the farms and villages south of the James River.

A proud father on the steamer lifts his five-year-old for waiting relatives to admire. "My, but he's grown!" an aunt shouts from the dock as the gangway is rolled into place and passengers begin to surge ashore. "Hold him up again!"

Thus it began—the magic interlude of Christmas in the country. In the simpler days when Woodrow Wilson sat in the White House, river boats carried many holiday homecomers to farms along the rivers running inland from the Atlantic. In retrospect they now seem splendidly romantic days, for bridges and automobiles would soon replace the white gothic river steamers and the horsedrawn vehicles which met them at the dock. Never since in America has life seemed quite so leisurely.

The arrival of the boat was Smithfield's chief weekday diversion in those days. Her "Here-I-come" toot at Red Point at 5:27 each afternoon was a signal to stevedores, farmers, and the idly curious to amble to the wharf and see just who and what came in that day from Norfolk or Newport News. The skipper, Captain Gordon Delk, was the idol of every child in town. He and his ship were Smithfield's link with the glamorous world of department stores and movie houses which lay across the wide James River and Hampton Roads.

To the homecoming stranger, Smithfield offered a fragrant welcome. The whitewashed smokehouses along Pagan River exuded the hickory scent of a century of ham curings. The warehouses of Mr. Pembroke Decatur Gwaltney and Colonel Charles F. Day bulged with the fall peanut harvest from miles around. Richard Jordan's livery stable added its earthy ambience, while Shivers' Market displayed in the open air the day's offerings of oysters, rockfish, croakers, and catfish.

From Berry Hill farm, my grandfather had sent Willie Bailey, a strapping farm hand, to load our luggage into the surrey and drive us to the farm. Strong arms were needed, for a horse sometimes bolted when it crossed the clattering wooden drawbridge at Wright's Point. Once or twice when a horse acted skittish, Willie dismounted and led it across.

December in southern Virginia is generally mild, though the sting of winter is usually felt during Christmas week. The last yellow leaves cling to maple and oak while red berries on the holly warn that cold winds will soon scour the trees. Thick growths of mistletoe are exposed in the crotches of leafless trees, waiting for nimble boys to shinny up and collect them. Rows of cedar trees divide recently-dug peanut fields, and pines look black against the pale winter sky. The gaudy profusion of summer is reduced to the cold geometry of fences and roads.

In the early 1920s, large flocks of migrating ducks still clustered in the blackwater creeks which drain from southside Virginia into the James, flying up with a great roar of wings as we approached. Now and then a rabbit or fox would dart across the sandy road, startling the horses. An occasional blue jay or squirrel chattering in the treetops mocked the sound of our excited voices and the steady rasp of the wagon rims as they cut through the sand.

Then we reached Berry Hill. There in the yard stood Grandfather, calling out, "Dismount! Dismount!" Grandmother was at his side, her thin white hair pulled upward and pinned in a knot above her head. Close behind came uncles, aunts, a profusion of cousins, and the black farm boys, Willie Boy and Albert, who were dear friends and constant companions of my brothers and me. (It was years later before we knew my Grandfather had paid them to watch us and teach us to ride and hunt.) At first, Willie Boy and Albert could only stand and grin, but their embarrassment left them when the grownups turned us loose to play outside.

How many things there are to do in a week

on the farm! We learned to eat persimmons ("No good till the first frost hits 'em"), to catch rabbits in a baited poke, to curry horses, to ride bareback and with a saddle, to find the eggs of renegade hens. We milked a cow, caught bull gudgeons in the creek, and did a thousand other things—some useful and some destructive.

If the weather turned cold, we sometimes helped with hog-killing, though one bloody experience was usually enough. To make short work of it, all the men from the farm's half-dozen tenant families worked from sunrise to sunset to kill, scald, cut up, and salt the hogs which had been raised the preceding summer. They were amazingly skillful, for southside Virginians have perfected hog raising and curing since their fertile lands were first settled by Englishmen.

After the men had done their work, my grandmother directed the hired women in the making of sausage, cracklings, and the heavy gray soap which they compounded of hog fat, lye, and other ingredients.

Once the hams and shoulders of the hogs were dressed, my grandfather had them treated in the time-honored Smithfield fashion. First, they were salted in a large pot and left covered a day or so in the brine. Then the hams and shoulders were cleaned, oiled, and hung in a draft. The procedure is similar to that which the Roman writer Cato the Elder described in his *De Re Rustica,* written 149 years before the birth of Christ and recently rediscovered by Miss Bess Wright, a retired professor who lived in Smithfield. "On the third day," Cato wrote, "take them down, rub them with a mixture of oil and vinegar, and hang them in the meat-house. Neither moths nor worms will touch them."

After this treatment came the process of smoking the meat over a steady smoky fire in a curing house. This was accomplished with green hickory logs, which had been cut and stored outside the old brick smokehouse to await their hour of need.

While we youngsters were enjoying the outdoors, the ladies for several days prepared a

Christmas in the 1920s was spartan by today's standards but exciting for youngsters.

memorable Christmas feast. In those days "getting ready for Christmas" primarily meant cooking, for prepared foods did not then exist. The big woodstove in the kitchen was kept busy from morning until night for days at a time. Fruit cakes and plum puddings must be made and drenched in brandy. Smoked hams must be soaked and baked, black walnuts must be shelled for cakes, and hard sauce must be made of butter, powdered sugar, and brandy. The jobs were endless.

A holiday ritual then as now was the cheering cup before sitting down to dinner. Southerners called it a toddy and made it usually of corn whiskey or bourbon, water, and a teaspoonful of sugar. At Berry Hill a Victorian shibboleth prevailed against women drinking. Therefore, my grandfather invited only the menfolk to gather in his room before dinner to quaff the welcome mixture before an open fire. A grandson had to be well along in college before being welcomed to the group.

Traditions in Christmas fare differ from house to house, but in southern Virginia in 1920 a Christmas dinner always included more food than any mortal could do justice to. At Berry Hill a ham graced my grandfather's end of the table and a goose my grandmother's. Between them ranged such heavenly fare as creamed sweet potatoes, baked tomatoes, creamed onions, corn pudding, watermelon-rind pickle, green-tomato relish, homemade pickle, cornbread, hot rolls, and whatever else came to my grandmother's mind.

With so many to be fed at once, Christmas at Berry Hill filled the big dining room with tables and chairs. Though grandmothers in Calvinist households might make the youngsters wait for a second sitting (it was "good discipline"), my kindly grandmother would not hear of such inhumanity. She insisted that all the family sit down for one blessing, the adults at one table and the children at another. With Addie and Mary Polly in the kitchen, a relay constantly

175

shuttled new provender into the crowded dining room.

As with any holiday feast, dessert was an important part of Christmas dinner at Berry Hill. Much advance work went into the mixing valiantly transferred the mixture to a lard tin, half-submerged this in a wash bucket of ice and brine, and vigorously turned it a half-hour with his hands until it froze. That, Addie explained, was the way poor people made their ice cream.

Kenneth Harris watercolor from author's collection

Around a bend from the James was Smithfield's Pagan River, where steambboats once docked.

and baking of fruit cakes, which were soaked with brandy and placed with an apple to provide moisture while they aged for several days in the basement cool room. Another favorite was frozen custard made up of cream, milk, many eggs, sugar, and vanilla. Frozen in a large ice cream freezer just before dinner, it was dished out and rushed on trays from freezer to table to prevent melting in the warm dining room. Once, when the freezer broke, a farmhand

Southerners undeniably have a sweet tooth. New Orleans is famous for pralines and pecan pies and Charleston for its Huguenot puddings and pastries. Virginia is no exception. In those day, before calorie-counting clouded our enjoyment of such sweets, our region seemed especially fond of grated sweet potato pudding or pie, made rich with butter and aromatic with bourbon and nutmeg. A showier dessert was tipsy cake or pudding, which had evolved from

England's traditional tipsy squire and syllabub (meaning "silly stomach"). It is less common today, perhaps because few of today's housewives have the leisure needed to bake sponge cake, blanch almonds, make brandy- or sherry-flavored custard, and whip the heavy cream which tops this heavenly edifice. Such chores call for abundant "kitchen help."

The holiday week between Christmas and New Year's day brought many other pleasures. Quail shot on one day's hunt turned up as next day's breakfast. Squirrels were boiled until tender and then combined in Brunswick stew, a Brunswick County, Virginia, concoction of vegetables and meat stock with cured pork for seasoning.

The hickory fire in the smokehouse produced other rewards besides the celebrated Smithfield ham. The classic Berry Hill breakfast was lean slices of Smithfield shoulder fried in a skillet with scrambled eggs and served with eggbread. (Spoonbread and hominy grits, which usually accompany fried ham in the Deep South, were not common in Virginia until recently.) Another smokehouse product was link sausage, called "dandoodles," which, when aged, became so strong and hard that it had to be parboiled before being split and fried. Its ugliness was deceptive.

Berry Hill's kitchen was housed in a long wing at the rear. Thanks to this fact, the Berry Hill kitchen could safely indulge some of the family's taste for the malodorous and often maligned salted herring. Caught by Chesapeake Bay net fishermen each spring, these roe-bearing fish were cured in brine and smoke before making their way to the table in autumn. A night's soaking in water—sometimes with several changes—was necessary to desalt them for the skillet, where they sizzled and popped dangerously until ready to be borne into the dining room amid mixed cheers and protests.

The time-hallowed New Year's day meal in some southern Virginia and North Carolina households is black-eyed peas and hog jowl, which Southern soothsayers say brings good luck in the months to come. This cherished dish was never evident at Berry Hill, nor were collard greens, which are often served with such "soul food." Instead, New Year's breakfast brought us goose hash and waffles, or calves brains and eggs. Whatever it might be, it was rich, delicious, and abundant.

It was fortunate that Christmas vacation from school then lasted only a week. Even with a daily hunt through the fallow fields and the forests to whet one's appetite, it was impossible to do continued justice to such fare. Looking back after a half-century, it's a wonder we survived!

But in those days it seemed the right and proper way to enjoy Christmas. It was always with sadness that we bade Willie Boy and Albert farewell on the afternoon of New Year's day. Then, as we waved goodbye to my grandparents while they stood smiling and beckoning from the porch—no doubt exhausted but still enthusiastic—we drove down the lane toward town and the waiting steamer.

Today, a half-century later, the smell of hickory smoke coming from an open hearth fire brings Christmas at Berry Hill vividly back to me. The dear faces, the riverboat, the surrey—most of them have long gone. But happy memories from childhood survive undimmed. Those first Christmases at Berry Hill will always seem the ideal which each family should try to achieve: a Christmas which abundantly fills the heart and richly and innocently gratifies the senses.

44. *The World of Pier A*

ONE of the busiest spots in the Newport News of the 1920s and '30s was the long wooden dock at 25th Street and the James River, called Pier A. That's where the water taxis operated to carry crewmen and pilots back and forth from their anchorage to shore. And that's where the produce of farmers and fishermen was sold, wholesale and retail, from the decks of river boats to customers on the dock.

More important, Pier A was the terminus for the Old Dominion Steamship Company's passenger steamer *Smithfield,* plying between Smithfield, Newport News, and Norfolk. It also berthed Captain A. F. Jester's small but feisty mail boat, *Oneita,* which competed with the *Smithfield.*

A 1920s photo shows mounds of watermelons on the dock and a string of produce boats alongside. In the background are the casino and a part of the post office nearby at 25th Street and West Avenue.

Until the James River Bridge opened in 1928, my family and other natives of southern Virginia crossed frequently from Newport News to Battery Park and Smithfield. I well remember boarding the Smithfield boat in the 1920s. It arrived at Pier A from Norfolk about 4 p.m. and took on cargo and passengers for about a half hour. Stevedores hurriedly pushed or carried cargo aboard—autos, farm equipment, hardware, and groceries. My parents held us children tightly till we were safely on the passenger deck, looking down.

My parents knew the captain and the purser, who punched our tickets. In fact, they seemed to know everybody, for the boat *Smithfield* operated from Smithfield and its officers were important men in the 1920s town. My family had moved to Newport News in 1918, three years after I was born, but they returned with their children to their birthplace for weekends, holidays, and vacations. A lot of other Southsiders who'd moved to World War I Newport News also traveled on the boat.

The trip up the James and into the Pagan River to Smithfield took a little more than an hour and got you there by suppertime. My brothers and I happily ran around the decks with our dog, while we waited for the loud ship's horn and the captain's loud "All a-a-a-a-b-b-o-o-o-a-r-r-r-d."

Once she set sail, she passed close to the Warwick Machine Shop pier, now torn down,

*Produce vendors in the 1920s brought their fare to sell
at Newport News's Pier A on the James.*

and then skirted the shipyard before moving up
the river off our familiar North End shoreline.
Several miles further along, she made the familiar port turn past Eclipse and then up the winding Pagan to the village of Battery Park.

The *Smithfield* and her competitor, the
Oneita, were Smithfield's only commercial ties
with the world before autos, for the town had no
railroad. In the old days, before 1875, a sailing
schooner had moved the town's peanuts, cured
meat, corn, and truck crops. It was the three-
masted *Three Sisters*, owned by Captain O.G.
Delk and by peanut processor P. D. Gwaltney,
Sr., father of the P. D. who founded the ham
curing firm.

Then, about 1875, Captain Delk joined the
Old Dominion Line and took command of its
steamboats.

A Smithfield lady named Dorothy Robbins
wrote her recollections of the steamers in 1947,
and I've saved her affectionate account. "Captain Delk loved his boats," she wrote, "and
when the Isle of Wight, loaded to the water's
edge with peanuts, burned at the dock on a
morning in the '90s, he wept like a child."

Dorothy Robbins wrote lovingly of the Sunday school picnics and moonlight excursions
the *Smithfield* also made. Its dining room
served breakfast en route to Newport News in
the morning—"crisply fried oysters or Ocean

Author's collection

Through Newport News's Victory Arch
townspeople drove to shop
on Pier A's produce boats.

View spots, Smithfield ham, and scrambled eggs, accompanied by hot biscuits and strong coffee."

My parents often recalled Smithfield's Sunday school picnics and moonlight cruises by steamboat back in the horse-and-buggy days. Dorothy Robbins wrote that "The moonlight trips were highly popular with the younger set, and some would bring along guitars to strum while the others sang, but many were content merely to hold hands and listen to the water swish."

Captain Delk was a celebrated figure in my parents' Smithfield, for he'd been born there and was kin to the Gwaltneys and other prominent families. While he sailed the *Accomac,* she collided in Hampton Roads with the *Luray,* another James River ship, and sank. However, Captain Delk was exonerated and served the Old Dominion Line 26 years, retiring at 62.

When the state of Virginia began to build hard-surfaced highways in the 1920s, trucks took over the water-borne commerce of the James and other rivers. Pier A declined as a passenger and produce center. Finally, the Old Dominion Line began to lose money and ended its Smithfield service. But the little farm town didn't give up its ship easily. A Smithfield Boat Line was formed under the leadership of John I. Cofer, Jr., and a Captain Winder was hired as skipper of its last ship, the *Hampton Roads.*

In a few years, however, even the local company had to give up. After the opening of the James River Bridge, my family never sailed on the *Hampton Roads,* but drove to Smithfield via the bridge.

Pier A lingered on for a while, but today it's gone. The 1920s photograph recalls a colorful landmark of the vanished steamboat era.

45. *The Bridge Changed Everything*

ONE of the grand moments on the James when I was young was the opening of the James River Bridge. It happened on November 17, 1928 —a year before the stock market crash—and it opened up a new world for a lot of people.

That narrow bridge livened up Southside as it had never been before. Over the years it created trade between the merchants of Newport News and the farmers of Isle of Wight. It brought to the Peninsula a lot of business which before 1928 had gone to Norfolk.

If you'd been there for the opening, you wouldn't forget it. The star was Woodroof Hiden, a shy girl of 18, dressed in peach silk. She cut the ribbon that opened the bridge, wielding a huge pair of scissors (wood, painted gold, with steel cutting edge).

The ceremonies took place around the toll plaza which had been built at the juncture of Warwick Boulevard and the bridge approach. Woody Hiden was "Miss Virginia," with a "court" of teenagers. The band played, and Governor Harry Byrd made a speech.

The big moment was when President Coolidge pressed a button in the White House to raise the bridge span. It went 147 feet above the water—then one of the highest bridges in the country.

Once the ribbon was cut, half of Newport News rushed to cross the river. The owners opened it free for the rest of the day, and traffic was bumper-to-bumper. Lots of Boy Scouts hiked over, but I rode in my family's Model-T. We took advantage of the free trip to Smithfield to see relatives.

Those were days of big risks. Investors who invested money knew it was a long shot, and they were right. After the 1929 crash, times really got tough for the bridge. A lot of investors lost their shirts. Finally, the state bought the system in 1949, paying for it with tolls. After the bonds were paid off in 1976, the bridge was made free.

The bridge was then the second longest in the country, spanning 4.9 miles and exceeded only by a bridge from Key West to the next Florida key. Everybody in those days talked about the $5.2 million it cost, though that seems a drop compared to what its replacement cost.

A group of Tidewater businessmen had conceived the bridge and formed a corporation to sell bonds to build it. Philip W. Hiden, ex-mayor and father of Woodroof, was one.

Another was Albert Sydney Johnson of Smithfield, who became manager.

The corporation built smaller bridges over Chuckatuck Creek and Nansemond River to create a route from Newport News to Portsmouth and Norfolk. The James River span put Southside closer to Newport News than to Norfolk. So Smithfielders began coming to Newport News to shop, see doctors, and eventually to play golf and go to cocktail parties. (Early tolls discouraged such frivolous trips.)

All of that changed the pattern of life in

Daily Press

The James River bridge at Newport News in 1928 helped build the city into a metropolis.

Smithfield and Battery Park. The steamboat from Smithfield to Newport News and Norfolk went out of business after the bridge opened. So did Captain A. F. Jester's mail boat and his car-ferry from the Boat Harbor to Chuckatuck. Instead of shipping watermelons by boat to Pier A at 25th Street, farmers sent them over by truck. A lot of Newport News people were partial to Smithfield-grown kale, turnip salad, sweet potatoes, side meat, and other edibles now low-rated as "soul food."

The bridge brought other changes. More Southsiders commuted to the shipyard and to Peninsula military bases. Shipyard traffic each afternoon loaded the bridge for an hour or so after 4. It has become part of Tidewater's lifestyle for people to live in the boondocks, where they can enjoy hunting and fishing when they get home from work. Some commuters plant a few acres, or raise chickens or even set a few traps for muskrats.

Another benefit of the bridge was to enable young couples and retirees to buy houses on the Southside, where real estate and taxes in 1928 were cheaper than on the Peninsula.

Today Southside is full of "come-heres," like all of rural Tidewater. Even Albert Sidney Johnson's old house on Smithfield's Church Street was bought by people from Newport News. William and Mary professors also discovered the area and commuted to the college.

In time, the bridge raised population, land values, and taxes in the black belt south of the James. The black people of Southside particularly benefited from the Peninsula job market and from the new money coming into Isle of Wight and Nansemond.

Southside Virginians took the initiative in the 1940s to have the state buy the span and reduce tolls. Senator A. E. S. "Gi" Stephens had a lot to do with the state's purchase, and Delegate Mills Godwin of Chuckatuck, later Virginia's governor, did a lot to reduce tolls, persuading the state to eliminate them first at Chuckatuck and Nansemond.

When Mills Godwin ran for governor in 1961, he advocated elimination of the final toll remaining on the James River span, which was done during his second term in 1976. By that time, tolls had paid off the indebtedness on the James River, Yorktown, and Rappahannock bridges, together with the Hampton Bridge Tunnel. Now they are free.

It was a long wait, but a few of us who were present at the opening in 1928 have survived to enjoy the freebies.

Daily Press

The original James River bridge segment no longer serves automobiles, but fishermen.

46. *Obici, the Peanut King*

AMERICAN towns, unlike European ones, don't have saints or guardian angels. But many have one outstanding benefactor. The dominant spirit in Suffolk, a prosperous city of 60,000, is Amedeo Obici, an Italian immigrant, who made Suffolk the "Peanut Capital of the World" before he died in 1947.

Planters is still a big part of Suffolk, where peanuts mean money. Virginia is the upper end of a southern goober belt that extends across the continent to Texas and California. Georgia may sell the most peanuts, but Virginia "big pearl," or "ballpark" nuts, bring the highest prices.

To Suffolk's Planters factory each year come endless truckloads of peanuts from Virginia and North Carolina. Expanding world demand for peanut products keeps the industry profitable and farmers happy.

How did a penniless Italian immigrant make Planters a worldwide name? And how did he happen to live in Suffolk?

Obici emigrated from Italy to Scranton, Pennsylvania, as a boy of 12 back in 1888, when many Europeans were emigrating. He went to work in Scranton at his uncle's fruit stand, where he roasted peanuts at night and sold them next day. Sales were so good he transferred to a push cart, yelling "Come get your hot roasted peanuts!" Soon, he opened a fruit and peanut stand in Wilkes-Barre.

In 1906 Obici and his future brother-in-law formed a firm to sell peanuts across the nation. They chose the trade name "Planters." A few years later they adopted the trademark figure of Mister Peanut which had been proposed by a Suffolk schoolboy in a Planters contest. Obici and his partner chose Suffolk as their factory site in 1913 because that's where they bought the best peanuts. After that, Suffolk rapidly outgrew such other James River peanut markets as Smithfield, Franklin, Ivor, Sedley, and Wakefield.

By 1925 Planters was bringing $8 million yearly into Suffolk. Today the figure is much higher.

Obici made Suffolk his manufacturing base, but Planters's executive and sales offices remained in Wilkes-Barre. However, Obici and his wife, Louise, moved to Suffolk and spent part of each year on their Bay Point dairy farm on the Nansemond River near Driver. Obici took pride in his dairy cows, which supplied milk to subscribers among his truck routes around Suffolk.

Much of Obici's success grew from his use

Ted LoCascio

Amedeo Obici was an Italian immigrant who made Suffolk "Peanut Capital of the World."

of advertising, which was developing in the 1920s to promote once local products for a nationwide market. The Italian immigrant sold his goobers in a 5-cent glassine bag all over the nation at candy stands, drugstores, and newsstands. Obici called them "The Nickel Lunch."

When the Depression came, Obici sold increasing numbers of penny and nickel bagged peanuts. In 1930 he began the sale of peanut oil. He also pushed a new food called peanut butter, which rapidly became a grocery staple around the world.

Up until Obici's time, peanuts had been roasted in their hulls and sold in paper bags at sports events. Many theaters, like the Newport News Academy of Music, had low priced peanut galleries where patrons munched peanuts before the acts.

Obici is remembered in Suffolk as a simple and democratic man. He was 40 when he married matronly Louise Musante, who had also operated a Wilkes-Barre confectionery. They had no children. He joined the Masons and the Elks, and he and Louise were active in Suffolk charities. He served as a member of the board of the College of William and Mary, and contributed funds for teaching Italian.

In 1936 Louise expressed the desire to give a hospital to the town, which had none. Four years after her 1938 death, her husband built that city's Louise Obici Memorial Hospital and nursing school.

After Obici's death, Planters Nut and Chocolate Company was bought in 1960 by Standard Brands, now part of RJR Nabisco. But Obici's imprint remains in Suffolk. After all, he and Mister Peanut put Suffolk on the map.

47. *Show Boat on the James*

I can see it in my mind's eye: "James Adams's Floating Theater," a fat, two-story houseboat, tied up at the foot of Wharf Hill in Smithfield. That was 1925, and for a week it offered glorious performances of tearful melodramas.

Today most of the showboat's patrons have died, but a few still remember the floating opera house that toured the waters of Chesapeake Bay and Albemarle Sound for years before 1939.

Edna Ferber spent four days on the Adams's boat in 1924 to collect background for her novel, *Show Boat,* which Jerome Kern and Oscar Hammerstein II made into a great musical comedy. More recently, John Barth of Maryland's Eastern Shore has written a novel, *The Floating Opera,* based on his memories of its visits to Easton, Maryland, when he was a boy.

The Adams showboat was one of many floating playhouses which roamed coastal and inland waters of the United Sates early in this century. Many people from tidal Virginia remember visits to the James, York, Rappahannock, Piankatank, and Eastern Shore. It even spent three weeks each November in Washington, D. C., long before the Kennedy Center and

Wolf Trap Theater catered to more sophisticated playgoers.

James Adams's Floating Theater had no competition in the Chesapeake and played to good houses for nearly 30 years, each year at a profit. It represented an investment of $70,000, which was big money before Franklin Roosevelt got hold of the dollar.

When the Depression of 1929 came along, Adams's profits were cut. In 1939 Edna Ferber reported that Adams's Floating Theater had sunk with all scenery, costumes, and stage sets on board. The cast and crew escaped. Only then did the owner finally cash the check Miss Ferber had sent him years earlier in appreciation for his help to her with *Show Boat.*

Unlike the "Cotton Blossom" showboat on the Mississippi, the Adams Floating Theater didn't even look like a boat. It was a square, white clapboard house on a rectangular barge, 34 feet wide, 122 feet long, and drawing 14 inches of water. It was built at Little Washington, North Carolina, shortly after 1900.

I never witnessed a performance on the showboat, for my parents thought me too young, but I know that its auditorium was like any small opera house of its day, with tiny stage, orchestra pit, 700 seats, and a rear balcony. Two small boxes flanked the stage, which was 19 feet wide and 15 feet deep.

The Floating Theater would tie up at Smithfield for a week in July or August, moving on to its next stop on Sunday. Its stock-in-trade was old-fashioned melodrama. Its orchestra played on the Smithfield dock before each performance, drumming up a crowd. Then the musicians filed into the pit to perform mood music throughout the show.

A week's bill in 1925 lists "The Balloon Girl" on Monday night. (A circus performer, the heroine, was dropped by a parachute trapeze on the roof of a handsome bachelor preacher.) Tuesday night brought "Pollyanna," Wednesday night "Tempest and Sunshine," Thursday night "A Thief in the Night," Friday night "Sooey-San," and Saturday night "Mystic Isle," in which two aviators crash-land on an island in the Gulf of Mexico amid bootleggers, smugglers, and opium runners.

Other Adams offerings were "Grandmothers and Flappers," "Gossip," "Mr. Jim Bailey," "The Girl Who Ran Away," "Peg o' My Heart," and "S'manthy." It was unsophisticated stuff for people who rarely went to the theater. Many were farmhands.

After the play you could pay an added admission to see the cast perform vaudeville acts and an old-fashioned minstrel show, which seemed to amuse blacks in the audience as much as whites. Impresario Adams and his chief assistant, Charles Hunter, were careful to avoid smut, sex, or high living. They knew rural Baptist and Methodist audiences.

Mrs. Hunter was the former Beulah Adams, James Adams's youngest sister. She was pretty and took the lead in showboat plays for 17 years, winning the title of "the Mary Pickford

Daily Press

James Adams's Floating Theater was a two-story barge towed to Tidewater towns each summer.

The show boat produced romantic melodramas to please unsophisticated audiences.

of the Chesapeake." Her husband had learned showboating on the Ohio River and was her stalwart leading man. Virtue always triumphed on the showboat, and the villain was always killed, convicted, or publicly disgraced.

The company compelled its actors and musicians to behave themselves and to avoid intimacies with patrons. Edna Ferber recalled that when she went ashore to an ice cream parlor in 1924 at Easton, Maryland, with the Adamses and Hunters, they were shocked when she started to light a cigarette.

The arrival of the Floating Theater at Smithfield livened up the town. The craft was towed in by two tugs, *Elk* and *Trouper,* owned by Adams. As soon as she tied up, the crew put on bright uniforms, got out band instruments, and began to play the usual free waterside concert to signal their arrival. Playbills advertising the week's shows were distributed on Smithfield's streets.

Virginia stops of the Floating Theater included Deep Creek on the Inland Waterway, Gloucester Point, Urbanna, Tappahannock, several Eastern Shore towns, and Alexandria. In Maryland it visited such places as Annapolis, Easton, and Crisfield. Finally, it returned to North Carolina for the winter, stopping at Edenton, Little Washington, Hertford, and Plymouth before laying up in December in Elizabeth City.

Besides the two Hunters, the company included an ingenue, a male juvenile lead, a "character" team of comedians, a "general purpose" team, a "heavy" or villain, and a "general utility man."

Like the pre-1930s passenger and river boats of Tidewater, the Floating Theater finally succumbed to the automobile and modern highways. After the boat was sunk in the 1930s, the owners decided against trying to refloat or replace it. It was also done in by talking movies, which began in the 1930s with Emil Jannings in "The Patriot" and Al Jolson in "The Singing Fool."

James Adams foresaw the change when he printed in his 1930s theatrical program a defense of his showboat. "If the time comes," he wrote, "that our public prefers mechanical entertainment, we will bring it to you. But until that time comes, we shall continue to bring you our company of 30 people, flesh and blood actors and musicians, which we believe is of more benefit to your community than 5,000 feet of celluloid and a phonograph."

The showboat wasn't art, but it was mighty popular entertainment.

48. *"The Sick, Sad, and Sorry"*

IF you drive your car aboard the Jamestown ferry from the Surry County side, you can look off to the shallow water near the ferry pier and see the broken pilings of a long-abandoned wharf.

That's all that remains of the Surry, Sussex and Southampton Railway, which once shipped vast amounts of timber to European and American ports from its rail dock, which it called Scotland Wharf. From 1885 until it disbanded in 1930, the SS&S (Southsiders called it "the Sick, Sad, and Sorry") and its Surry Lumber Company brought millions of dollars into the three counties they served. That meant a good living to Southside's farmers, landowners, loggers, lumbermen, and rail workers.

Surry's lumber railroad symbolizes the transition of post-Civil War Tidewater from a broken-down farm economy in 1865 to an industrial one 50 years later. Since then we've broadened into tourism, military bases, and greatly increased technology.

The homely story of the narrow-gauge SS&S was told by Temple Crittenden, a railroad buff, in *The Comp'ny,* published in 1967. The author talked to dozens of Surrymen, now dead, to put together his tragicomic saga of the post-Civil War period. His book is full of rail mishaps, practical jokes, and homely asides.

A group of Baltimore men started the project, but it became a Tidewater affair. Mrs. Linwood Holton, wife of a Virginia governor, is a member of the Rogers clan who ran it. Others from the Surry area, the Morris, Edwards, Whitley, Causey, Faison, and Pretlow families, got involved. The SS&S hauled timber for competing Southside mills like Camp Manufacturing Company at Franklin and Gray Lumber Company at Waverly. Both are large industries.

Surry is quiet today, but it was busy in its timber years. As Crittenden says; "The largest enterprise ever operated in Surry County was the Surry Lumber Company. It was the largest producer of yellow pine lumber in the East. It was among the largest railroad-logging companies in the country. It created communities, built roads, strung telephone lines, established stores and banks, sold electric power and ice, but above all it created jobs that raised the living standard of a large number of people."

Actually, Surry's lumbering industry goes back before the Civil War to Major William Allen who owned Claremont Manor on the James and was Virginia's richest planter. Allen

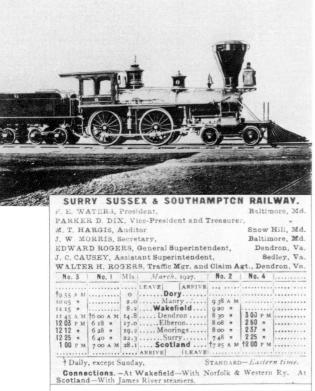

SURRY SUSSEX & SOUTHAMPTON RAILWAY.

F. E. WATERS, President,   Baltimore, Md.
PARKER D. DIX, Vice-President and Treasurer,   „
M. T. HARGIS, Auditor.   Snow Hill, Md.
J. W. MORRIS, Secretary,   Baltimore, Md.
EDWARD ROGERS, General Superintendent,   Dendron, Va.
J. C. CAUSEY, Assistant Superintendent,   Sedley, Va.
WALTER H. ROGERS, Traffic Mgr. and Claim Agt., Dendron, Va.

No. 3	No. 1	Mls.	*March, 1927.*	No. 2	No. 4	
			LEAVE ⟨ARRIVE			
†9 55 A M		0	......**Dory**........			
10 05 „		2.0	.....Manry........	9 38 A M		
11 15 „		8.2	...**Wakefield**....	9 20 „		
11 45 A M	†6 00 A M	14.8	.....Dendron	8 30 „	3 00 P M	
12 03 P M	6 18 „	17.0	.....Elberon......	8 08 „	2 50 „	
12 12 „	6 28 „	19.2	....Moorings.....	8 00 „	2 37 „	
12 25 „	6 40 „	22.3	.....Surry.......	7 48 „	2 25 „	
1 00 P M	7 00 A M	28.1	.... **Scotland**	†7 25 A M	†2 00 P M	
			ARRIVE⟩ ⟨LEAVE			

† Daily, except Sunday.   STANDARD—*Eastern time.*

Connections. —At Wakefield—With Norfolk & Western Ry. At Scotland—With James River steamers.

Author's collection

Three James River counties depended on the logging railroad for transport till its 1931 end.

owned 365 slaves, and he kept them busy in the 1850s and early '60s cutting pines for railway ties and cordwood, which he shipped from the Claremont dock, then called Sloop Point.

To get the lumber from forest to river dock, Allen built an iron-railed tramway near the town of Spring Grove. When war came, he pulled up his rails and gave the steel to the Confederate cause. After Appomattox he revived his lumbering, but without slaves or his defunct tramway. He sold rail ties to the Prussian government in the Franco-Prussian War of 1870–71, plus cordwood shipped to Norfolk, Richmond, and Baltimore.

Northern lumbermen came south in numbers after the Civil War to buy cheap land and produce lumber for the nation's expanding economy. In the 1870s, several Maryland and Dela-

ware operators descended on Surry, some of them uniting in 1885 to create the Surry Lumber Company, with a capital of $500,000.

To haul pines from Southside forests, the company built a narrow-gauge railroad. At first it ran only a few miles and hauled only lumber. But as it prospered it added a little coach primitively divided to carry passengers, mail, and freight, including livestock. Eventually the toy-like trains operated from Scotland Wharf southwestward through Surry, Sussex, and Southampton counties, a distance of over 50 miles.

A tiny donkey engine drew the SS&S trains. The narrow-gauge tracks ran mostly through forests, often marshy and uneven. Much of the terrain was what woodsmen called "pocosin" or "poquoson," a word from the Indians meaning low-lying. Cows and deer often crossed the tracks, and heavy rains sometimes undermined the rails. Derailments were frequent, but the

Thomas L. Williams from U.S. Park Service

Cypress trees, once profuse along the James, still dot the shoreline of the lower river.

The logging railroad's Surry dock, close to that now used for the ferry to Jamestown.

train traveled only 15 to 30 mph and fatalities were few.

The railway's main stops were the headquarters town, called Dendron (from the Greek for "tree") which it had created, and Scotland Wharf. There passengers, lumber, and other cargo boarded river steamers like the *Pocahontas* and *Ariel,* which plied the James, stopping at Jamestown, Carter's Grove, Newport News, and several dozen small wharves to exchange passengers, mail, and cargo.

Eventually a drop in lumber demand conspired to kill the company and its Toonerville Trolley railroad. The company stopped on July 31, 1930, selling what equipment it could. The rest, like Scotland Wharf, just rotted away. "Today," Crittenden wrote at the end of his book, "practically nothing remains to show there ever was a lumber company or a railroad up in that territory. Nature is slowly restocking the cutover land. Some of the towns that existed along the railroad are completely gone, vanished, and even Dendron is a ghost of its former self."

When I first went to Scotland Wharf in the 1930s, the deserted lumber dock was standing. Now it's gone. I still think of it when I cross the ferry. Surry has never been the same without its lumber company and "the Sick, Sad, and Sorry."

Minnie Moger Corson described Crittenden, a fishing village near the James.

Esther Hillyer

49. *Crittenden, A Fishing Village*

THE fishing villages of the Chesapeake look very much alike. White frame Victorian houses, built by nineteenth-century fishermen and merchants, face the water. Boatyards and marine railways line their shore, with boats being overhauled on the ways.

Projecting into the water are piers with oyster and fishing boats moored alongside or anchored in deep water.

That's my early memory of Eclipse, a fishing village at the juncture of the James River and Chuckatuck Creek, in what used to be Nansemond County, now Suffolk. Eclipse (pronounced E-clipse, accenting the E) adjoins two other little towns on Chuckatuck Creek. They are Crittenden, for James Crittenden, its early postmaster, and Chuckatuck, which borders Route 17 and has an early Indian name.

I've just read about these towns in a nostalgic memoir by Minnie Moger Corson, lifelong resident of Crittenden. She was "Woman of the Year" in Nansemond County, lauded by Mills Godwin. A spirited lady, Mrs. Corson penned her book in her 90s, while blind, deaf, and wearing a pacemaker. She was a triumph of age over ailments, and her memoirs are lively and

up-to-date, full of names and places. She has since died.

Born of parents who moved from Fox Hill to Crittenden in 1894, Minnie Corson grew up among oystermen, fishermen, and crabbers. Her father ran a Crittenden boat railway, which repaired many of the 200 James River oyster boats that operated in 1904.

The James is the most prolific oyster spawning ground on the East Coast; seed oysters from its muddy oyster grounds are annually transplanted to other rivers. Despite the recent decline in oysters, seed oysters are in great demand.

I've often passed Eclipse and Crittenden on the water, looking like a watercolor by Barclay Sheaks. Once they were isolated towns, but now they're commuter suburbs for Suffolk, Newport News, and Portsmouth.

In a dozen brisk chapters, Mrs. Corson recreates the life she knew in the Chuckatuck Creek area for nearly a century. She writes well. You can sense the full lives led by these hardworking people.

Mrs. Corson notes that Eclipse began about 40 years after Jamestown. It had only three or four houses until the Civil War, owned by the

Grays, Lewises, Adamses, and Moores. After the Civil War, Northerners came in to buy and to sell the area's oysters. That's when the Barcalow, Corson, and Haughwout families arrived. The area's older history was lost when Nansemond courthouse at Suffolk burned in 1860.

The Mogers lived on the waterfront at Crittenden. There Lorenzo Dow Moger, the author's father, overhauled workboats, lifting them out of the water with a cradle and "treading machine" powered by a docile horse named

The former public school at Crittenden was closed when Nansemond schools merged.

Frank that circled a capstan to lift the heavy boats. Workers' pay was $1.50 to $2 a day in 1900, but more later. Boys worked for 75 cents a day.

"The only Crittenden livelihood," writes Mrs. Corson, "was oystering, fishing, crabbing, and farming. Almost everyone worked in the river from a boat."

As I read on, my mind went back to Battery Park, a similar fishing town on the Pagan River, where the steamer from Smithfield to Newport News stopped. As I leaned over the steamer's rail to watch stevedores haul barrels of oysters on board, I could read the names of the little

workboats along the shore: Mary, Sally, Irene— always women's names.

On the shore were oyster shucking houses. Behind green lawns stood wooden houses, with gingerbread railings and roof decorations. A church or two stood nearby, usually Methodist or Baptist.

"Shad fishing started in February and lasted through April," Minnie Corson writes in her book. "In the summer men went crabbing for hard and soft-shelled crabs. Sometimes the

The big farmhouse of Minnie Moger Corson at Crittenden looked onto Chuckatuck Creek.

hard-crab market was so flooded that they sold for fifty cents a barrel." To sell oysters commercially in recent years, the shells had to be three inches or longer. Smaller ones were shoved overboard.

Mrs. Corson paints a familiar picture of rural peace. "Most of the people owned their homes," she wrote. "There didn't seem to be any real poor people here. Some of them liked their whiskey, however, and it could be bought for $1 a quart."

Despite her age, the memoirist remembered nearly everybody who grew up in Crittenden and Eclipse in her lifetime. The most memorable was Dr. Leslie L. Eley, who moved to Crittenden in 1896, after graduating from the University of Maryland medical school. He was the area's revered doctor until he died in 1954. Mrs. Corson quotes Governor Mills Godwin's tribute to Dr. Eley: "He was a doctor for everything and everybody—colored and white, rich and poor." When the doctor was ill, his wife took medicine to his patients.

At the end of her book, Minnie Corson wrote, "I hope I haven't overlooked any close friends, and if I did, it was not intentional."

The little fishing villages of the James are no longer the homes of boat builders or fishermen, but they provide attractive homes for many retirees and newcomers.

Daily Press

*Chuckatuck oystermen in winter used to bring up the catch
and wash the shells before culling out the marketable bivalves.*

50. *Contrasting Shores of the James*

To me, the James divides Virginia into Today and Yesterday. Today is the Peninsula, stretching from Newport News to Richmond, jumping with traffic. Yesterday is Isle of Wight, Surry, Prince George, and Chesterfield counties—that rich belt of pine forests and farmsteads that runs south to the Dismal Swamp and North Carolina.

It's specially purdy (Southside for pretty) in the spring, when trees are leafing, and farmers plant corn and peanuts.

I can sense the change in regional spirit when I cross the Jamestown ferry—Old Unreliable—to Scotland Wharf, where the dock creaks and the sea gulls squint lazily on the railing. You can smell Southside in that indolent, pine-scented air. On the Surry shore, life is calmer, slower, more friendly.

The ferry itself suggests the slower pace of Southside. As the last of its kind in tidal Virginia, it has become an issue with Virginians, some of whom want a bridge to replace it.

That piney flavor I identify as Deep South. In Isle of Wight, Sussex, and Prince George, blacks make up 70 percent of the population. The pattern is paternalistic and conservative. Blacks do a lot of the peanut-picking, hog-rais-ing, ham-curing, and timbering that make up this land of pines, peanuts, and pork, as Surry-men like to call it.

Driving along Route 10, which runs along Southside from Richmond to Portsmouth, you see cute little nineteenth-century farmhouses, junked cars, fruit trees, pigs, grazing cattle. The land is flat and unromantic, but nowhere do pine trees grow faster, peanuts grow bigger, or tobacco better flavored.

The part I know best lies around Smithfield, that tiny, proud Pagan River port. When I knew it as a child, farmers tethered horse-drawn wag-ons and jumpers to hitching posts along Main Street while they went into Delk's or Betts's general stores and Simpson's or Parrish's drug-stores. It was a drowsy village then, but now it rumbles with trucks hauling pigs in to its slaughter houses or cured or fresh meat—Gwaltney's, Luter's, or Joyner's—out to the big grocery chains.

I like Smithfield's jumble of old and new, rich and poor, gracious and garish, black and white. It has the charm that comes from slow growth and a beautiful waterfront location.

The old houses aren't as restored or as well-kept as Williamsburg's, but they're haunted by

Daily Press

*During spring's annual herring migration up the James
to spawn, fishermen enjoy sport at Walker's Dam.*

Virginia Commission of Game and Inland Fisheries

*Fishermen along the upper James cast for
shad and herring, to be salted down for winter.*

legends of sea captains, ham shippers, peanut kings, and steamboat skippers who built them. Some are now owned by commuters who teach in Norfolk or work in Newport News.

Like all of Southside, Smithfield enjoys the folksy, democratic familiarity of rural places. Many of its people descend from old settlers and know the sins and eccentricities of everybody in town. Who can be high hat in such a place?

Smithfield residents still sit on front porches. Town ladies still walk uptown each morning to a tea room to drink coffee and cokes and trade news. Most businessmen go home to lunch, but you'll see a few in the Smithfield Inn, which still serves Smithfield ham lunches despite the decline in traffic since the state built a Route 10 bypass around town.

Southside has never tried to sell itself to tourists, but it has things worth seeing. None of Smithfield's fine old eighteenth-century houses is open to the public, but its now vacant Isle of Wight courthouse occasionally is. Open daily also is St. Luke's Church, thought to have been built beginning in the 1630s.

Surry County, not far from Smithfield, offers Bacon's Castle and the Warren House (once called the Rolfe House), both owned by the Association for the Preservation of Virginia Antiquities. Down a Surry road to the James River you'll encounter Chippokes plantation, which preserves both eighteenth- and nine-teenth-century houses. There the state of Virginia runs a riverside nature park, exhibiting ancient farm equipment and a beautiful crape myrtle garden.

Southside is a serendipitous place, dotted with unexpected discoveries like the Surrey House restaurant, Wakefield Diner, Blackwater Swamp, old Burma-Shave signs, and roadside flower gardens that delight the eye. If you have time, Petersburg offers Victorian architecture and Civil War history. Farther south lies Dismal Swamp, but the only way to see it is to go down its canal in a sightseeing boat.

What I like best about Southside is its unpretentious style. "Nobody over here puts on airs," a Smithfield dowager once told me. Few lures or come-ons are aimed at tourists. Its attitude seems to be, "If you want to come, come on, but we don't want to grow crowded."

Someday the world will discover Southside. Then the state will have to build another bridge and maybe even a high-speed highway. That's just what those folk fear most. At heart, they like their pines, peanuts, and pork just the way they are.

Photo by J. J. Shoman from Virginia Commission of Game and Inland Fisheries

The James attracts many varieties of fish, changing with the seasons.

Net fishermen on the James below Richmond show big shad, once abundant but now declining.

Left and below, Virginia Commission of Game and Inland Fisheries

Photo by L.G. Kesteloo

Spawning runs of shad have declined in recent years.

Shad like these are cooked over open flames at Tidewater spring shad plankings.

Daily Press

All-purpose fishing boats used on the James River are typical of Chesapeake fishermen.

Left and above, Virginia Commission of Game and Inland Fisheries

Shad and herring are salted in James River households to supply winter breakfasts.

Daily Press

James River crabber shows hardshells he caught in wire traps which he set on river bottom.

51. *Patton's Army Sails for Battle*

ONE of the dramatic moments in the life of the James is barely known because of wartime secrecy. It was the departure of General George Patton and his army of 34,000 men from Newport News at dawn on October 24, 1942, to stage the invasion of North Africa. The convoy movement was kept secret until after the war.

The African campaign, under command of Dwight Eisenhower of the United States and Harold Alexander of Great Britain, led to Allied victory over Nazi General Rommel's powerful Afrika Corps and to the subjugation of Vichy French forces.

Newport News was a city at war. After the attack on Pearl Harbor, Hampton Roads became a port of embarkation, with a New York Irishman, Colonel John R. Kilpatrick, as its commander. He'd been manager of Madison Square Garden and knew a lot of politicians, sports greats, and entertainers.

The army put its headquarters in the old C&O building at 24th Street. Nearby it rebuilt temporary offices and barracks from 23rd to 25th streets and from the James River to Jefferson Avenue. These were manned by 1,000 army personnel and over 1,500 civilians.

General Patton boarded the cruiser *Augusta* at Newport News a day before departure. At other docks, 28 navy transport and cargo ships loaded 31,831 enlisted men and 1,188 officers. The battle ship *Massachusetts,* the cruisers *Wichita* and *Tuscaloosa,* and many destroyers accompanied them.

Patton then was a 57-year-old major general, rugged and trim. Already he had the nickname, "Old Blood and Guts," because of his tough talk. On the *Augusta* he shared flag officer quarters with Rear Admiral Henry K. Hewitt, whose job was to land Patton's army at undisclosed enemy beachheads. Few officers except Patton and Hewitt knew that the destination of the armada was the Moroccan coast. They were one of several convoys from East Coast ports which, a week later, would meet in the mid-Atlantic, under U. S. aircraft protection, and file into the Mediterranean at night through the Strait of Gibraltar.

Patton's army was the first major convoy to sail from Hampton Roads in World War II. It required months of planning, for the ships had to be divided on D-Day among several beachheads. As the landings would be made through surf, combat vehicles had to be waterproof, their electrical equipment protected against short-circuiting.

Newport News and Norfolk lacked sufficient berths for so many ships, so navy transports were loaded and then anchored in Hampton Roads to await sailings. As the loading progressed, it became clear that some transports could not carry the loads assigned to them. One transport, the USS *Lee,* developed engine trouble after loading. In only 31 hours her cargo and men were taken off and put aboard the USS *Calvert.*

At the last moment, the slow ex-merchant ship *Contessa* was added to the convoy. When it was found that the ship lacked a full crew, prisoners in Norfolk's jail were given opportunity to volunteer. Eighteen did so, but when it was realized the *Contessa* could not keep up with the convoy, she had to sail the Atlantic unaccompanied. Her hectic voyage to Port Lyautey in Morocco was later described in the *Saturday Evening Post* and on the "Cavalcade of America" radio program.

Once in the Mediterranean, Patton's men were told they were about to engage France's army in Morocco. Patton urged them on in a broadcast: "We are now on our way to force a landing on the coast of Africa. . . . We will be opposed by units of the French African army."

Patton's army went ashore at the Moroccan towns of Safi, Port Lyautey, and Cape Fedhala. Soon the feisty general was headquartered in offices abandoned by the French in Casablanca. The rout of the Axis had begun. Before the war's end, Patton had become one of its great generals.

Today, few evidences of World War II survive in Newport News. The C&O piers and the warehouses which the army leased for the war have reverted to peacetime use. The Nansemond Hotel at Ocean View, where Patton, General Lucian Truscott, and other army and navy invaders drew up plans for the operation, has been torn down. So also has Camp Patrick Henry, where most of Patton's troops waited to board their ships.

Someday I hope the spot where the USS *Augusta* embarked General Patton for World War II will be marked on the Newport News waterfront.

Daily Press

General George Patton, center, sailed from Newport News in World War II to invade Africa.

52. *President Truman Takes A Trip*

A lot of Americans remember Newport News as the port they sailed from in World War II, but not many are aware that President Truman embarked there during the pre-dawn hours of July 7, 1945, and sailed for the Potsdam Conference to resolve the fate of Europe.

Do you remember 1945? It was one of the most eventful years in American history. In the midst of our war with Germany and Japan, Franklin Roosevelt died on April 12, Germany surrendered on May 7, and the Allies then turned all effort to defeating Japan and bringing peace. Just a month before we dropped the first atomic bomb on Japan in early August, the United States, Great Britain, and Russia held their last wartime conference at Potsdam, near Berlin.

Because Japanese subs still roamed the seas, Truman's trip from Washington to Potsdam had to be protected. The president came to Newport News by overnight train, got off at the C&O docks, and immediately boarded the USS *Augusta,* which sailed in the early morning through the capes, accompanied by the USS *Philadelphia.*

Potsdam was an important challenge for the untried Truman, so he took 52 State Department and military advisers with him. Secretary of State James Byrnes was one, along with Admiral William Leahy, Truman's chief of staff, Charles Ross, his press secretary, and General Harry Vaughan and Captain James Vardaman, aides. Twenty reporters were also passengers.

The leading specialist on Russia present was Charles Bohlen, later U. S. ambassador to Russia.

Truman told his staff it was his first ocean voyage since he had returned from France as a captain after World War I. During the eight-day voyage to Antwerp, the president strode the *Augusta's* deck, wearing a loud sports shirt and sailor's cap. He occupied the admiral's quarters and ate with the crew from aluminum trays in the mess several times during the voyage. He had strong appeal as an average man who had succeeded through merit.

Truman's whereabouts weren't made known to the world until July 10—three days after he had sailed. Then the press revealed that he was aboard the *Augusta* in mid-ocean. "Starting with his arrival at Newport News," the Associated Press reported, "the president has been up and about every day no later than 6 a.m."

The dispatch went on to say that "wearing a sporty cap cocked jauntily on the side of his head, the president seems to feel the peace of his journey may augur well for the outcome of the rendezvous in mid-July in Potsdam."

conference, which lasted from July 17 to August 2, 1945.

During the Potsdam Conference, British elections unseated Churchill's Conservative Party and replaced it with Clement Attlee's

Daily Press

Harry Truman, center, sailed from Newport News to Antwerp to confer with Clement Attlee and Josef Stalin at Potsdam.

After the *Augusta* reached Antwerp, the president was welcomed by General Eisenhower, the supreme Allied commander in Europe. Ike took Truman on a tour of war-bombed Berlin, which had not then been divided between the Americans, British, French, and Russians. Then Truman proceeded to Potsdam for the

Labor Party. Attlee was then flown to Potsdam and succeeded Churchill at the table for the latter sessions.

Stalin was a day late reaching Potsdam because of a heart attack. When he arrived, Truman found him appealing. "I had an instant liking for this man," Truman wrote. "There was something very open and genuine about the way he greeted me. I liked to listen to him talk." He later was less enthusiastic.

Churchill in turn found Truman "gay, precise, with a sparkling manner and obvious power of decision."

Despite Stalin's "charm," Truman and Churchill failed to reach agreement with him over Poland's future or over the fate of Romania, Bulgaria, and Hungary. All soon came under strong Russian influence, termed by Churchill in his Fulton, Missouri, speech as "behind the Iron Curtain." The Potsdam Conference was a disappointment.

Soon thereafter, Newport News was crowded with transports bringing American fighting men back from Europe and from Japan.

Many World War II combatants, some of them later famous, trained and embarked for combat on the Peninsula. Someday, a record of them should become a part of Newport News's history.

53. *"Smokey Joe's" Last Run*

SHIPS come to have a personality almost human. That was the case of the SS *Virginia*, a sleek white riverboat which carried several million passengers from Newport News to Norfolk and vice versa from 1902 till she was retired in old age in 1949.

The James River knew the *Virginia* as the C&O's passenger ferry in the days when the railroad hauled passengers from the Great Lakes to Hampton Roads and back. In fact, everybody in Newport News knew the familiar ship that backed into the James River from the C&O passenger depot three times daily.

Newport News people called her "Smokey Joe" because she belched clouds of smoke. We didn't know till later that was because she burned low-grade coal that gave off a lot of waste.

The 47 years of the *Virginia*'s service spanned years of growth for Newport News. However, by the time the ship was laid up, the city's waterfront was declining. Passenger train service was abandoned in the 1950s by the C&O and other lines, some of it to be carried on by Amtrak.

I often saw the *Virginia* at her dock on 23rd Street or underway in the channel. Sometimes I rode her to Norfolk—a rare Saturday outing in my youth. I remember going over with Charlie Epes to see "The Ten Commandments" at the Norva theater on Granby Street. My mother and other ladies often went to Norfolk to buy clothes at the House of Arthur Morris or at David Rawles's. In those days, we would dine at Colonel Consolvo's Monticello Hotel, which he had built for the Jamestown Exposition of 1907, or maybe at Parks's Seafood Restaurant.

The *Virginia* was so punctual that businessmen claimed to set their watches by her. And the C&O passenger depot was an important Peninsula junction, where Norfolk passengers arriving by "Smokey Joe" would join others from the Peninsula to entrain to Huntington, Charleston, Toledo, Cincinnati, and Cleveland.

The *Virginia* made three round-trips daily from Newport News to Norfolk and Portsmouth. Then she laid up at Newport News overnight awaiting the next day's runs. In her 47 years she made about 100,000 crossings and covered 1.3 million miles. That's over 54 trips around the world.

The *Virginia* was built for the C & O in 1901-02 in Richmond by the William R. Trigg Com-

*Passenger service from Newport News to Norfolk was provided
for many years by the ferry steamer* Virginia.

pany, whose shipways were on the James. She was a one-stacker, capable of 18 knots. In a race with the New York, Philadelphia, and Norfolk steamer *Pennsylvania,* which plied from the Eastern Shore to Old Point, "Smokey Joe" easily triumphed.

The C & O charged 36 cents for the 57-minute voyage to Norfolk. A side run to Portsmouth required another 10 minutes.

The C & O steamer succeeded four earlier vessels on the Norfolk-Newport News run. The first was *Ariel,* which Collis Huntington engaged in 1881. Two years later, in 1883, the

C & O chartered two sidewheel steamers, *Northampton* and *Luray,* to make the run. In 1884, the railway bought the sidewheeler *John Romer,* which served off and on until 1902, when "Smokey Joe" took over.

The *Virginia* was 200 feet long with two propellers, a steel hull, and a superstructure of steel and wood. She had inside seating for 198 but during World War II could carry up to 841 servicemen standing and sitting.

The vessel often encountered rough water off Point Breeze, at the lower end of the Peninsula, where the new bridge-tunnel is. Conflicting currents and winds at that point sometimes buffeted the ship.

From December 1917 till February 1918, when Hampton Roads froze over in one of the coldest winters of this century, the *Virginia* had to miss trips, but she kept running as long as she could. Said the Newport News *Times-Herald* of January 4, 1918, "All water transportation to and from Norfolk was temporarily cut off when the Virginia, Chesapeake and Ohio ferry, for the first time in her career started from Norfolk this morning and had to turn back at Craney Island on account of the ice."

During the hurricane of August, 1933, the *Virginia* rode out the storm at her dock in Norfolk. In 1948, "Smokey Joe" was in collision with the SS *Nettie B. Greenwell* off the New-port News coal piers. The *Greenwell* sank, but "Smokey Joe" was exonerated.

Hauling soldiers and sailors across Hampton Roads in World War II proved the *Virginia's* hardest duty. In 1944, the C&O bought the SS *Wauketa*, a former Great Lakes steamer, to augment the *Virginia's* service. Five years later "Smokey Joe" was removed from service, leaving only the *Wauketa* running. She made her last trip June 4, 1950. The C&O had lost most of its passengers.

If you revisit the Newport News dock area today, you find little you can recognize. "Smokey Joe," the depot, and everything else from the 1940s has disappeared. But to me, they were the real Newport News.

The Jamiesons have restored and promoted Berkeley to high rank among James River houses.

Berkeley

54. *Reviving Berkeley Plantation*

IN a long lifetime you'll find few men who work as hard as Malcolm Jamieson. He's the owner of Berkeley plantation in Charles City County, one of the more popular tourist sites in Virginia. How Mac and Grace Jamieson have saved the home of the Harrisons is a Cinderella story.

Mac Jamieson is 80, but you wouldn't know it. He's up often at 5 a.m. to pay his bills and get things moving before his farm workers arrive at 7:30. It takes work to keep 600 cleared acres and 400 acres of woods in show-place condition for Berkeley's 80,000 annual visitors, but work is Mac's passion.

As a plantation owner, Mac is an awesome figure. He's shown owners of historic sites they can attract year-around paying crowds if they show enough imagination and energy.

The story of Berkeley is one of surprises. Unlike his neighbor, Hill Carter of Shirley plantation, Mac wasn't born with a background of James River ancestry. Instead, his father, a New York City builder, bought rundown Berkeley house and lands in 1907 for $17 an acre, partly for its timber. Son Malcolm inherited a third when his father died in 1929, moved into

the decrepit mansion, and, in 1938, bought out his siblings' shares.

Mac credits his wife, Grace, for much of Berkeley's restoration and refurnishing. When they opened Berkeley's first floor to the public, Mac and Grace and infant son, Jamie, now in his 40s, lived on Berkeley's second and third floors. Jamie has since married and moved to another house on Berkeley's land. He has joined his father in devoting his life to the place.

It's hard to believe that the beautiful brick manor house built by Benjamin Harrison IV left Harrison family ownership back in 1842.

Twenty years later the estate was overrun by federal troops of General George McClellan after Robert E. Lee had turned back the Army of the Potomac from Richmond. That occupation began its long decline.

That's when Mac Jamieson's father—teen-age Scottish immigrant John Jamieson, who was a drummer boy in the Union army—encamped at Berkeley in the Civil War. Presumably, father Jamieson saw President Abraham Lincoln land at Harrison's Wharf and meet with McClellan there. In any case, John

Jamieson fell in love with Berkeley.

Years later, the ex-drummer learned the estate was for sale and bought it for a song. Young Mac summered there as a boy, camping out with his mother, brother, and sister. He liked it so much he decided to spend his life restoring the house and opening it to the public.

Mac went to work. He plowed and planted crops and hundreds of trees and boxwood. After studying animal husbandry at Rutgers, he moved to Berkeley in 1929. He brought his bride there in 1933. She was Grace Eggleston, daughter of a Richmond lawyer, who took a while to adapt to Charles City's rural pace. She and Mac still spend much time in Richmond.

"When I first saw the place, it was so terrible you wouldn't think you could do anything with it," Grace recalls. "Besides, I hated bugs and I hated the outdoors in the country—I'm allergic to everything. But when you're in love you forget about those things. I was crazy about Mac."

Hostesses take visitors through Berkeley's first floor, and then an orientation film in the basement recites more history. Finally, visitors wander past the Harrison tombstones to the James River, where Berkeley's first settlers landed in 1619.

Mac loves to tell what he's learned of Berkeley since those 38 Englishmen came ashore and created a farm settlement called the Berkeley Company. Each November he welcomes several thousands to the re-enactment "First Thanksgiving," reviving the observance prescribed by the Berkeley Company's English charter on the anniversary of its landing. He reminds the world that it was "before Plymouth's Thanksgiving."

Three years after the Berkeley landing, the Indian massacre in 1622 nearly wiped out the settlement. Then, in 1691, the land was bought by Benjamin Harrison II, whose grandson, Benjamin IV, built the present house. The builder's son, Benjamin V, signed the Declaration of Independence, was three times Virginia's governor, and fathered President William Henry Harrison, who was born at Berkeley.

William Henry wrote his inaugural address in the second story room the Jamiesons use as their bedroom.

Mac Jamieson also revels in Berkeley's Civil War history. While McClellan occupied it in 1862, Lincoln visited it twice. Union officer Oliver W. Norton composed "Taps," the Army's lights-out tattoo, there.

Dementi Studio, Richmond

Grace and Malcolm Jamieson began restoring Berkeley, now widely visited, in the 1940s.

Young Jamie Jamieson, who will inherit the plantation, is as enthusiastic as his father. He farms its 600 open acres in hay, corn, and pasture. He also raises boxwood and maintains roads, rental cottages, and an emergency airport. Like his father, he wouldn't trade places with anybody.

As Mac Jamieson puts it, "Berkeley needs me and I need Berkeley." You can't dispute that.

55. *Exploring the Black Belt*

IT'S peanut and tobacco-growing season in Southside Virginia. That was clear to me as I drove down Interstate 85 through the counties of the Black Belt, to visit friends in Durham.

If you're rooted in Southside, you know the peculiar, old-fashioned appeal of that region. It has no real cities except Petersburg and Danville, for most of its people make their living on the land. Being a city boy, I wouldn't want to live there myself, but it's a welcome change now and then from the hustle of city streets.

From the time you cross the James to Scotland Wharf, in Surry, the air begins to change. This is the way I described it in *Below the James Lies Dixie* in 1969:

> The minute the ferry from Jamestown noses in to the Surry County dock, you sense you're in another world. The wooden planking creaks lazily as your car rolls toward the pines along the shore. Ker-plock-a, ker-plock-a, ker-plock-a. Sea gulls squint from roosts on the pilings. A hint of indolence is in the air.
>
> This is Southside Virginia, where the

South really begins. This is the northern boundary of a rural world that time and machines have failed to destroy in 350 years. Here, below the James, lies the gen-u-ine, old-time, pre-Civil War South.

This summer the corn and peanuts of Surry look unusually green. We creep along Route 10, past Surry Courthouse to Spring Grove, and we see houses where various Savedges, Barhams, Holloways, Edwardses, and others of my family have lived. At Spring Grove we turn onto shady Route 40, which runs westward through pine forests and blackwater swamps about 50 miles before it joins I–85 at McKenney, a crossroads village in Dinwiddie County, close to the dirt-brown Nottoway River.

Nothing pleases the eye more than to see rows of corn or tobacco, bright green and lush, stretching from the highway to the woods on the horizon. Route 40 is made up of such fields. Huge trees overarch the road, providing shade from the summer sun. The only town you encounter is Waverly, sitting astride the Norfolk and Western in Sussex County.

Many houses have been built along Route 40 since I last traveled it. Most are ranch style, which seem to me less suited for rural living than the old-style farmhouses of my youth, with their screened porches and breezeways for outdoor living. But I guess air-conditioning has killed porch sitting. Nobody builds porches anymore.

Household gardens are important on the Surry-Sussex-Southampton circuit. With grocery prices high, nearly every commuter comes home after a day's work to tend his snapbeans, onions, and tomatoes.

Flowers are abundant, and many roadside dwellers put them out front for motorists to see.

I see roses, snapdragons, bergamot, day lilies, geraniums, and petunias galore. It's a good year for gardens, with plenty of rain.

Once we get onto I-85, the atmosphere changes. Traffic is heavier. Drivers go faster. There isn't much to see, for interstates have limited access restrictions which discourage abutting houses and businesses. Along I-85 you can see none of the little towns whose exit signs you read: towns like Alberta, Lawrenceville, South Hill, or La Crosse. I miss seeing them, but it takes too long to reach them from the interstate.

Colonial Williamsburg

Music of river plantations is performed in Williamsburg's black history program.

The Tobacco Belt has lost some of its charm, too. No longer do you see picturesque old tobacco sheds and drying houses in the middle of tobacco fields, veterans of years of droughts and floods. Woodcut artist J. J. Lankes, who once lived on the Peninsula, loved to portray those tobacco barns, sometimes made in log cabin style, with a leaning chimney of mud, stone, or eroded brick. I see only one or two.

Nowadays tobacco is cured differently. Gone are the flue-curing houses and even the big tobacco storage warehouses that dominated onetime market towns like South Hill and Clarksville. In the old days each was lettered with the warehouseman's name—Boyd or Harrison or Brodnax—and with some such motto as "The Grower's Friend" or "Best Prices." Tobacco storing and buying have become centralized in cities.

For years the cultivation of tobacco has been declining in Virginia, but it is still an important crop along the Buggs Island Dam and its lakes.

Virginia Gazette

Cypress grow in the James and adjoining creeks and marshes, sometimes harboring eagles.

The dam system has replaced the once destructive Roanoke River along the border counties of Greensville, Brunswick, Mecklenburg, Halifax, Pittsylvania, and Henry. It has altered the appearance and economy of a wide area.

Once you cross the state line into North Carolina, tobacco is more abundant. The longer growing season further south has increased cultivation in North and South Carolina and Georgia. The Carolinas' tobacco growth has also been promoted by those states' tobacco ports, which have taken business from Newport News and Norfolk. Another factor in Virginia's tobacco decline is the competition of other Tidewater industries. Even with government support, tobacco growing is a boom-or-bust investment. Many men prefer industrial jobs.

Even so, the Tobacco Belt is one place where the small farmer seems to be surviving. Many farmers around the Bugg's Island Dam area work the same fields their grandfathers worked 50 years ago. Because tobacco requires much hand labor, the small tobacco farm has not had to give way to the giant mechanized farm as in the west or deep south.

As my wife and I mosey through Mecklenburg County, we remember trips we each had made there with our parents when we were children. My family's object was to visit relatives in Boydton. Whenever we went in fall, we were invited to a Brunswick stew, which took place around some rural tobacco barn when the fires were going to dry the tobacco strung up inside.

It was pleasant in those days to eat ears of corn roasted in the ashes of the curing house fire. Meanwhile, a large vat of Brunswick stew was cooking over a nearby open fire. A skilled stew maker—often the county sheriff or some other political figure—would preside over the stew making.

Down in the Tobacco Belt they claim the stew originated in Brunswick County, but this is contested by Brunswick, Georgia. My Southside friends insist the dish was first recorded in 1830 by Dr. Creed Haskins at his home on the Nottoway River. That first stew is said to have been served at a rally held at Dr. Haskins's plantation, called Mount Donum, attended by Virginia's Governor Littleton Waller Tazewell.

Whatever its origin, rural dwellers in the Virginia-Carolina Tobacco Belt still gather each fall to ritually make their stews. As everybody must know, it was originally concocted with squirrel, but chicken is now usually substituted. Other ingredients are onions, cured pork, potatoes, corn, tomatoes, butter beans, and lots of butter.

As we approach Durham, I–85 widens into a busy urban thoroughfare. We come back to the present with a jolt. Our refreshing journey through the past ends in a throng of converging traffic lanes, like those of any growing city.

Somebody once wrote, "Cities are the brains of a nation, but the country is its heart." It's pleasant now and then to drive south across the James River and contemplate the contrast.

56. *Along the John Tyler Highway*

OST of the James River's historic roads have succumbed to billboards and service stations, but a few gems survive. One of them is Route 5, which runs from Williamsburg past Jamestown and the Chickahominy River westward to Charles City County and Richmond. It's called the John Tyler Highway because President Tyler was born and lived much of his life along that plantation road.

I frequently drive from Williamsburg to Richmond over the picturesque road. It's easier than Interstate 64 and it's more pleasant. In fact, when the oaks and maples turn yellow and red in the fall, it's a sightseer's delight. Along the road sit more eighteenth-century Virginia plantations than you can find along any other 50-mile road in Virginia. Besides Tyler's Sherwood Forest, it has Berkeley, the Harrison plantation; Westover, the Byrd estate; and Shirley, where the Carters hold forth. Other less-celebrated houses lie hidden down country lanes.

Some of the houses are open to the public. And many venerable old places are visible from the road. They include Greenway farm, where President Tyler was born, Westover Church, a

colonial survival; and Charles City Courthouse, one of the nation's oldest.

What pleases me especially about Route 5 are its fields and forests, little changed over 300 years. If you like neatly planted fields, Route 5 is the place to see them. It was a favorite drive of John D. Rockefeller, Jr., in his twice-yearly visits to Williamsburg when he was restoring that town. Many sightseers follow it from Jamestown to get a look at a route that has been travelled by coastal Virginians since that peninsula was the site of Virginia's capital.

In recent years Route 5 has had its troubles. Many of its forests are being cut for timber. Now Charles City's planning commission wants to create a preservation zone along the road, hoping to keep it rustic and also to attract appropriate tourist facilities to encourage visitors. But the James City end is endangered.

Says Hill Carter of Shirley plantation, a member of the Charles City board of supervisors, "The idea is not to have a bunch of golden arches lining Route 5." County Attorney Randolph Boyd further explains, "The planning commission wants to limit development to uses that are aesthetically compatible with the area's

Virginia Department of Transportation

The newest James River crossing is the Interstate 295 bridge near Hopewell, serving north-south traffic.

Tugboats nudge vessels bearing raw materials into Hopewell's James River factory docks.

Hopewell Promotions and Tourism Office

current historical and scenic beauty. You could put a restaurant in an old mill, for example, but would want to limit the construction of fast food restaurants."

Travelers who use the road are rewarded for their pains. They find a picturesque country road surviving between the bustling communities of Richmond and Williamsburg. The problem is that few out-of-state visitors know about Route 5 or how to find it. It's fairly easy to get on at the Williamsburg end, but it's harder in Richmond, where it joins the faded downtown industrial area through a maze of railroad sidings.

Stanley Abbott, a far-sighted landscape planner who headed the Colonial National Park several decades ago, urged that Route 5 be protected by historic easements. However, that upset Route 5's landowners who discouraged James City, Charles City, and Henrico from acting. Now it is heartening to see one of those counties thinking about the problem.

The John Tyler Highway is unique in linking Virginia's three capitals at Jamestown, Williamsburg, and Richmond. From the time of John Smith, pioneers followed its route west to the fall line at Shockoe, later named Richmond. Along its winding course eighteenth-century planters built some of the handsomest houses in America. There Sir William Berkeley put his great house, Green Spring. Further up the road Thomas Jefferson wed Martha Wayles Skelton.

I'm glad Charles City is concerned about Route 5. It has few equals, though there are a few charming country roads along the upper James. They take a little time, but they're worth it.

Daily Press

*Ferries cross the James from Jamestown to Surry County
to speed travelers southward into Carolina.*

57. *Wildlife on the Lower James*

Virginia Commonwealth University student boating on the James in 1977 made a discovery: In the trees of Eppes Island, offshore from Shirley in Charles City County, he found the nests of several dozen exotic long-legged birds. He reported it to his teacher, biologist Charles Blem of the university, who identified them at cattle egrets.

Cattle egrets? It's hard to believe, for the big birds are natives of Africa—the ungainly white fowl you sometimes see pecking insects from the backs of hippos, elephants, and other animals in African TV movies. Yet since that day, other bird-watchers have confirmed the egrets' invasion, and many have come to see them.

Recently the egrets returned to Eppes Island to nest, this time accompanied by a dozen or so double-crested cormorants, which also raised families. When members of the Lower James River Association boated downriver from Hopewell to Jamestown, they got a view of the aviary and its denizens.

Ornithologists have come forward with data on cattle egrets. For centuries they were presumably content to live in Africa, but in 1930 a flock of them flew westward across the Atlantic and landed in British Guiana. In the next 20 years the birds spread to Surinam, Venezuela, and Colombia.

Twenty-two years after they reached South America, the egrets showed up in North America—another miraculous flight. They were recognized first in 1952 in the Sudbury Valley in Massachusetts, near the Atlantic. Since then they have spread in successive summers along the Atlantic from Florida to Prince Edward Island, Canada. Their James River nesting ground was farther from the Atlantic than any others reported thus far.

Other cattle egret colonies have been reported near Wilson Creek in Gloucester, on the Eastern Shore of Virginia, in coastal Florida, and in the lower Mississippi River. Though they feed in fields, the birds stick close to the water.

The cattle egret is one of 64 known species of herons, egrets, and bitterns. Herons and egrets are long-legged, long-necked wading birds with lean body lines and graceful movement. However, egrets are the showier of the two because of their plume-like curved feathers,

Photo by L. Kesteloo

A solitary egret keeps watch above a marsh along Mill Creek near Jamestown.

called aigrettes, which trail down their backs. Once in demand in Mae West's day as the source of plumes to trim women's hats, the birds are currently protected by law.

Now that they are no longer an endangered species, cattle egrets are multiplying and spreading through the western hemisphere. In case you see one, the bird is about 20 inches long, with a yellow bill and a tall, angular shape. It is stockier than other herons, with a short neck, lacking the graceful curve of other members of the heron-egret family. A dirty white during most of the year, mature birds develop rusty buff feathers on breast, back, and head during breeding.

Ornithologists are seeking more information on the cattle egrets' long migrations by capturing and banding the young birds. It is thought that those which nested on Eppes Island fly south in winter to Florida and thence across the Florida keys to Cuba or South America.

One fact seems clear, says Frederick R. Scott, an amateur ornithologist from Richmond:

The species frequents coastal places and eats insects common to meadows and cow pastures. Thus, says Scott, it occupies a "food position" in the animal world not occupied by any other bird. Furthermore, some insects it eats are harmful to man, making the cattle egret a welcome immigrant.

A resident along the James called me recently to say that a flock of whistler swans had lighted on his waterfront and seemed happy. He was anxious to do anything he could do to make them stay. I suggested he feed them corn and let them alone.

On my walks around Jamestown, I've seen wild geese far overhead, flying south. In the woods around the James hoot owls rend the nightly quiet with mating calls. It's winter, and I can see the birds and beasts trying to cope with the cold, like me.

It's been a long time since I was a Boy Scout, but I like wildlife and want to see it survive. The James and its creeks have been home to many species of life since prehistoric time. Now civilization is challenging many species. Every time we fell a tree or dump chemicals in a creek, we make it harder for plants and animals to survive.

I remember the unspoiled James in the 1920s. Eel grass and seaweed then abounded, providing a haven for crabs and other shellfish. In summer you could catch several dozen soft

Dorothy Grubbs

The James from Newport News to Richmond is dotted with plantations, many on exhibit.

crabs in an hour or so of low tide off 59th Street in Newport News.

The river offered real sport for handline fishermen. Those were the days of big croakers and gray trout, plus lots of spot, sun perch, hogfish, and black willies. August brought what we called dogfish—small sharks that fought like demons and often broke your line. My brothers and I occasionally pulled up bluefish, mullets, and eels.

Then came an epidemic of blowtoads—ugly brown-skinned fish which looked a little like mudtoads but could be skinned to yield tasty boneless filets that restaurants called "sea squab."

Gradually I saw many of those other species disappear from the rivers after the 1920s. Like other saltwater fishermen, I gave up the sport because there weren't enough fish.

We don't usually realize it, but a lot of coastal Virginia wildlife has already disappeared or been driven away. The wood pigeons that were so common in colonial Virginia are gone. So are most sturgeon, once prized for their caviar. Eagles are endangered, along with many shorebirds that can't find quiet places to nest in summer.

It's hard to believe, but even buffalo ranged over parts of Virginia in colonial times. They were described as similar to those of the western plains, but smaller. The last one was killed in Virginia in 1804. Fortunately, the western plains buffalo has survived.

Similarly, most of the larger game animals once abundant along the James have been killed off: bobcats, black bears, and wild turkeys. Of the larger species, only the Virginia or white-tailed deer abounds. I see them often bounding over fields or across Route 5 in James City and Charles City counties.

A few other wild animals, evidently as adaptive as deer, seem to have survived in numbers despite shrinking James River forests and heavy hunting. I'm impressed by the squirrels, rabbits, and songbirds I see in my walks. On Jamestown Island, I've encountered a huge

Author's collection

Seafood from the James and nearby rivers began to be shipped on refrigerated trains and later trucks.

population of raccoons, which have prospered like the deer on that 1,500-acre Park Service game preserve.

Raccoons are a nuisance in many James River suburbs, where they forage in garbage.

Two other survivors are skunks and possums. I seldom see them on my walks because they're night prowlers, but their carcasses litter the highway to show they abound.

I would guess that the songbird population of the Peninsula has been increased by the many bird lovers who provide feeders for them all year round. I know several Peninsula birders who go to great length to keep squirrels from their feeders, even trapping them in SPCA-approved traps and taking them to the woods to

Virginia Institute of Marine Science

James River soft crabs are flown to the Orient to meet gourmet demands.

turn them loose. "Would you believe, I see the same ones right back in my yard next day," one incensed trapper told me.

Pretty soon it will be time for flights of grackles and blackbirds to come swarming over the gray winter fields, assailing our ears with their coarse chatter. But I don't mind even grackles any more. As I get older, I can see with Albert Schweitzer that every living thing has its role in the world. Why should man want to destroy creatures that don't bother him?

I've even begun to miss the screech owls that kept me awake those nights after I moved to Williamsburg in 1951. They're very different from hoot owls. A screech owl emits a soprano blast like a trumpet, whereas a hoot owl sings bass. I used to think screech owls were female and hoot owls male, but nothing is that simple.

Anyway, I hope those whistler swans are still on the river. At least, they were when I last looked.

Williams' Dam above Richmond feeds James River water into a seven-mile canal around rocky falls.

Valentine Museum

William Snyder observes life on Powhatan Creek from his rural home near Jamestown.

58. *A Twentieth-Century Thoreau*

ONE of the busiest retirees anywhere is Bill Snyder, who lives near Jamestown and keeps his eyes on the world around him. A native of Newport News, he worked 40 years in the shipyard before moving to his woodland retreat in James City County.

Like Thoreau, whose pleasure was living in a cabin on Walden Pond and watching the seasons change, Snyder's passion is nature. He's wandered all over James City and York counties, noting the migrations of birds and the haunts of eagles, beavers, deer, and many other creatures.

"We Peninsulars are surrounded by a wealth of birds and animals that we must protect," Snyder says.

He's written two books about birds, animals, and plants of the James River, and he conducts guided tours for amateur naturalists and historians. At 75, he's vigorous and active.

Many species of animal life are increasing, Snyder tells me, including wild turkeys, deer, raccoons, and squirrels. He credits that fact to our increasing awareness of nature and to Virginia's 1982 Non-Game Wildlife and Endangered Species Program. He's not opposed to hunting but prefers animal-watching. He keeps notes of his observations and gives these to wildlife agencies.

I met Bill Snyder when I ran Jamestown Festival Park. He lives on Powhatan Creek. He's read the accounts by John Smith, George Percy, and other Jamestown settlers, and he marvels at the persistence of the wildlife the first settlers noted on their arrival from England.

If you like birds and animals, Snyder recommends any of a dozen preserves where you can see them on the James and nearby. They include Jamestown, Newport News City Park, Williamsburg's Waller Mill Park, Hog Island in the James, the Chickahominy Wildlife Management Area in Charles City, and the Ragged Island Wildlife Management Area near the James River Bridge.

Of all nearby game preserves, Hog Island is probably the most exciting. An estimated 10,000 wild geese and many more ducks winter there, flying south from Canada in fall and returning in summer. Rarities like goshawks and barnacle geese are spotted there. Many raise young along Hog Island's streams and on the James.

Another wildlife area is Jamestown Island. Swampy and picturesque, its marshes along the Thoroughfare and nearby Powhatan Creek are full of muskrats and shore birds. On an outing there, I saw several varieties of osprey plus many mallards that have been fed by shore dwellers and domesticated.

Snyder tells me the protected 1,550 acres of Jamestown contain about 1,000 deer. Some venture close to the Visitor Center at dusk. There are also night-prowling raccoons, possums, muskrats, woodchucks, and rabbits. A five-mile wilderness road around the island brings you upon nesting wildfowl. Red-headed woodpeckers, ospreys, and an occasional eagle nest on the island.

Virginia Gazette

Seagulls keep vigil at Jamestown ferry dock.

Virginia Gazette

Deer are protected on Jamestown Island but are hunted elsewhere.

In John Smith's history of Virginia, he listed himself as seeing "conies" [rabbits], deer, turkeys, bears, foxes, squirrels, otters, waterfowl, and wild pigeons. He described Chief Powhatan as "hung with manie chaynes of great pearles about his neck and covered with a great covering of raccoon skins and all the tayles hanging by."

Virginia's first settlers found many buffalo and wild pigeon. William Byrd II in the eighteenth century described the buffalo as "an animal with a hump on its back, of an enormous and terrible size, has long curly hair, from which the Indians make many things and Europeans [make] mattresses."

Wood pigeons, also called passenger pigeons, which were a favorite game of early Americans, have been wiped out.

Two other endangered species have revived under protection laws. One is the beaver, whose pelts were long valued for men's hats. A beaver dam may be seen on the Chickahominy. The other once-endangered species is the wild turkey, now protected by a limited shooting season.

James River dwellings increasingly attract deer, raccoons, squirrels, and song birds, which used to feed on crops that are no longer planted. Many households begrudge them their expensive backyard azaleas, tulips, and lettuce, but Audubon societies oppose the use of most poisons and traps. It's becoming an issue everywhere.

As for Bill Snyder, he's clearly on the side of the animals.

Virginia Gazette

Herons and duck blinds are numerous on the James.

59. *Pilots on Bays and Rivers*

I
T'S a rough day on Virginia's coast. Just outside the capes a huge Greek collier battles the waves toward the CSX coal piers at Newport News, where she'll take a load of coal.

Out of the morning blackness races a tiny boat. A half hour earlier it had left the Virginia Pilot Association's dock at Lynnhaven Inlet, guided by radio from the incoming ship. Now, as the pilot boat sights the collier, the boat makes for a rope ladder dangling to the collier's water line. Deftly, the pilot boat sidles up to the rope. The pilot leaps from the boat and scrambles up the swinging ladder.

Hundreds of times each year Virginia pilots meet ships like this at the capes and steer them to the James, or wherever they're headed in Virginia's waters. If a vessel is bound for Maryland, a pilot from that state meets it at the capes.

Since colonial times, mariners versed in the channels of the Chesapeake have brought ships into port. In 1661, the Virginia legislature named the first "official" pilot to bring ships up the James River. In 1866, the state chartered the Virginia Pilot Association to direct Chesapeake ships—a self-perpetuating body that pilots all visiting ships. It's still very much alive.

Few people know much about the 54-member association headquartered at Lynnhaven Inlet. About 25 of them live in Hampton-Newport News, and the rest in Norfolk-Virginia Beach. All serve five years as apprentices and a sixth year as "sharemen," receiving a two-thirds salary until they are voted in by fellow pilots.

The VPA is a semipublic organization, which divides its receipts among its pilots. Its rates and conditions are set by the State Corporation Commission.

Two-way radio and radar have simplified the Chesapeake transit of deep-draft foreign and American ships. Hampton Roads ships' agents notify the Pilot Association of the estimated arrival time of any foreign ship they represent. Then, as the ship gets within four or five hours of Cape Henry, it establishes radio contact with the Pilot Association at Lynnhaven.

The Lynnhaven center operates radio and pilot boats throughout the year. Its building contains bunks for pilots waiting in rotation for ships. Each pilot boards his ship from the pilot boat, about two miles off Cape Henry Light in the bay entrance.

The pilot is responsible for the safe transit of the ship to its dock or anchorage in Norfolk, Newport News, Portsmouth, Richmond, York-

*Pilot R.B. Holland climbs aboard to bring
an incoming ship into the Chesapeake.*

*Virginia's pilots now await calls in
headquarters at Lynnhaven, built in 1985.*

Until recent years Virginia's pilots waited on its headquarters boat inside the capes for vessels needing pilotage.

town, or Alexandria. The job is hardest with big tankers, freighters, or aircraft carriers drawing 30 feet or more.

All foreign ships are required to take pilots, as are all American ships going to or from a foreign port. However, U. S. naval vessels may take a pilot or not, though most of them do since the grounding in the 1940s of the battleship USS *Missouri* near Old Point. She was proceeding without a pilot.

Since it was organized, the Virginia Pilot Association has gained hefty political influence. Its members also earn good incomes. Its lobbying of the General Assembly in past years led to jokes about the "Virginia Pirates Association," but people rarely question the pilots' skills. They're professionals.

The pilot must know not only the Chesapeake's sea lanes but also its shoals. Channels

often grow shallow through silting, especially after storms. The pilot must know this, as well as the location of underwater wrecks, and the clearance of bridges. He must know the location of anchorages for vessels under quarantine, for naval ships with ammunition, and for incoming vessels awaiting dock.

Aboard a foreign vessel, the pilot must quickly adjust to its language as well as to its different navigational equipment, terms, and practices. He must know navigational buoys, lights, and tidal movements.

Virginia pilots were said to have helped Admiral de Grasse's fleet when he defeated the British in the Chesapeake in 1781. Other Virginia pilots helped navigate the CSS *Virginia* —formerly the *Merrimack*—in her 1862 Hampton Roads battle with the USS *Monitor.* They have a long and impressive record.

60. *Over and Under a River's Mouth*

TAKE it from the big boss of the Newport News-Suffolk bridge-tunnel project: the $400 million job will greatly ease traffic problems around the James River and Hampton Roads.

The big boss is Jerry K. Morrison, and he oversaw a dozen major contractors who worked all along the route, from its elevated Interstate 664 approach road at the Newport News Boat Harbor to its underwater tunnel to South Island and its southside highway through rural Suffolk and Chesapeake to Norfolk. It's intended to reduce traffic on the Hampton Roads Bridge-Tunnel and the James River Bridge, providing a fast route to southside Virginia and coastal North Carolina. "It can do nothing but good," Morrison says.

I paid a visit to Jerry in his office at the Boat Harbor, close to the north approach to the colossal tunnel. The approach lies between the C&O's James River coal piers on one side and Boat Harbor seafood retailers on the other. It's a busy place, with hardhats coming and going by work boats that shuttle between Newport News and Suffolk.

Morrison knows more about the project than anyone else. He started it 11 years ago, when the Virginia Department of Transportation made its first studies. "It's something a man will only do once in a lifetime," he told me.

The tunnel has four traffic lanes—two each in separate conduits. "By the year 2000 we estimate 80,000 cars will use it daily, or about 40,000 each way. It will greatly aid Newport News shipyard workers coming from Southside. That will deflect much traffic from the James River Bridge, averting commuter stackup there," Morrison told me.

Since it is 33 years newer than the first Hampton Roads Bridge-Tunnel 10 miles away, the new bridge-tunnel improves on it in many ways.

From bridge portions at Newport News and Suffolk, the crossing dips below water to carry cars through 15 segments of tunnel that whisk motorists 60 feet beneath the main channel, from Hampton Roads into the James River.

"The Corps of Engineers dredged a channel 1,100 feet wide, but it is marked for ship traffic at 800 feet," Morrison said. "That's more than wide enough for the biggest aircraft carriers going to the shipyard and for coal carriers docking at CSX coal piers."

The channel at its deepest point above the tunnel is 50 feet, allowing ample room for the deepest-draft vessels, which draw 43 feet. "Big aircraft carriers are no problem," Morrison assured me. "The new USS *Lincoln* went through on her way from and to the shipyard recently," he said. It draws 37 feet.

The tunnel was made in sections by Bethlehem Steel in Maryland and floated down the Chesapeake Bay to be submerged and joined together. Part of the work was done by Interbeton, a Dutch firm which builds many European tunnels. "We sank the final tunnel section June 17, 1989," Morrison says. "Then we started

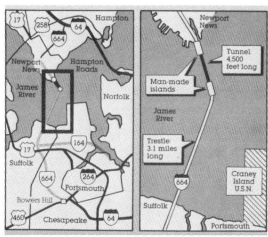

Virginia Department of Transportation

1991 bridge-tunnel at Newport News goes under the James River channel to reach Suffolk.

Jamestown ship Godspeed *visits USS* Theodore Roosevelt *near the new bridge-tunnel.*

Newport News Shipbuilding

applying inside tile walls, working from the South Island end toward Newport News. We also built the tunnel sidewalk and ledges."

At the Boat Harbor and on South Island are ventilation buildings which control airflow in the tunnel. The ventilation was awarded to the Geste Newberg and Hardaway Contractors firms for $57 million. The ventilator at the Boat Harbor rises five stories.

I asked Morrison if any crises had arisen, but he said no. "Laying the tunnel was complicated because the underwater route had a soft mud bottom," he explained. "We took that out and dumped the spoil on Craney Island, near Norfolk. Then we replaced it with sandy material that had been dredged from Thimble Shoals channel and from Shirley Plantation," on the James River in Charles City County. The tunnel was laid on this sand over the river's firm bottom.

Morrison agreed that sinking the 15 prefabricated tunnel tubes and aligning them underwater was the most exacting part of the project. "When they shipped that first tube from Baltimore," he says, "we were more than ready. I waited for it all day, and when it arrived I was like a kid with a new toy."

Each tube section is 300 feet long, 80 feet wide, and 40 feet high. Before the construction crew sank each, they reinforced it with concrete to make it heavier. Before easing it in place underwater, they had to position the tube precisely between two construction barges, held parallel by overhead beam. With the aid of underwater constructors, this giant catamaran lowered each section into its trench.

Linking the 15 tubes was another precise operation. The end of each section had a protruding lip with a massive rubber gasket. These gaskets of adjoining sections were pressed together to create a seven-foot chamber of water. Once in place on the bottom, each section's chamber was pumped dry, creating a vacuum that sucked the gaskets together.

Morrison thinks the project's $400 million in a few years will seem like a bargain. "The Chesapeake Bridge-Tunnel cost $247 million 20 years ago, and today it would cost $1.8 billion," he told me. I believe anything that man says.

61. *Farewell to a River*

THE marshes and flatlands of the James River region support a myriad plant and animal life. It ranges from Cape Henry's Spanish moss and live oaks to the mountain laurels which spill down from Lynchburg. Because the Gulf Stream buffers the Atlantic winds a few miles off Virginia's coast, the river region enjoys mild winters and normally generous rainfall. Plants, trees, and birds of semi-tropical variety abound in fields and forests.

Like all natural resources, the James River is increasingly threatened by the spread of man and his machines. The James has suffered a Kepone crisis and many legal battles over threats to water purity and seafood resources. But thanks to the missionary work of federal, state, and local agencies, it is holding its own. These friendly forces include the Lower James River Association, the Chesapeake Bay Foundation, and the Virginia Institute of Marine Science.

The loblolly pine is the giant of the landscape. What the palm is to Florida and the spruce to New England, this abundant gaunt tree is to the James River. It towers like a king over the forests, sheltering hardwoods and smaller scrub pines in its shade. Many a Virginia landowner lives comfortably from the sale of fast-growing pines to feed voracious paper mills. Taller specimens are used for masts. English shipyards imported them for just this purpose in Virginia's first years.

A wealth of dogwood enamels Tidewater with porcelain whiteness each April. Other plants contribute to spring's symphony: the dainty shad-blow, the white-flowering plum, the magenta Judas tree, and the yellow Scotch broom, whose seed is said to have come from Scotland in forage for British horses in the Revolution. Tropical brilliance radiates from purple wisteria and from yellow Carolina jasmine, both of which climb over trees and buildings. Later in summer, the spiky yucca, or Spanish sword, sends up a showy stalk of white flowers that looks like the cactus of the Southwest. Magnolias recall the sentimentalism of the South "before the War."

Repeated planting of tobacco impoverished the James River area in the eighteenth century, and many planters moved to new land. However, crop rotation and fertilization have now restored soil productiveness. The pressing farm problem today is labor cost.

The animals and birds of the region, which flourished on the agricultural economy, are finding life more difficult as Tidewater industrializes. The decline in catches of fish, crabs, and oysters has led to state controls. The wild game population has suffered less. Virginia white-tailed deer are abundant in many areas. Ducks, geese, rabbits, squirrels, and partridges provide sport for huntsmen from neighboring states. The red fox has been hunted almost to extinction, which accounts for the decline in fox hunt-

Of all James River neighbors, the Dismal Swamp provides the widest variety of wild life. This humid forest extends southward across the North Carolina line from the city of Chesapeake. Its thick and impenetrable depths are haunted with mystery. They also shelter black bears, wildcats, and other predators which have become extinct elsewhere in the east.

Virginians, who are used to living among the landmarks of three-and-a-half centuries, develop a curious unawareness of time. A man who

Virginia State Library

Lexington, with Washington and Lee and VMI in mist, was linked by Maury River canal boats to Lynchburg.

ing in Tidewater. Not so the dull witted opossum and skunk, which frequently fall victim to automobiles on highways.

Tidewater's richest wild life is its birds. Along the swamps fly bald eagles whose nests can be seen high up in waterfront trees. Feeding largely on fish, these magnificent predators have felt the damage wrought to sea life by pollution. Rare cranes and ospreys also live along the James, while woods and meadows all summer long are enraptured with the cadenzas of mockingbirds. Many birds fly south from northern climes to winter in the Chesapeake region.

has seen the friends of his youth grow old continues to think of them as the young men he once knew. So it is with a born-and-bred resident of Tidewater. Its history is a contemporary landscape which he cannot divide into "old" and "new."

The events which have swept over Tidewater since 1607 seem a living and continuing present to the dyed-in-the-wool Virginian. If he himself has not witnessed all of it, at least he has heard so much about it that it seems part of his experience.

In this century the pulse of the James has begun to beat at a quickened rate. Two World

Wars have changed it. Its face, too, has altered more in the 50 years since the introduction of the automobile than in the whole 300 years before it. The river has ceased to be a channel of communication. Expressways have wakened rural Virginia from a lethargy. Cities have dominated the countryside for miles around. Bridges and tunnels have removed barriers

One of the James River's last ferries is moved by hand-ground cable.

*As it passes through the Allegheny Mountains, the James narrows
between limestone hills.*

which for 300 years discouraged commerce.

In a warlike age, the armed forces have
ringed Hampton Roads with defenses. Factories have moved in, pulling farm dwellers to the
cities. In a pattern established in the North a
century earlier, Tidewater has felt the urbaniza-
tion of life.

With industry has come a revolution in relations between whites and Negroes. In the last
generation the James has seen the integration of
its schools, even in counties where Negroes out-
number whites. This was the final blow to
paternalism. Like all social change, it sacrificed
one ideal for another: in this case, the equalitar-
ianism of the machine age for the concept of
leadership by an educated elite. The long
ascendancy of white Anglo-Saxon Protestants
which produced Virginia's eighteenth-century
golden age is giving way to a pluralistic Great
Society.

In this transitional age, the James River is a
paradoxical paradise, midway between present
and past.

APPENDIX to Chapter 15: 'Dynasties of the James'

Virginia's 100 Wealthiest Planters

The wealthiest and most influential of Virginia's planters were concentrated along the James, Rappahannock, and Potomac Rivers on the Northern Neck. Based on tax returns, here are the 100 wealthiest as listed by Professor Jackson T. Main.

Richard Adams of Richmond city, William Alexander of Princess Anne, William Allen of Surry, John Ambler of James City, John Armistead of Caroline, Roger Atkerson of Dinwiddie, Henry Banks of Richmond city, Burwell Bassett of New Kent, Edmund Berkeley of Middlesex, Robert Beverly of Essex, Theodorick Bland of Prince George, William Blunt of Sussex, William Brent of Stafford, Cuthbert Bullitt of Prince William, Lewis Burwell of Mecklenburg, Nathaniel Burwell of James City.

Joseph Cabell of Buckingham, William Cabell of Amherst, Charles Carter of Charles City, Edward Carter of Albemarle, George Carter of Lancaster, John Carter of Loudoun, Landon Carter of King George, Robert Carter of Westmoreland, Robert W. Carter of Richmond county, Archibald Cary of Chesterfield, Wilson Miles Cary of Elizabeth City, William Churchill of Middlesex, Allen Cocke of Surry, Chastain Cocke of Powhatan, John Cocke of Surry, John Hartwell Cocke of Surry, Francis Corbin of Middlesex, Gawin Corbin of Caroline, Richard Corbin of King and Queen, John Parke Custis of New Kent.

Nicholas Davis of Bedford, Francis Eppes of Chesterfield, Francis Eppes of Amelia, George Washington Fairfax of Fairfax, Henry Fitzhugh of King George, Thomas Fitzhugh of Stafford, William Fitzhugh of King George, William Fitzhugh of Stafford, Muscoe Garnett of Essex, Philip L. Grymes of Middlesex, Benjamin Harrison of Charles City, Carter H. Harrison of Cumberland, Nathaniel Harrison of Prince George.

James Henry of King and Queen, Patrick Henry of Prince Edward, Adam Hunter of Stafford, Thomas Jefferson of Albemarle, Joseph Jones of Dinwiddie, Peter Jones of Amelia, Robert Lawson of Prince William, Henry Lee of Westmoreland, Richard Lee of Westmoreland, William Lee of James City, Warner Lewis of Gloucester, William Lightfoot of Charles City, George Mason of Fairfax, Stevens Thomson Mason of Loudoun, Joseph Mayo of Powhatan, Daniel McCarty of Westmoreland, Thomas Nelson of York, Thomas

234

Nelson of York (another of the same name), Wilson Cary Nicholas of Albemarle.

John Page of Gloucester, Mann Page of Spotsylvania, John Paradise of James City, David Patterson of Buckingham, Edmund Pendleton of Caroline, John Perrin of Gloucester, Edmund Randolph of Richmond city, Peyton Randolph of Powhatan, Thomas Randolph of Henrico, Thomas Mann Randolph of Chesterfield, William Randolph of Charles City, Thomas Roane of King and Queen, William Ronald of Powhatan, David Ross of Richmond city, Edmund Ruffin of Prince George.

Henry Skipwith of Buckingham, Sir Peyton Skipwith of Mecklenburg, Alexander Spotswood of Spotsylvania, James Southall of Williamsburg, John Tabb of Amelia, Richard Taliaferro of James City, John Taylor of Richmond county, John Taylor of Caroline, Alexander Trent of Cumberland, George Turberville of Westmoreland, John Turberville of Westmoreland, Robert P. Waring of Essex, George Washington of Fairfax, and Ralph Wormeley of Middlesex.

Acknowledgements

Anyone who writes about Virginia's waters is bound to be in debt to Alexander Crosby Brown, the prolific Newport News scholar who has written more about our ships, our rivers, and our canals than anyone else in Virginia's history. I also acknowledge my gratitude for Robert Burgess, formerly of the Mariners Museum, and to Lon Dill of West Point, both industrious researchers.

I would also like to credit the many contributions of the Reverend Pierce Middleton, author of *Tobacco Coast,* of the late Edward Miles Riley, longtime research director of Colonial Williamsburg, of Malcolm Jamieson of Berkeley plantation, Hill Carter of Shirley, Lewis Kirby of Claremont Manor, Mrs. Virginia Eley of Mount Pleasant, Mr. and Mrs. Harrison Tyler of Sherwood Forest, Ross Weeks of the Jamestown-Yorktown Foundation, Paul Murphy of Charles City County, Robert Wharton of Flowerdew Hundred, William Martin of Downtown Petersburg Inc., Brenton Halsey of the James River Corporation, Lawrence Lewis, Jr., of Weyanoke, Stuart D. Layne of the Virginia Department of Transportation, Dale Wiley of Richmond, and Patti Jackson of the Lower James River Association.

Most of the material in this book appeared originally in the *Newport News Daily Press,* to which I am indebted for many kindnesses, including the use of many illustrations herein. There I am particularly grateful to Jack Davis, editor, and to Will Molineux, editor of the editorial page. I also appreciate the cooperation of the *Virginia Magazine of History and Biography,* the *Naval Institute Proceedings*, *Chesapeake Bay Magazine*, and *Early American Life*, wherein some of this material had earlier appeared.

For illustrations I am grateful to the Colonial Williamsburg Foundation, the College of William and Mary, the Virginia State Library, the

Valentine Museum, the CSX and Norfolk-Southern railway systems, and the Mariners Museum. At Colonial Williamsburg I thank Pearce Grove, James Garrett, Suzanne Brown, and Audrey and Ivor Noël Hume. At Fort Eustis I thank Richard Ivy and Carl Cannon of the Archeological and Historical Society there.

For much incidental help along the way, I am grateful to Segar Cofer Dashiell of Smithfield, the late Charles E. Hatch, Jr., of Yorktown, Ted LoCascio of Suffolk, Kay Domine and Margaret Cooke of the Swem Library at the College of William and Mary, and Paul Hudson, William Snyder, and Judge Robert T. Armistead of Williamsburg. Many photographs were generously provided by Catherine A. Long of the Association for the Preservation of Virginia Antiquities in Richmond.

Lastly and especially, I appreciate the many kindnesses of my wife, Betsy Gayle Rouse, and of Sonnie Rose, Richard Stinely, Tom Ford, and August Dietz III in seeing this book to publication.

Bibliography

Allan, Mea. *The Tradescants: Their Plants, Gardens, and Museums, 1570–1662.* London, 1965

Corson, Minnie Moger. *Living Memories of Crittenden and Chuckatuck.* Suffolk, Va., 1984

Crittenden, Temple. *The Comp'ny.* Parsons, W.Va., 1967

Green, Bennett Wood. *A Word-Book of Virginia Folk Speech.* Richmond, 1899

Hilldrup, Robert. *Upper Brandon.* Richmond, 1987

Jester, Annie Lash. *Newport News, Virginia, 1607–1960.* Newport News, Va., 1961

Lavender, David. *The Great Persuader.* Garden City, N.Y., 1970

Lewis, Clifford, and Loomie, Albert J. *The Spanish Jesuit Mission in Virginia, 1570–1572.* Chapel Hill, 1953

Lossing, Benson. *The Pictorial Field-Book of the War of 1812.* New York, 1868

Noël Hume, Ivor. *Martin's Hundred.* New York, 1982

Swem, Earl Gregg. *Brothers of the Spade.* Barre, Mass., 1957

True, Ransom B. *Plantation on the James.* Richmond, 1986

Vollertsen, Arthur H. and Dorothy F. *The Carys and the Peirces: Mulberry Island Families.* Yorktown, Va., 1985

Yonge, Samuel H. *The Site of Olde James Towne, 1607–1698.* Richmond, 1926

Index